Definition and Dispute

Definition and Dispute

A Defense of Temporal Externalism

DEREK BALL

Great Clarendon Street, Oxford, OX2 6DP,
United Kingdom

Oxford University Press is a department of the University of Oxford.
It furthers the University's objective of excellence in research, scholarship,
and education by publishing worldwide. Oxford is a registered trade mark of
Oxford University Press in the UK and in certain other countries

© Derek Ball 2024

The moral rights of the author have been asserted

All rights reserved. No part of this publication may be reproduced, stored in
a retrieval system, or transmitted, in any form or by any means, without the
prior permission in writing of Oxford University Press, or as expressly permitted
by law, by licence or under terms agreed with the appropriate reprographics
rights organization. Enquiries concerning reproduction outside the scope of the
above should be sent to the Rights Department, Oxford University Press, at the
address above

You must not circulate this work in any other form
and you must impose this same condition on any acquirer

Published in the United States of America by Oxford University Press
198 Madison Avenue, New York, NY 10016, United States of America

British Library Cataloguing in Publication Data

Data available

Library of Congress Control Number: 2023945037

ISBN 978–0–19–890618–6

DOI: 10.1093/oso/9780198906186.001.0001

Printed and bound by
CPI Group (UK) Ltd, Croydon, CR0 4YY

Links to third party websites are provided by Oxford in good faith and
for information only. Oxford disclaims any responsibility for the materials
contained in any third party website referenced in this work.

Contents

Acknowledgements	vii
1. Introduction	1

I. CONSERVATISM ABOUT PRACTICE AND MEANING SAMENESS

2. Verbal Dispute and Metalinguistic Negotiation	21
3. Conceptual Engineering: Ambitious or Anodyne?	31
4. Why Are Paradoxes Hard? On the Explanatory Inefficacy of Inconsistent Concepts	46

II. TEMPORAL EXTERNALISM

5. Definition: What and When	71
6. Stipulation Reconsidered: Temporal Externalism	90
Appendix A: A Case Study	105
7. The Metaphysics and Epistemology of Backwards Determination	111
8. Contextualism, Relativism, and Metasemantics	134
9. Temporal Externalism, Context Sensitivity, and Matters of Taste	151
10. Temporal Externalism: Choice Points	166
Bibliography	189
Index	197

Acknowledgements

I have been fortunate to have the opportunity to discuss the views developed in this book with many people. I especially remember conversations with and comments from Nate Charlow, Josh Dever, Esa Diaz Leon, Andy Egan, Matti Eklund, Patrick Greenough, Simon Hewitt, Torfinn Huvenes, Manuel Gustavo Isaac, Henry Jackman, Steffen Koch, Ethan Landes, Lixiao Lin, Bryan Pickel, David Plunkett, Brian Rabern, Mark Richard, Amr Salih, Paolo Santorio, Sarah Sawyer, Tim Sundell, Kevin Scharp, Rachel Sterken, Ravi Thakral, Emanuel Viebahn, and Emilia Wilson. Indrek Reiland, Roy Sorenson, and the referees for Oxford University Press gave very helpful written comments. Kirsty Graham helped prepare the index. I owe a special debt to Herman Cappelen, who provided helpful and encouraging feedback on a number of occasions. And I am extremely grateful for the support of my family, including Kat Fox, Laurie Ball, Cy Ball, and Ansel Ball-Fox.

1
Introduction

People talk. We agree and disagree, communicate and argue, in classrooms and lecture theatres, in bars and kitchens and beds, about all sorts of things: about matters of fact, as when I think that it will rain and you think it won't, or when I think the Crimean War ended in 1856 and you think it ended in 1865, or when I think most English speakers use "vermillion" to pick out a shade of green and you think that they use it to pick out a shade of red; and about what to do, as when I think that we should have a picnic and you think we should go to a restaurant, or when you maintain that we should not use "hopefully" to mean "it is to be hoped that", and I think this use is acceptable.

We also talk about things that are not so easy to classify—things that do not seem simply to be matters of fact, but also do not seem simply to be matters of what we should do—and those things are the subject of this book. Here is an example. We read a book on the history of art in the twentieth century. Along with the paintings of Picasso and Dali, and the sculptures of Rodin, the book describes Marcel Duchamp's famous "readymades", such as his *Fountain*—a urinal—as well as Chris Burden's 1971 performance piece *Shoot*, in which an accomplice shot him in the arm. You ask me: "These things are just awful. Isn't art supposed to be beautiful? Are these things really *art*?" I reply: "Plenty of famous artworks are not intended to be beautiful. These works are part of an important cultural tradition—the tradition that is represented in museums, galleries, discussed by critics, and so on—and that is all it takes to be art."

Anyone who has attended a course in the philosophy of art will be familiar with sophisticated variations on debates of this kind: they are, after all, the philosopher's stock-in-trade. But they will be no less familiar to teenage coffee shop patrons the world over, and more generally to any thoughtful person exposed for the first time to the art world and its recent history. And lest it be thought that debates of this kind are a matter exclusively for the ivory tower, even the European Commission has weighed in, ruling that works by the sculptor Dan Flavin (disassembled for shipping) are "lighting fittings" (rather than art)—a decision with real-world significance as lighting fittings and art are subject to different tax regimes. The Commission gave two arguments: first, that "it is not the installation that constitutes a 'work of art' but the result of the operations (the light effect) carried out by it"; and second, that the work has "the characteristics of lighting fittings ... [and] is therefore to be classified ... as wall lighting fittings" (European Commission, 2010).[1]

Discussions of art of this sort are typically described as being about the *definition of art*. They are complicated for several reasons, but one is the variety of things that seem to be at issue. On the face of it, we appear to be talking about *art*; we are thinking about a collection of objects, events, and practices in the world—as it might be, the *Mona Lisa* and Rodin's *The Thinker* in Paris, Burden's performance in mid-twentieth-century America, prints from Hiroshige's *One Hundred Famous Views of Edo* in various museums, and so on—wondering whether they all belong together and what they have in common. But it also appears that our dispute may turn on how we define the word "art"—what we mean by that word—and that at least part of what we are concerned with is how we ought to talk. To make matters worse, in addition to this, we are sometimes concerned with practical matters such as what belongs in museums, or who should pay which taxes.

Disputes of this general kind—disputes that seem (in some sense) to turn on matters of definition—are common, especially in philosophy but also in politics, the law, and ordinary life. Is same-sex marriage, or non-religious marriage, or marriage after divorce, possible? Is a human foetus, or a corporation, or a chimpanzee, a person? Is alcoholism a disease? What about obesity? Gambling addiction? Is Pluto a planet? Is caffeine a drug? Is oral sex sex? Is free will compatible with determinism? Can computers, or non-human animals, think? Is knowledge compatible with the possibility of error? And of course, discussion of related questions about gender, race, and other phenomena of social and philosophical interest are very widespread. We will call them *definitional disputes*; the detailed account given in Chapter 5 will make it clear why this label is justified.

We also argue about whether spicy food is tasty, whether the room is cold, and whether vulgar comedy is funny. In each case, similar issues arise: are these questions about what we should believe, about how we should use words like "cold" and "funny", or something else (such as whether we should turn up the thermostat or what we should watch this evening)? As we will see in Chapter 9, it will turn out that these disputes share crucial features with definitional disputes, and can also be regarded as definitional disputes in an extended sense.

We will discuss many of these examples in more detail in subsequent chapters of the book. But I hope that enough has been said already to motivate the idea that there is a puzzle here. These debates often matter deeply to us: our views about marriage, about disease, about our own identities, shape our lives. They can determine not only what taxes are due but also who can form lives together, and who gets medical treatment. Even debates about whether the house is cold or whether Thai food is tasty can make a big difference to our home lives and

---

[1] I learned of this example from Lopes (2014, 5).

relationships! But it is not even clear what we are debating about. Are we talking about some fact? Is it what we mean, or should mean? Or is it something else?[2]

The view to be defended in this book can be seen as the conjunction of three claims:

1. *Conservatism about Practice.* The way we typically engage in definitional disputes makes sense, and is not confused or in need of wholesale revision; and there is (in typical cases) no better way of engaging with these issues.
2. *Meaning Sameness.* Parties to a definitional dispute typically mean the same thing by their words, and the meanings of words do not typically change over the course of or as a result of the dispute.
3. *Temporal Externalism.* Facts about what happens at later times can play a role in determining the meaning of our words (and the contents of our mental states) at earlier times. In particular, definitional disputes can play a role in determining meaning, even though they do not involve change of meaning.

The aims of the rest of this introductory chapter are to develop these claims in a bit more detail, and to introduce some technical terminology that will aid later discussion. In order to do this, the next section develops another example of a definitional dispute.

1. Malcolm on Knowledge

I woke up early this morning, ate breakfast, and am now sitting in front of a computer—or so it seems to me, anyway. Should I be so sure? Do I really know even simple truths about my environment, or about the recent past? The sceptic says no: after all, how can we rule out the claim that we are dreaming, or that we are mere brains in vats fooled by an evil demon or a powerful supercomputer? And if we cannot rule out these claims that are obviously incompatible with what we ordinarily take ourselves to know, how can we claim knowledge?

And so we are off on one of philosophy's oldest problems: a problem that, in many traditional discussions, turns in large part on the definition of *knowledge*.

---

[2] Because (I will contend) similar cognitive and linguistic factors are at work in abstract philosophical disputes (for example, about the nature of truth) and in local disputes about matters of taste as are at work in the disputes that shape our lives, we discuss all of these, sometimes together. In so doing, we do not diminish the importance of the disputes that matter deeply; on the contrary, it is important to understand these disputes precisely *because* they matter deeply. Nor do we express any moral approbation of the views expressed in the various disputes. One morally ought not to hold certain views about (say) marriage or race; it may even be that one *ought not* to raise certain questions about these issues. The fact remains that bad views are held and defended, and we need to know what is going on when they are.

Can this old problem be answered by looking at how we use the word "know"? The suggestion may be surprising, but Norman Malcolm (1949) claimed that it can. Malcolm's key observation is that we only use the word "know" when there is genuine doubt about an issue. This observation is based on an examination of the kinds of circumstances under which "I know" seems like a sensible thing to say:

> We are seated in the audience at an open-air theatre, the stage of which is bordered by trees. The stage scenery is painted to represent a woodland, and the painting is so skilfully executed that we are in doubt as to whether that which we see on one side of the stage is a real tree or a painted tree. Finally one of us exclaims "I know that that is a real tree, because just now I saw the leaves move in the breeze." This would be a natural use of language. (1949, 203)

By way of contrast, suppose the tree were in plain view. Even so, the sceptic may say: "You do not know that that is a real tree. After all, you might be dreaming!" Malcolm's response is that the claim is inappropriate. It would only make sense to say "You know that that is a real tree" or "You do not know" when there is some real doubt about whether it is a real tree. We might feign doubt at the thought that we might be dreaming, but our doubt is not genuine; there is no serious issue about whether the tree is real. (As Malcolm says, "The sort of circumstances in which it would be unnatural to say of a man that he 'doubts' that there is a fire are the very circumstances in which that man might express a philosophical doubt as to whether there is a fire!" (1949, 205).) Therefore, Malcolm concludes, the sceptic is mistaken: since the sceptic's arguments introduce no genuine doubt, her claim is not true. To say "I do not know, because I might be dreaming" is a linguistic error.

On Malcolm's view, it is not just that the sceptic is defeated: the whole philosophical project of studying, or even discussing, scepticism is one that makes no sense. Moore, who famously offered his knowledge that he had hands as more certain than the premises of any sceptical argument to the contrary, and Descartes, who famously claimed to prove that scepticism could not be true because God would not deceive us, are no less mistaken than the sceptic. (Indeed, it is Moore (not the sceptic) who is the main target of Malcolm's argument in the article from which the above passages are quoted.[3]) Malcolm's contention is not that we can respond to the sceptic by claiming that we know; it is that the question of whether we know or not is a mistake, because neither the word "know" nor the phrase "do not know" is not correctly applied in this kind of case.

---

[3] Malcolm changed his mind on this point; in earlier work, he had held that Moore was correctly observing ordinary usage: "By reminding us of how we ordinarily use the expressions 'know for certain' and 'highly probable,' Moore's reply constitutes a refutation of the philosophical statement that we can never have certain knowledge of material-thing statements" (1952, 355).

2. First Main Theme: Conservatism about Practice

Malcolm's contention is an instance of a kind of reaction to definitional disputes with which many may have some sympathy: that there is something wrong with them. Even those who are not sympathetic to Malcom's proposal might suggest at least that typical definitional disputes are going awry because the parties to the dispute are failing to understand each other; they are talking past each other; the resulting dispute is 'just semantic' or 'merely verbal'. We should not be trying to make sense of the disputes, except perhaps by way of diagnosing why the parties to them are making the mistakes they are. Perhaps we should abandon the disputes entirely: definitional disputes are hopelessly confused and there is just nothing interesting to discuss. Or perhaps we need to reconsider the kinds of arguments we are making in order to come up with better ways of engaging in definitional disputes. (For example, perhaps we should stop trying to give theoretical arguments for our proposed definitions of knowledge or of art, and should stop trying to give counterexamples to others' definitions; instead, we should give pragmatic arguments to the effect that one or another way of using a word would serve certain purposes better than others.) Call the view that we need to abandon definitional disputes, or substantially change the way we engage in them, *revisionism about practice*.

I think that we should view revisionism about practice with suspicion. Definitional disputes are common and really matter. It seems to many of us (myself included) that what we are doing in engaging in such disputes is worthwhile. The conclusion that we are so confused about something so common and important would be a serious cost of any view. We should therefore try to develop a theory that can make sense of definitional disputes as they are carried out. That is, we should look for a view that satisfies Conservatism about Practice:

Conservatism about Practice   The way we typically engage in definitional disputes makes sense, and is not confused or in need of wholesale revision; and there is (in typical cases) no better way of engaging with these issues.

My defence of Conservatism about Practice comes in three parts. First, the best-developed proposals of ways that we ought to revise our practice fail. In particular, as I argue in Chapter 3, proponents of *conceptual engineering*—the idea that we ought to "assess and improve our representational devices" (Cappelen, 2018, 148)—have not described a practice distinct from ordinary theorising. In particular, proponents of conceptual engineering have not described an alternative methodology for engaging in definitional disputes. Second, prominent motivations for thinking that what we are doing when we engage in definitional disputes is fundamentally confused are unsuccessful. In particular, as I argue in Chapter 4, the persistence of definitional disputes is not explicable in terms of some inconsistency or incoherence in our language or concepts. Third, there is a plausible way of maintaining Conservatism about Practice. Defending this claim is the work of Part II, where I defend *Temporal Externalism*, the third major theme of this book. In order to introduce temporal externalism, and to clarify the second major theme—*Meaning Sameness*—we will need some technical terminology; introducing this terminology is the task of the next section.

3. Semantics and Pragmatics

Malcolm's basic strategy is to move from observations about how we use the word "know" to a claim about the *meaning* of "know", and then to the claim that a certain philosophical position or debate is a mistake. In particular, he moves from claims like (1) to claims like (2) and (3):

(1) We would not ordinarily use the word "know" to describe a case about which there is no real doubt.

(2) The meaning of the word "know" is such that applying "know" to cases about which there is no real doubt is incorrect.

(3) An assertion of "I know" or "I do not know" in a case where there is no real doubt is not true.

The move from (1) to (2) and (3) should excite suspicion. After all, no one would conclude from the fact that we would not use the word "fart" in front of the queen that the meaning of the word "fart" precludes its application in the presence of the queen, or that an assertion made using that word in the presence of the queen could never be true. So Malcolm's move could be resisted if we had some reason to think that the fact that we do not say "I know" when there is no real doubt is due to some factor other than the meaning of "know".

Paul Grice (1989a) gave a reason to resist Malcolm's attempt to read our reticence to use "know" about uncontroversial matters into the meaning of the word.[4] Grice's thought is that talking to each other is a cooperative endeavour. In general, when we speak we are trying to do something useful; this usually entails not only telling the truth and being clear and unambiguous but also giving only information that is relevant. This explains why we do not go around saying things like "I know that is a real tree", except in cases where there is genuine doubt. If there is no doubt, we do not say "I know", not because saying so would be incorrect or untrue but because it would be irrelevant; in ordinary cases (where we are in the

---

[4] Grice does not provide a detailed discussion of Malcolm's view of knowledge, though he indicates that Malcolm is one of his targets (Grice, 1989c, 5).

vicinity of a plain tree in good lighting, with no reason to suspect shenanigans), you will take it for granted that the tree is real and that I know that it is. Telling you that I know is odd because it gives you no useful information and so contributes nothing to the conversation.

So the dispute between Malcolm and Grice goes something like this. Malcolm claims that way we use "know" shows that the meaning of the word is more complicated than many philosophers have supposed; an account of the meaning of "know" must allude not only to evidence, justification, reliability, truth, and the like but also to the existence of genuine doubt. But Grice responds that the complication is unnecessary: the facts about our use of "know" can be explained on the view that the meaning of "know" is simple, given an independently motivated view of how language is used.[5]

To be clear about exactly what is at issue, we need to introduce some technical terminology. Utterances of declarative sentences (made in appropriate circumstances, with appropriate intentions, and so on) are true or false, and whether an utterance is true or false is in part a matter of what that utterance means. If I say, "Grass is green", I am speaking truly, and this is because grass is green; given what "Grass is green" means, my utterance is true if and only if grass is green. So the meaning of a declarative sentence must be, or at least be something that determines, the conditions under which utterances of the sentence are true.[6] (To do justice to views like Malcolm's, we should note that some theories will want to distinguish different ways of failing to be true; for example, being false, and being neither true nor false (but entirely inapplicable or nonsensical). But this complication won't be relevant to most of the discussion to follow.) I propose to call a theory that gives a systematic description of the conditions under which utterances of declarative sentences are true a *semantic* theory.[7] No doubt, there is

---

[5] Charles Travis (2008) advances a bolder reading of Malcolm, on which his claim is not just that words like "know" and "certain" require doubt but (roughly at least) that no sentence has truth-conditional meaning except when used in relation to a particular line of inquiry, and it must be conceded that this view is suggested by some passages in Malcolm's later work (e.g., Malcolm, 1970, 42–43). On this interpretation, Malcolm's observations about the use of "know" can be used to defend a position which radically questions the distinction between semantics and pragmatics sketched below. Full treatment of this style of view would take us far afield from the primary issues to be discussed, and I therefore propose to set it aside. I respond to the kind of view Travis attributes to Malcolm in Ball (2018b); see also the discussion of meaning variation in Chapter 10, Section 2.

[6] Should a semantic theory deal with utterances, as opposed to sentences-in-context or something similar? Little turns on this for our purposes in this chapter; we revisit the choices we are making here in Chapter 8.

[7] There is, of course, much controversy about meaning and semantic theorising; the view of semantics just suggested is a gesture at one mainstream perspective on these controversies (it is a core element of the otherwise diverse views of Davidson (2001); Montague (1974a); Lewis (1983a); Larson and Segal (1995); Heim and Kratzer (1998); Borg (2004); among many others). Another way of using the terminology would have it that a much wider array of phenomena should count as semantic or as matters of meaning. For example, one might say that anything conventionally encoded in language is semantics (where this might include matters of e.g., conventional implicature, presupposition, information structure, and so on, which arguably go beyond truth conditions). I have no objection

more to meaning than semantics in the sense described. (For one thing, we have said nothing about the semantics of non-declarative sentences.) But when we go on to talk about meaning in later parts of this book, it is semantics in this sense that we will have in mind.

With this terminology in place, we can pause to make two of Malcolm's assumptions explicit.

First, Malcolm is assuming that all parties to the dispute—himself, the sceptic, anti-sceptical philosophers such as Moore—are using the word "know" with the same meaning, and no one is advocating a change of meaning. Call this claim *meaning sameness*. The assumption of meaning sameness is crucial to Malcolm's case: if the sceptic were using "knows" with a different meaning, it might well be the case that an utterance of "I don't know whether I have hands" by the sceptic is true, even if a homophonic utterance by Malcolm is untrue.

Second, Malcolm is assuming that semantics is connected to our linguistic behaviour in a very simple way. At least roughly, Malcolm assumes that if a sentence has certain truth conditions, and those conditions obviously obtain, then it will be appropriate to use the sentence to make an assertion; so that if it is not appropriate to use the sentence under certain circumstances, we may infer that the sentence is not true under those circumstances.

What Grice points out is that the relation between truth conditions and conditions under which it is appropriate to use a sentence is more complicated than this. A sentence will not be used if there is no point in using it—even if it is true. (And of course, Grice further suggests that a sentence may sensibly and cooperatively be used even when using it involves speaking falsely, for one's hearers may be able to reason from the fact that one uttered the falsehood and the hypothesis that one is being cooperative to some useful truth.) So Grice points out that the conditions under which a sentence could be uttered truly need not be the conditions under which the sentence is actually used; even if we are given a semantic theory, we have further questions to answer about when and how sentences with the given semantics are used. I propose to call a theory that purports to explain how and why sentences with given truth conditions are used a *pragmatic* theory. A pragmatic theory, in this sense, will typically make claims about why people say the things they do—why their actions are reasonable and what they aim to achieve.

The need for a pragmatic theory shows that Malcolm's simple idea about the relation between semantics and linguistic behaviour is too simple. More subtle pragmatic theories can also call into question meaning sameness. We turn to these theories in the next section.

---

to this way of using the terminology, but I adopt the truth-conditional notion in order to simplify discussion; it should be understood as a stipulation to get us started.

4. Second Main Theme: Meaning Sameness

Malcolm assumed that all parties to discussions of knowledge agree about what their words mean, and it is plausible that something like this assumption is true in many ordinary cases of communication. If I tell you, "The Crimean War ended in 1864", it's natural to think that you understand me just in case you understand that I am using "The Crimean War" to talk about the Crimean War, and "ended in 1864" to predicate of the Crimean War that it ended in 1864; if you think that I am using "The Crimean War" to talk about something else, or "ended in 1864" to predicate something else, you are misunderstanding me.

But people speak for a variety of reasons. We might be faced with a situation in which a good pragmatic theory will hold that a speaker is trying to communicate something about how we ought to speak—what we mean or ought to mean—or to bring about a change in the way that we speak. And a number of theorists have defended this kind of pragmatic theory in the case of definitional disputes.

A. J. Ayer provides a good example of this strategy in action. Ayer claimed that a theory can be true only if it is empirically verifiable, and that philosophical claims—including his own claim that truth requires empirical verifiability—are typically not decidable on empirical grounds (Ayer, 1940, 55). This position appears incoherent, since by his own lights the claim that truth requires empirical verifiability is not empirically verifiable, and hence not true. He concludes that philosophers are not in the business of making true claims. What, then, are they doing? Ayer's alternative is that they are making proposals for how to use language: "what we here have to consider is not a number of alternative hypotheses concerning the nature of the empirical facts, but a number of alternative recommendations concerning the way in which we are to describe them" (Ayer, 1940, 55).

Now it is easy to see Ayer as grasping at straws in the face of a very deep problem in his position, and perhaps there is an element of truth in this thought. But Ayer is appealing to a deeper methodological principle than "save your own skin". It is a piece of common sense that we should try to interpret the words and actions of others charitably. Whether and how this piece of common sense can be precisely formulated is a good question, but its application in particular cases seems clear enough. Ayer's strategy is essentially to apply charity to himself;[8] when his view seems to predict that he is speaking nonsense, he suggests that he ought to be interpreted as doing something else: making a proposal about what we

---

[8] On one conception of charity, charity is a matter of maximising agreement: I interpret someone charitably just in case I make their beliefs match mine to the maximum possible extent (Davidson, 2001). On this conception, self-charity is trivial and always achieved. I am suggesting that Ayer should be read as aiming for something more than this: he wants to tell a story on which the speech acts he makes in the course of defending his philosophical position—for example, saying "Truth requires verifiability"—can be understood as reasonable means to a reasonable end. Thanks to Roy Sorenson for discussion of this point.

should do rather than an assertion about how things are. This can be seen as an application of Grice's strategy: although Ayer is not saying something true, he is still doing something that makes a cooperative contribution to the conversation by communicating how we ought to use a word. We need to look beyond the semantics of sentences like "Truth requires empirical verifiability", and focus on giving a pragmatic theory, a theory of how they can be used.

Later philosophers used other kinds of consideration to motivate the idea that something like this strategy has a prominent role to play in understanding definitional disputes, especially in philosophy. Alice Ambrose (1952, 1992, 1970) and Morris Lazerowitz (1952, 1964) point to the fact that philosophers often, and with apparent sincerity, advance claims that are inconsistent with obvious facts that they are in a position to know to be true. The defender of scepticism is arguably a case in point: Ambrose and Lazerowitz (following Moore) take it to be abundantly clear that I am in a position to know that I have hands, that I am standing before a desk, and so on. When the sceptic denies that she knows anything, she is denying perfectly obvious facts. The situation is even worse with respect to philosophers such as F. H. Bradley, who claimed that space and time did not exist. Ambrose and Lazerowitz point out that Bradley knows that he had breakfast *before* he had lunch, and that this entails that time exists. How can it make sense to deny perfectly obvious known facts?

If we have taken on board Grice's idea that conversation is cooperative, we should be looking for a way that Bradley's falsehoods can be interpreted charitably as making a helpful contribution to the conversation. Ambrose and Lazerowitz suggest that the best way of doing this is to regard philosophical claims as linguistic proposals: suggestions that we should speak in certain ways. "Time does not exist" as we use it now is inconsistent with "I had breakfast before I had lunch"; Bradley's willingness to assert both just goes to show that he was not using "Time does not exist" in the ordinary way. Instead, Ambrose and Lazerowitz claim, Bradley was suggesting that we use "time" in such a way that "Time does not exist" comes out true. Similarly, when the sceptic says, "We know nothing", she is making a suggestion about how we should go about using the word "know"—and when Moore or Descartes argues that we know plenty, they are making a counter-suggestion.

In the contemporary literature, this kind of pragmatic story about what is going on in definitional disputes is called *metalinguistic negotiation*. Proponents of metalinguistic negotiation typically accept Conservatism about Practice; they think that definitional disputes, conducted in broadly the way we normally do, make sense, and they aim to establish this by providing a pragmatic theory according to which parties to definitional disputes disagree about what they ought to mean by some word. On this view, resolving a definitional dispute will typically mean that at least one party to the dispute changes what they mean by the word.

I reject pragmatic theories of this kind. The second main theme of this book is that the best way of understanding typical definitional disputes will not involve such changes in meaning:

Meaning Sameness Parties to a definitional dispute typically mean the same thing by their words, and the meanings of words do not typically change over the course of or as a result of the dispute.

In Chapter 2, I show that metalinguistic negotiation is incompatible with Conservatism about Practice; if Meaning Sameness is false, then the ways in which we engage in definitional disputes are confused.

On some views, it is possible that two people might mean the same things by their words, while possessing different concepts, or thinking thoughts with different contents. In order to keep discussion simple, I am ignoring this complication for now, and I am framing the key themes in terms of linguistic meaning. I would defend analogous views about concepts and mental contents: parties to definitional disputes typically possess the same concepts, their concepts have the same contents, and neither concepts nor contents change over the course of the dispute; and moreover, temporal externalism is true for mental contents. I will return to this issue explicitly in Chapter 10, Section 1.

5. Third Main Theme: Temporal Externalism

But Meaning Sameness poses a puzzle. In the discussion of conceptual art sketched above, the person who denies that so-called conceptual "art" is really art thinks that to be a work of art is to be an object that has been created with a certain aesthetic intention. The person who thinks that conceptual art is art thinks that to be a work of art is to be the product of a certain cultural tradition. It looks like the two parties are focused on different phenomena: one is trying to talk about one thing, the other is trying to talk about something different. How can it be that they nonetheless succeed in meaning the same thing?

Developing this puzzle in detail is one main task of Chapter 5. For now, I want to sketch the view that I think best answers it.

Semantic features are not fundamental features of the world. Wherever we have semantic facts, it makes sense to ask: in virtue of what do these semantic facts obtain? Why are the semantic facts the way they are? Questions of this kind are called *metasemantic*.

The final key theme of this book—in many ways, the most distinctive feature of the view to be developed—is that the best complete answer to these questions will appeal not only to what I (and perhaps also my interlocutors and my community) believe, intend, and do *now* but also to what we go on to believe, intend, and do *later*:

Temporal Externalism (TE)   Facts about what happens at later times can play a role in determining the meaning of our words at earlier times.[9]

One philosophical project is to give a *complete* metasemantic theory: a theory that would explain how anything that has truth conditions has the truth conditions it does.[10] But we can also do less ambitious metasemantic work; we can formulate a *partial* metasemantic theory. Temporal externalism describes one factor that can play a meaning-determining role in some cases. There is no reason to expect a simple metasemantic theory; in any given case, multiple factors might be relevant to meaning, and different factors may be at work in different kinds of case.

The most prominent defence of temporal externalism in literature to date is in the work of Henry Jackman (1999; 2004; 2005; 2020). In the next section, I show that Jackman's case for temporal externalism is incomplete, and his version of temporal externalism does not cover all of the cases of definitional dispute in which we might be interested.

6. Jackman's Temporal Externalism

Jackman develops temporal externalism in response to cases such as the following, which Jackman draws from Wilson (1982):

> the term 'Grant's zebra' was introduced around 1820 for a type of zebra native to Kenya. A few years later, the term 'Chapman's zebra' was introduced for a morphologically distinct type of zebra found in present-day Zimbabwe. Later still it was discovered that the two types of zebra interbred near the Zambezi river and that, morphologically, one gradually faded into the other. Grant's and Chapman's zebras both turned out to be a races [sic] of the species *Equus burchilli* [...] it is merely a *historical accident* that the term ['Grant's zebra'] has the extension it does. If the taxonomists had investigated the area around the Zambezi river *before* they hit deepest Zimbabwe, they probably would have 'discovered' that

---

[9] Previous defences of temporal externalism include Ball (2018a, 2020b,c); Collins (2005); Ebbs (2000); Haukioja (2020); Jackman (1999, 2004, 2005, 2020); Stoneham (2003); Rouse (2014); Tanesini (2006, 2014). The views defended in Wilson (1982), Richard (1995), and Sainsbury (2005) also have temporal externalist elements. Criticisms of temporal externalism can be found in Brown (2000); Bantegnie (2020), and Sawyer (2020b). Jackman (2004), Stoneham (2003), and Ball (2020c) respond to some of these considerations.

[10] Cf. the project of "naturalising intentionality" (e.g., Dretske, 1991; Millikan, 1989).

Grant's zebra could be found through most of East Africa, gradually changing into a different sub-species as it drifted south. In such a case, 'Grant's zebra' would have picked out the entire species, not just the race found in Kenya.

(1999, 159–160)

Jackman's view of the case is this. Suppose that in 1820, just after introducing the term "Grant's zebra", someone says (demonstrating a particular animal), "That is a nice-looking Grant's zebra". Now we need to contrast the actual case, in which taxonomists next travelled to present-day Zimbabwe and introduced the term "Chapman's zebra" for the animals that lived there, with a counterfactual case in which taxonomists proceed to the Zambezi river and continue to use the term "Grant's zebra" to talk about the zebras they saw, despite the gradual change in morphology. In the actual case, Jackman thinks, the utterance of "That is a nice-looking Grant's zebra" is true just in case the animal referred to by "that" is a nice-looking member of the race or subspecies of *Equus burchilli* native to Kenya. In the counterfactual case, Jackman thinks the truth conditions of the utterance of "That is a nice-looking Grant's zebra" will be different; that utterance will be true just in case the animal referred to by "that" is a nice-looking member of the species *Equus burchilli*. So, the truth-conditions of the utterance depend in part on what happens after the time of the utterance. Thus temporal externalism is true.

Why does Jackman endorse this view? It is useful to see him as presenting three mutually supporting but independent arguments: the *Argument from the Metaphysics of Practices*, the *Argument from Indeterminacy*, and the *Argument from Attribution*. In what follows, I present each of these in turn. Although I am sympathetic to Jackman's view, I criticise the first two arguments and suggest that the third is in need of further development.

The Argument from the Metaphysics of Practices
Jackman's first argument turns on two claims. The first is that particular utterances of a word are parts of larger practices of using the word, and that the practices play an important role in determining the meaning of the utterances. For example, "Grant's zebra" means what it does in virtue of (at least) the history of applications of the word, dispositions to apply it, patterns of correction of speakers by other speakers, related beliefs, and other features. The second claim is that we ought to endorse a view of the metaphysics of practices on which practices extend into the future: "It would be arbitrary to insist that our usage is part of a temporally extended practice that ends with our current utterance. [. . .] When we make an utterance, we often commit ourselves to future refinements in communal usage because these refinements determine just what linguistic practice our usage is (and has always been) a part of" (1999, 160).

We may regiment this argument in the following way:

Premise 1 Utterances of words mean what they do at least partly in virtue of the practices of which they are a part.
Premise 2 Practices extend into the future.
Conclusion Therefore, utterances of words mean what they do in virtue of things that happen in the future.

The argument is suggestive. Ultimately, however, the conclusion does not follow from the premises. The problem is that facts may depend on only part of a practice, and in particular that facts that depend on a practice that extends into the future may depend only on the past part of that practice.

Here is an example. The fact that I have a certain sum in my bank account depends on all sorts of human economic practices: practices related to the use of currency and record keeping; my practice of coming in to work and my employer's practice of paying me for it; the bank's practice of paying interest; and so on. Many of these practices extend into the future. However, it does not follow from this that the fact that I have a certain sum in my bank account depends on things that happen in the future. My bank balance depends on my practice of coming into work, and that practice will likely continue; but my bank balance depends only on the past part of it, not on the future part. Likewise, it might be suggested, meaning might depend on the past part of our practice, not on the future part; and this suggestion might not seem arbitrary to someone worried about the apparent metaphysical peculiarity of future facts determining present meaning (an issue we revisit in Chapter 7).

The Argument from Indeterminacy
Jackman's second argument begins with the fact that it can turn out that our beliefs and dispositions about the correct application of a word—including both our general beliefs about the correct application, and our dispositions to apply the word to particular cases—cannot all be correct. For example, we may believe that "Grant's zebra" is correctly applied to *this* animal, that "Grant's zebra" is not correctly applied to *that* one, and that "Grant's zebra" is correctly applied to all and only the members of a certain species; but it may turn out that this animal and that one are members of the same species. In this kind of case, Jackman claims, there are typically multiple ways in which our practice might evolve. We might give up the claim that "Grant's zebra" is correctly applied to that animal, or we might give up the claim that "Grant's zebra" is correctly applied to all and only the members of a certain species; nothing in our previous practice dictates that one or the other response is uniquely correct. Therefore, if our past practice is the only factor that determines what we mean, then what we mean is often indeterminate. Since, Jackman assumes, what we mean is determinate, future practice must must

play a role in determining what we mean. "It is fortunate that we incorporate social and historical usage into the practices we take part in. Otherwise what we mean would often be indeterminate. Much the same can be said for future usage, since future usage is often required if we are to arrive at a determinate extension for our terms" (1999, 161).

The fact that Jackman motivates his temporal externalism by appeal to indeterminacy limits its potential application to definitional disputes. On Jackman's view, past and present usage may settle some aspects of meaning and leave others open. Future usage can only close what past usage left open; departure from what past usage has settled results in meaning change (Jackman, 1999, 163, 167). But in many cases, a party to a definitional dispute may aim not to resolve something left open by past usage but to overthrow past usage. For example, it could be that examining the use of "art" and art-related beliefs prior to 1900 would reveal firm and determinate dispositions to withhold "art" from things like Duchamp's *Fountain*, to judge that such things are not art, and so on—and that there were no countervailing dispositions and judgements. In that case, Jackman would have it that past use settled that "art" is not correctly applied to *Fountain*, and, barring change of meaning, "*Fountain* is art" is not true.

But it is by no means clear that we ought to accept this verdict. After all, perhaps it was precisely the aim of conceptual artists to challenge these entrenched dispositions and judgements. And perhaps we all come to agree that they were right. An account of definitional disputes should accommodate cases of this kind as well. (See Chapter 10, Section 3 for further discussion.)

So this style of motivation for temporal externalism would need supplementing in order to handle the full range of cases. But in any case, the argument is problematic. Abstracting away from some details, we may represent it as follows:

Premise 1 There are cases in which past and present facts are insufficient to give our words determinate meaning.

Premise 2 Our words have determinate meaning.

Conclusion Therefore, future facts must play a role in determining meaning.

This argument is unlikely to carry much dialectical weight. Premise 2 is controversial; there are familiar reasons to doubt that any facts about our beliefs, dispositions, or patterns of usage can provide a determinate meaning (e.g., Quine, 1960; Kripke, 1982; Putnam, 1978). Appeal to future facts will not resolve these familiar sources of indeterminacy. And it is plausible that whatever resources we may appeal to in order to resolve this indeterminacy could also resolve Jackman's kind of indeterminacy. For example, one popular line of response to many forms of indeterminacy is to appeal to *metaphysical naturalness* (Lewis, 1984; Sider, 2011). On this kind of view, certain entities are simply more apt to be referred to than others; roughly, if our practice does not determine which of several candidates is the unique meaning of a given expression, then if one candidate is more natural than the others, it will be the referent. (As it is sometimes put, the natural entities are "reference magnets".) If we appeal to metaphysical naturalness to resolve other forms of indeterminacy, then (on the assumption that species is a more natural categorisation than sub-species), it is plausible that we should say that "Grant's zebra" as used in 1820 refers to the species because the species is the more natural candidate referent.

In short, the suggestion is that resources needed to defend Premise 2 from other challenges are apt to undermine Jackman's defence of Premise 1.

The Argument from Attribution

Finally, Jackman appeals to our practice of attributing attitudes and speech acts to ourselves and to other speakers. It would be natural, for instance, to use the expression "Grant's zebra" in attributing attitudes and speech acts to speakers in 1820; for example, we might report that they said that Grant's zebra is a distinct species from Chapman's zebra. These attributions seem to presuppose that what speakers in 1820 meant when they said "Grant's zebra is a distinct species from Chapman's zebra" is what we would mean if we uttered the same sentence. (If "Grant's zebra" as we use it means something different, then it seems that a report like, "Speakers in 1820 said that Grant's zebra is a distinct species" would be inaccurate; after all, they did not have a word that means what "Grant's zebra" means now, and so presumably did not say anything about Grant's zebra.) But our word means what it does in virtue of things that happened after 1820. Therefore, the word meant what it did in 1820 partly in virtue of things that happened after 1820. Here is Jackman's succinct statement: "when we interpret the past use of other speakers (and even ourselves), we help ourselves to subsequent specifications which were not determined by the facts available at or before the time of utterance" (1999, 160).

We may summarise this argument in the following terms:

Premise 1 In a range of cases, we make attributions of attitudes and speech acts to speakers in the past, and these attributions are true only if our words mean the same the same as the words of the speakers we are reporting.

Premise 2 In some cases of this kind, the meaning of our words is determined in part by things that happened after the attitudes and speech acts we are reporting.

Premise 3 In some cases of this kind, our reports are true.

Conclusion Therefore, the meaning of words as used by speakers in the past is determined by things that happened after those uses.

Premise 1 raises a number of issues, but is plausible if we restrict our attention to cases in which our purposes require very precise reports of what was said. (See Chapter 7, Section 5 for further discussion.) But the opponent of TE might argue that Premise 2 and Premise 3 should not both be accepted, on the grounds that if Premise 2 is true, then the most plausible interpretation of the case is as one in which the meanings of our words have changed and Premise 3 is false. For example, it might be insisted that although twenty-first-century reports like "Speakers in 1820 said that Grant's zebra is a distinct species" may be appropriate in contexts where only a loose sense of what was said in 1820 is required, such reports are not true in contexts (a courtroom, perhaps) where we are trying to capture exactly what was said.

One way of rebutting this line of resistance to the Argument from Attribution would be to provide independent evidence against the idea that cases of this kind involve meaning change. Part I of this book defends Meaning Sameness and so provides such evidence. Another way of rebutting this line of resistance would be to defend the idea that in many contexts, our retrospective reports and evaluations (of what we or others said and thought, and why) are strictly correct and do not need to be interpreted as a kind of loose speech. I defend this view in Chapter 6, Sections 1 and 4 (and see also Chapter 7, Section 5). I therefore think that some version of the Argument from Attribution can be made acceptable (and our reporting of past speech acts and attitudes will play a role in the discussion in Chapter 6). But at a minimum, Jackman's case for TE needs supplementation, both to make a fully convincing case that TE is true at all, and to develop a version of TE that fits the full range of definitional disputes.

7. Summary

Let's return to Malcolm's view in order to summarise some of the themes that we have introduced. We can usefully present Malcolm's view as being a combination of two elements. The first element is a claim about what determines meaning: Malcolm thinks that the semantics of "know" can be read off of people's speech behaviour—what they say and what they refrain from saying—in a straightforward way; in particular, he thinks that the fact that people refrain from saying "I know" in certain circumstances is very good evidence that the word "know" cannot be correctly applied in those circumstances. Second, Malcolm takes for granted that our aims in theorising should be descriptive: we are bound by what "know" means given the way we speak now, and are not in the business of trying to shape what we mean.

Both elements of Malcolm's view should be rejected. There is no simple recipe for reading off what people mean from their present speech behaviours in the way Malcolm proposed. And it can be reasonable to interpret them as having revisionary aims. The temporal externalist view to be developed in what follows rejects both, but in a way that departs from the views of Ayer, Ambrose, and Lazerowitz discussed in this chapter: according to temporal externalism, what we say or are disposed to say *now* does not determine what we mean, because what happens *later* also plays a role; we may therefore aim to change each other's views and the ways in which we are disposed to speak, and doing so need not involve changing what we mean.

The case for TE to be made in this book is that it is the best way of vindicating Conservatism about Practice. Part II defends this claim in detail. The core of this defence is in Chapters 5 and 6, where we give an account of the kinds of definition that are at issue in definitional disputes. I will argue there that adopting the temporal externalist view that the conclusions of our inquiry plays a role in determining what we meant all along can help explain how thinkers with very different views about the definition of a word (and about the phenomenon under discussion) can nonetheless use the word with the same meaning, and this is crucial to making sense of definitional disputes.

Chapter 7 discusses issues in metaphysics and epistemology raised by temporal externalism; it argues that temporal externalism is compatible with a wide range of views about the metaphysics of time, that temporal externalism raises no distinctive epistemological problems about knowing what we think and mean, and sketches an account of meaning change that is compatible with temporal externalism.

The next two chapters turn to issues of context sensitivity in language. Our focus is on disputes involving gradable adjectives such as "tall", "flat", "tasty", and "funny". Chapter 8 develops a general framework for thinking about these issues, and argues against familiar accounts of what is going on in such disputes (including the relativist views of Richard, 2008; MacFarlane, 2014; Egan, 2010). Chapter 9 develops the temporal externalist alternative, focusing on explaining putative data about disputes about taste, including that such disputes involve a kind of "faultless disagreement".

Chapter 10 discusses a number of choice points for temporal externalist views. Temporal externalism says that future facts play a role in determining what we mean; but this leaves many open questions about which future facts matter, what they matter to, and exactly what role they play.

PART I
CONSERVATISM ABOUT PRACTICE AND MEANING SAMENESS

2
Verbal Dispute and Metalinguistic Negotiation

Chapter 1 considered a variety of disputes, including one about the nature of art. To return to the example introduced there, let's suppose that you say (referring to some conceptual "artworks"): "These things are just awful. Isn't art supposed to be beautiful? Surely these things aren't really *art*." I reply: "Plenty of famous artworks are not intended to be beautiful. These works are part of an important cultural tradition—the tradition that is represented in museums, galleries, discussed by critics, and so on—and that is all it takes to be art."

What is going on in a dispute like this? Part of what is at issue seems to be the meaning of the word "art"; and many philosophers have defended the idea that participants in definitional disputes—including many philosophical disputes—are fundamentally defending views about how we ought to use words. This is the Ayer/Ambrose/Lazerowitz view discussed in Chapter 1; in the contemporary literature, the idea is sometimes called *metalinguistic negotiation* (Plunkett and Sundell, 2013; Thomasson, 2016; Belleri, 2017).

The aim of this chapter is to develop this view, and to show that it cannot be correct. I begin (in Section 1) by giving an initial characterisation of metalinguistic negotiation before developing a more precise account, which distinguishes metalinguistic negotiation from other forms of verbal dispute, in Section 2. In Sections 3 and 4, I present two arguments that show that typical definitional disputes are not instances of metalinguistic negotiation.

1. Are Definitional Disputes about Words?

There are a number of ways in which the metalinguistic negotiation view can be developed. One view would adopt something in the spirit of Malcolm's epistemology of semantics, according to which what we mean can be read of off our speech behaviour in a straightforward way. On this view, the fact that you are inclined to say "Art is supposed to be beautiful" is good evidence that you are using the word "art" in such a way that it is correctly applied to things only if they are created with certain aesthetic intentions; and similarly, the fact that I am inclined to say "Art is the product of a certain cultural tradition" is good evidence that I am using the word "art" in such a way that it is correctly applied to things only if they are the products of a particular cultural tradition. (The view need not adopt Malcolm's idea that the facts about when we refrain from calling things "art" is good evidence.) This entails that we mean different things by our words; both our utterances are true, and what you say is consistent with what I say. Why then do we dispute? What could be at issue between us? One natural answer takes on board the Gricean insight that there are a variety of reasons that we might say the things we do. And it supposes that what we are trying to do in these cases is to communicate something about how we think we ought to speak. We disagree about how we ought to use the word "art", or what "art" ought to mean; that is what our dispute is primarily about.[1]

An alternative way of developing the metalinguistic negotiation view takes the relation between what we say and meaning to be somewhat less direct; on this view, there is a single communal meaning shared by all parties to the dispute. This means that at most one of us could be speaking truly; at least one of our utterances could not possibly be correct, given what "art" means. Let's suppose for the sake of discussion that you are right, and I am wrong. Then my position is not unlike the position Ambrose and Lazerowitz take Bradley to be in: I am saying something that is false, and that (assuming at least that I am in a position to know the meanings of my words) I ought to know to be false. How could I take this to be a cooperative contribution to the conversation? Again, one hypothesis is that I am making a proposal about what we ought to mean; I am being revisionary, trying to get you to adopt a new way of speaking, to use "art" with a new meaning.[2]

I think that both versions of the view are mistaken. But before I try to make this case, some clarification is in order: what does it mean to say that a dispute is a matter of metalinguistic negotiation, or is *about* how we should use a word?

2. Verbal Dispute and Metalinguistic Negotiation: What Is at Issue?

Plunkett and Sundell's account of metalinguistic dispute is the following: "When two speakers employ competing metalinguistic usages of a term to express a disagreement about how that term is used in the context, or how it ought to be used, we call that a metalinguistic dispute" (2021, 4). This account relies on the notion of a "metalinguistic usage", which Plunkett and Sundell characterise as follows: "A metalinguistic usage of a term is a case where that term appears to be used (not mentioned) to convey information about how that very term is or ought to be used in the context" (2021, 4). But this characterisation is unhelpful, since every assertion conveys information about how the words it employs are or

---

[1] I take this to be the view defended in Plunkett and Sundell (2013).
[2] I take this to be the view defended in Thomasson (2016).

ought to be used. If I say, "Grass is green", I am conveying the information that the word "green" is correctly applied to grass in this context; if I say, "That tree is three metres tall", I am conveying the information that "three metres tall" is correctly applied to that tree in this context; and so on. The proposal threatens to make every dispute—even about what seem to be the most ordinary empirical issues—a metalinguistic matter.

Plunkett and Sundell say more about what they have in mind in discussing an example:

> In Barker (2002)'s much-discussed example, someone asks you what counts as "tall" around here, and you reply, "Well, Feynman is tall" as you and your listener both look over at Feynman (Barker 2002). We could even imagine that Feynman just happens to be standing in front of a measuring stick.
>
> In this case, the central communicative upshot of your utterance is not new information about Feynman's height, which, after all, is mutually known by you and your listener. Rather, you've communicated information about language, and in particular, about the local height threshold for "tall". (2021, 146)

Plunkett and Sundell's idea (following Barker) is that, in this case, it makes little sense to suppose that the utterance of "Feynman is tall" primarily communicates something about Feynman's height. (After all, his height is plainly visible; what's the point in commenting on it?) Instead, they suppose, we need to think pragmatically about why the sentence is used; the "central communicative upshot" of the utterance cannot be understood purely in terms of the semantics of "Feynman is tall" but instead must be understood as saying something about how it is appropriate to use the word "tall"—roughly, how the word is typically used around here.

The problem with this characterisation is that it is no clearer than the notion of *central communicative upshot*. How can we tell what the central communicative upshot of an assertion is? Even if we find it plausible that the central communicative upshot is linguistic in Barker's case, it isn't clear what could decide what is the central communicative upshot in our dispute about art.

I suggest a different approach. Everyone agrees that one aim in typical disputes is to get people to change their verbal behaviours. The proponent of metalinguistic negotiation is pointing to the fact that there are two importantly different ways in which this aim can be achieved. In non-metalinguistic disputes, we (typically) want people to change their verbal behaviours *because they change their non-linguistic beliefs*. For example, if we are arguing about whether that tree is three metres tall, I may want you to stop saying "That tree is not three metres tall". But I will not be trying to change your views about (for example) what "tree" means. We agree that (given the context we are in) "That tree is three metres tall" means that that tree is three metres tall. What I am trying to convince you of is that that tree *is* three metres tall. Once you believe that, you will change your verbal behaviour—you will stop saying "That tree is not three metres tall"—but the change in non-linguistic belief comes first. Metalinguistic disputes are supposed to be different: in a metalinguistic negotiation, the first change is to your attitudes about how language is used. In some cases, there may be no change in non-linguistic belief; if there is a change in non-linguistic belief, it will come as a consequence of this change in attitudes about language.

Let's try to characterise the distinction between the two ways in which someone might change their verbal behaviours more precisely. Each party to a dispute will have certain aims, desires, and objectives in carrying out the dispute. If I tell you that the Queen's birthday is in April, under typical circumstances my aim is to get you to form the belief that the Queen's birthday is in April. If you disagree, and say so—you think that it is in May—under typical circumstances your aim will be to get me to give up my belief and form another. Of course, I may also want you to change the way you speak—for example, I may want you to stop saying "The Queen's birthday is in May"—but if so, my plan will be to get you to change your belief about the Queen's birthday first, and change your way of speaking because you have changed your belief. Let's say that in this case my *first aim* is to change your (non-linguistic) belief, and my *resultant aim* is to get you to change the way you talk.

The proponent of metalinguistic negotiation thinks that definitional disputes are not like this. On their view, we might share all relevant beliefs about the phenomenon you want to call "art", all relevant beliefs about the phenomenon I want to call "art", and even all relevant beliefs about how the word "art" is in fact used. In that case, the idea is, if you say, "Art is supposed to be beautiful", you are not trying to get me to believe that art is supposed to be beautiful; I believe that already. Your aim is to get me to use the word "art" in a certain way. You may also want me to change other beliefs—for example, you may want me to believe that conceptual art does not belong in the museum—but if so, your plan is to get me to change my way of speaking first, and change my belief because I have changed the way I speak (say, because I am in the habit of treating whatever I call "art" as important). Let's say that in this case your first aim is to get me to change the way I speak, and your resultant aim is to change my belief about what belongs in the museum.

In many cases, perhaps, our aims are confused; perhaps I regard myself as trying to convince you to adopt a belief even though we already agree on all relevant matters, or perhaps I have no clear conception of my aims at all (Plunkett and Sundell, 2021). So we cannot just read what a dispute is about off of those attitudes that we give voice to, or that are consciously accessible to us, in a straightforward way. Those who think that definitional disputes are a matter of metalinguistic negotiation think that we *should* be aiming to get our interlocutors to revise their linguistic practice: that's what we would do if we appreciated the situation. Let's say that any dispute of which this claim is true is a *verbal dispute*:

Verbal Dispute   A dispute is a *verbal dispute* if and only if: if the parties to the dispute were rational and understood certain facts about their circumstances (e.g., if they knew that they agree on relevant matters of fact), then they would make their first aim to convince their interlocutors to change how they talk.

The idea that typical definitional disputes are verbal disputes so characterised could be accepted by a range of theorists, including those who think that definitional disputes are "merely verbal" or "just semantic", and hence are hopelessly confused and ought to be abandoned, or ought to be pursued in a very different way than they in fact are. What distinguishes proponents of metalinguistic negotiation is that they do not advocate such methodological revision. Proponents of metalinguistic negotiation accept Conservatism about Practice. They think that the way we conduct our disputes—the arguments we give, the considerations we use to defend our positions and attack our opponents', and so on—is by and large okay; when we engage in such disputes, we tend to do things that make sense given that the reasonable thing to be trying to get our interlocutors to do is to change their ways of speaking. In short:

Metalinguistic Negotiation   Our actions in typical definitional disputes would make sense if our first aim were to convince our opponents to speak in certain ways; we act in ways that would be reasonable as attempts to achieve that aim.

I propose to understand the claim that definitional disputes are *about how to use words* as advocating the idea that they are verbal disputes as characterised above, and the claim that definitional disputes should be understood in terms of metalinguistic negotiation as advocating this idea as well as *Metalinguistic Negotiation*.

In the next section, I present a pair of arguments, one of which targets the idea that definitional disputes are about how to use words, and the other of which targets *Metalinguistic Negotiation*.

3. Definitional Disputes Are Not Verbal: The Wrong Kinds of Reasons Argument

Consider how debates about how we should talk normally proceed. If I am trying to convince you that you should talk in a certain way, I should provide considerations that support, or at least seem to support, talking in that way. For example, if I am trying to convince you not to say "ain't", I might claim that it is widely believed that people who say "ain't" are stupid or uneducated, so that if you say it you will be so regarded; if I am trying to convince you not to use "hopefully" to mean "it is to be hoped that", I might claim that this usage is likely to be misunderstood. Or I might advance other kinds of practical considerations: teachers reward children with grades and praise for adopting or giving up certain ways of speaking, and parents have been known to offer straightforward bribes of toys and cash.

Considerations of this kind are reasons to adopt a certain course of action—reasons to speak a certain way. If what is at issue in our debate about art were simply a matter of how we should define a word, one would expect the kinds of consideration we advance to be reasons to adopt a certain way of speaking. I might point out that the word "art" is commonly applied to things that are not intended to be beautiful, so that using the word differently might cause confusion or misunderstanding. I might offer you a cash bribe. If you catch me in the wrong mood, I might even threaten you with physical harm if you don't adopt my usage. And perhaps sometimes considerations like this are appropriate, at least in the sense that they bear on what is at issue in our discussion. But most of the considerations we advance in this kind of debate are quite different. Suppose I say:

(4) Surely it is possible for an artist to intend their work to be disturbing, or thought-provoking, rather than beautiful.

It does not seem that I am giving you a practical consideration that favours speaking in a certain way. I am not suggesting some benefit that would accrue to you if you apply the word "art" to certain objects. It looks much more as though I am just stating (what I take to be) a fact—something you should believe, but not something that immediately suggests any particular action.

But perhaps appearances here are misleading. After all, when I say (4), one of the conclusions you may draw is that I want us to use the word "art" in such a way that it may correctly be applied to objects that are disturbing but not beautiful; and this may give you reasons to act (if, for example, you want to help me satisfy my desires—or perhaps merely if you want us to coordinate on a common way of speaking in order to exchange information more efficiently). Isn't it possible that the point of my utterance is to convince you to speak in my way by suggesting reasons of this kind?

There are several problems with this thought. The first is that across a wide range of cases, explicit appeal to practical considerations that bear on how we should speak seems misplaced or inappropriate. Suppose, for example, I claim that if you use "art" to pick out objects that are intended to be beautiful, then people will regard you as stupid or uneducated; and suppose that it is important to you not to be regarded in this way, and justifiably so. This may be a decisive reason for you to speak in a certain way. But have I settled our debate about the nature of art? Or, to take a more egregious example, suppose the head of my department—a well-known but unscrupulous professor of aesthetics—promises great professional advantage if I use "art" to pick out objects that are part of a certain cultural tradition, and a grim future of endless administrative work if I do not. Again, this may be a decisive reason to speak a certain way. But has my department head settled the debate about art?

It seems clear that practical considerations like these do not settle a dispute about the nature of art. They are the *wrong kind of reasons*. Pascal famously argued that one should believe in God because if God exists the benefits of the belief are great. Though this is a powerful consideration in favour of adopting a certain course of action, there is an important sense in which Pascal is not giving us a reason to believe that God exists. It is a difficult matter to describe exactly what it is that Pascal's argument doesn't provide, but roughly the idea is that Pascal has given us no evidence, no information in virtue of which the existence of God seems more likely. And it seems that considerations such as being thought stupid, or getting professional advantage or disadvantage, fall clearly into the same category as Pascal's considerations. They likewise give us reason to adopt a course of action rather than evidence or information. It seems clear that considerations of this kind no more settle our debate about art than they settle the debate about whether God exists.

Some philosophers have concluded that all reasons to believe p are evidence for p (e.g., Shah, 2006; Way, 2016). But we do not need to endorse such a strong claim; it may be that in some cases there are practical reasons that are good reasons for believing (e.g., Greaves, 2013; Maguire and Woods, 2020, and see Chapter 3, Section 5 for further discussion). But it seems clear in other cases (like Pascal's) that particular practical reasons do not decide a question of what to believe. And this is the case with the definitional disputes we are considering: the practical reasons that bear on how to speak do not settle what to believe in definitional disputes. In short, the argument runs as follows:

The Wrong Kinds of Reason Argument

Premise 1 If definitional disputes are verbal—about how to use words—then the considerations that would settle definitional disputes are the same considerations that would settle disputes about how to use words.

Premise 2 In most cases, the considerations that would settle disputes about how to use words do not settle definitional disputes. (They are the wrong kinds of reason.)

Conclusion Therefore, in most cases, definitional disputes are not verbal; they are not about how to use words.

Now it might be objected here that practical considerations, even weighty ones, do not settle every debate about what to do. For example, the head of my department might offer me relief from administrative work if I murder the Dean: a weighty practical reason to be sure, but not one that should make me decide to do it. Analogously, we might doubt that relief from administrative work can settle the question about the definition of art, even if that is just a question of how to speak.[3]

The objection fails for at least two reasons. First, it seems clear that in the murder case, the potential relief from administrative work is a reason to act—a consideration that favours murder. It's just that other, far more powerful considerations speak against murder, so that all things considered, I shouldn't murder. The art case is different. It's not that relief from administrative work is a factor that bears on whether or not *Shoot* is art, but is outweighed by countervailing factors. Relief from administrative work just doesn't bear on the issue at all; it is irrelevant. Second, in a wide range of cases, relief from administrative work is a decisive reason to adopt particular ways of speaking; I would gladly use "art" in the way my colleague prefers in exchange for relief from administrative work. But even if I changed my way of speaking, I would not take this to settle the issue about the nature of art.

I conclude that typical definitional disputes are not verbal. Perhaps some definitional disputes really are about what we should mean, how we should use words. But most are not.

4. Definitional Disputes Are Not Metalinguistic Negotiations: The Argument Argument

The Wrong Kinds of Reason Argument tells against the idea that definitional disputes are verbal disputes. Since the claim that definitional disputes are metalinguistic negotiations entails that they are verbal disputes, we have significant reason to doubt that definitional disputes are metalinguistic negotiations. But it is also possible to target the claim that definitional disputes are metalinguistic negotiations more directly. The proponent of this claim maintains that definitional disputes are verbal disputes, but also maintains Conservatism about Practice. This section argues that these claims are incompatible: if definitional disputes are verbal, then the ways we engage in definitional disputes are generally ill-suited to our aims.

Consider my assertion of (4).

(4) Surely it is possible for an artist to intend their work to be disturbing, or thought-provoking, rather than beautiful.

On the assumption that this is an assertion one might make in a dispute about art, then *Metalinguistic Negotiation* predicts that it is reasonable. The assertion is

---

[3] Thanks to Nate Charlow for discussion of this point.

reasonable only if it is reasonable for me to think that there is some chance that it will promote my aim—that is to say, some chance that it will make you change your usage. This could be so under certain circumstances. For example, if I am an authority (either on art, or on lexicography) and you are a novice, my assertion would make sense: it would be reasonable for me to think that my utterance might inform you of how others use the word, and that you might have reasons (being understood, being clear, fitting in) to conform to how others use the word.

But suppose our debate is like this: we are both just folks; neither is an authority on art, still less an authority on lexicography. You have already made clear your view: you think that "art" should be applied to all and only those objects that are made to be beautiful. And you have made clear that you do not accept my incompatible proposal. Now I say (4). What should I expect the result to be?

I submit that it would not be reasonable for me to expect this utterance to change your usage. For what reason have I given you to do so? By hypothesis, I am not giving you any information about ordinary or expert usage; I have no more information than you about these matters. You are already familiar with my usage, and you have made it clear that you are not going to conform to it without some further reason. And it is hard to construe what I have said as giving you any such reason.

It is tempting to think that I might be trying to influence your usage indirectly by first changing your beliefs about art. (If I can convince you that art can be disturbing rather than beautiful, then if you agree that "art" picks out art, you should also agree that "art" can be applied to things that are disturbing rather than beautiful.) But though this thought is correct if definitional dispute is not about how to speak, it is not available to the proponent of *Metalinguistic Negotiation*, since to accept it is to give up on the idea that our dispute is verbal. If our dispute is verbal, then (according to *Verbal Dispute*), if I appreciated the situation, my first aim would be to change the way my interlocutor talks, and any further change in belief would be a result of this change. To accept the idea that we must first change non-linguistic beliefs is just to abandon this claim.

Perhaps the best that the proponent of *Metalinguistic Negotiation* can do is to claim that our arguments, too, should be interpreted metalinguistically. For example, if I say something like (4), I should be interpreted as putting forward something like the following claim:

(5) We should use the word "art" in such a way that that word is correctly applied to certain works that are created to be disturbing rather than beautiful.

Since (5) is inconsistent with your view about how "art" ought to be used, defending (5) would be a reasonable thing for me to try to do. But there are at least two problems with this way of understanding the argumentative moves in typical metalinguistic disputes. First, it is not clear why I would expect my opponent to accept (5). (5) is very close to the position that you deny; asserting (5) is uncomfortably close to begging the question against your position. Second, even if convincing you of the truth of (5) would be one way to get you to change the way you use the word "art", it isn't a particularly good way. In typical cases, you would be much more likely to change your usage if given some good practical reason to do so. (The bribes and threats that we have already discussed are one kind of example, but a wide range of normative or prudential considerations are likely to be more persuasive then the bare claim that you should.)

In short, then, the argument against *Metalinguistic Negotiation* is this:

The Argument Argument

Premise 1 If *Metalinguistic Negotiation* is true, then the ways we typically argue in definitional disputes are (in most cases) reasonable ways to achieve the goal of getting our interlocutors to change the way they speak.

Premise 2 In most definitional disputes, most of the considerations we raise provide our interlocutors no clear reason to change the way they speak.

Conclusion Therefore, in most cases, *Metalinguistic Negotiation* is not true.[4]

The argument generalises: across a wide range of definitional disputes, the majority of the conderations we advance will be facts that provide no clear reason to change the way we speak—unless it is by first changing our non-linguistic belief. The argumentative strategies we adopt are simply not effective if they are to be understood as serving the aim of changing how our interlocutors talk.

5. Conclusion

Proponents of the idea that definitional disputes are metalinguistic negotiations suggest that Conservatism about Practice can be maintained by denying Meaning Sameness, and adopting a pragmatic reinterpretation on which at least some parties to definitional disputes aim (or should aim) at changing what we mean. This chapter has argued that typical definitional disputes are not metalinguistic negotiations. We are therefore left with two options: reject Meaning Sameness and also Conservatism about Practice, and defend some alternative way to engage in definitional disputes; or defend Conservatism about Practice and Meaning Sameness together. In the next chapter, we consider and reject a leading defence of the former option: the idea that there is a distinctive methodology of 'conceptual engineering' that will address definitional disputes in a way that may result in change of meaning.

---

[4] I develop this argument in more detail in Ball (2020c).

3
Conceptual Engineering: Ambitious or Anodyne?

Chapter 2 argued that definitional disputes are not verbal disputes. The key argument was this:

The Wrong Kinds of Reason Argument

Premise 1 If definitional disputes are verbal—about how to use words—then the considerations that would settle definitional disputes are the same considerations that would settle disputes about how to use words.

Premise 2 In most cases, the considerations that would settle disputes about how to use words do not settle definitional disputes. (They are the wrong kinds of reason.)

Conclusion Therefore, in most cases, definitional disputes are not verbal; they are not about how to use words.

The argument does not explicitly include Conservatism about Practice as a premise. But someone who denied Conservatism about Practice might object that Premise 2 of the argument is false. Although it typically seems to us that the kinds of practical considerations that settle disputes about how to use words do not settle definitional disputes, this is because we are confused about what is at issue in definitional disputes. If we were to understand what is really going on, we would take the practical considerations that settle disputes about how to use words to settle definitional disputes. And so we ought to reform our practice; we ought to stop carrying out definitional disputes in the same old way, and develop a new methodology.

A number of contemporary philosophers have combined the idea that we ought to adopt a revisionary stance towards methodology with the idea that we ought to aim to promote changes to the way we speak and the meanings of our words. On their view, we ought to focus our attention on developing or "engineering" novel meanings or concepts. One prominent advocate of this view, Herman Cappelen, suggests that this *conceptual engineering*—the project of "assess[ing] and improv[ing] our representational devices" (Cappelen, 2018, 148)—should be regarded as "one of the central topics of philosophy, or perhaps even *the* central topic of philosophy" (Cappelen, 2018, ix).

Cappelen is methodologically revisionary; he is suggesting conceptual engineering as a *novel* and *distinctive* methodology, something that we should do when we are engaged in definitional disputes *in addition* to familiar theoretical activities such as gathering and assessing evidence. And Cappelen conceives of the kind of improvement of representational devices that he is interested in as involving meaning change. (So he rejects Meaning Sameness.)

Let's call the view that conceptual engineering is a novel and distinctive methodology that involves meaning change *ambitious conceptual engineering*. One might accept much of what Cappelen says in a more methodologically conservative spirit. A view of this kind might maintain that there is a sense in which the kinds of theoretical activities that we already engage in—gathering and assessing evidence, drawing inferences, and so on—are or involve assessing and improving representational devices; and that this kind of improvement need not require or involve meaning change. Call this view *anodyne conceptual engineering*.

The aim of this chapter is to show that amibitious conceptual engineering is false. There is no such disinctive activity. I begin my justification of this claim by discussing Cappelen's arguments for the importance of conceptual engineering. I will then (in Section 2) present a familiar metasemantic view—the Ramsey/Carnap/Lewis view of the meaning of theoretical terms—and show that, on that view, there is no room for ambitious conceptual engineering. Section 3 discusses the features of the Ramsey/Carnap/Lewis view that generate this result. In Section 4, I show that the version of temporal externalism that I defend shares these features. Section 5 addresses a further motivation for ambitious conceptual engineering: the idea that there are cases or examples of interesting ambitious conceptual engineering projects in the literature; I explain the temptation to describe cases in this way as a result of mistaken views about metasemantics.

1. Cappelen's Master Argument

The following is Cappelen's "Master Argument" "for why conceptual engineering is important for all parts of philosophy (and, more generally, all inquiry)" (2020, 132):

1. If W is a word that has a meaning M, then there are many similar meanings, $M_1, M_2, \ldots, M_n$, W could have.
2. We have no good reason to think that the meaning that W ended up with is the best meaning W could have: there will typically be indefinitely many alternative meanings that would be better meanings for W.
3. When we speak, think, and theorise it's important to make sure our words have as good meanings as possible.

4. As a corollary: when doing philosophy, we should try to find good meanings for core philosophical terms and they will typically not be the meanings those words as a matter of fact have.
5. So no matter what topic a philosopher is concerned with, she should assess and ameliorate the meanings of central terms. (Cappelen, 2020, 134)

The argument is closely related to what Cappelen (elsewhere) calls "the Prudential Argument"; there he refers to *the Revisionist's Basic Assumption*, which is in effect a version of Premise 2: "The terms or concepts which we use to talk and think about a particular subject matter can be defective and can be improved to address these defects" (Cappelen, 2018, 39). The Prudential Argument has it that if the Revisionist's Basic Assumption is true, we ought to assess and ameliorate the meanings of our words. My response to the Master Argument will be applicable to the Prudential Argument as well: I admit that the Revisionist's Basic Assumption is true, but deny that this entails that there is a distinctive activity—assessing and ameliorating the meanings of our words—that we ought to engage in. There is no such activity.

Of course, there may be various ways in which facts about our representational devices are significant to our theorising. (The development of suitable notation by Frege and others was crucial to the development of logic since the nineteenth century; the development of Braille has played an important role in theorising for many thousands of people.) But these are not the kinds of facts that Cappelen and other proponents of ambitious conceptual engineering have in mind. First, in at least the vast majority of cases, these kinds of facts are not especially relevant to definitional disputes. (There is not even prima facie a path to resolving questions about the definition of art by developing a new notation.) Second, Cappelen's focus is on the evaluation of *meanings* (rather than, for example, notations). The view to be defended in this chapter, then, is that there is no such activity as evaluating meanings which bears on the resolution of definitional disputes.

Let me anticipate where I think the Master Argument goes wrong. I grant that Premise 1 is true, and I also think that Premise 2 is true (although there is some need for care about exactly what it would be for one meaning to be "better" than another). The problem, in my view, is with Premise 3. In order to be clear about what is wrong with Premise 3, we need to say more about how Cappelen and others understand the process of "try[ing] to find good meanings" or "assess[ing] and ameliorat[ing] the meanings of central terms".

Cappelen speaks of the meanings of words, while other self-described conceptual engineers couch their theories in more mentalistic language—the language of concepts. In order to avoid any controversies here, it will be useful to have some neutral terminology. Let's say that all of the mental representations that constitute our beliefs (and knowledge), and all of the sentences that we sincerely assert or are disposed to sincerely assert, constitute our *full theory of how the world is*. It is controversial whether we ought to believe our best theories in science and in other areas of inquiry (e.g., van Fraassen, 1980); some maintain that accepting a theory may involve a weaker commitment than belief. If that is so, let our full theory of how the world is include those representations and sentences which we accept.

In what follows, when we speak of our *theories*, this should be understood as our full theories of how the world is.

Everyone agrees that we evaluate and revise our theories: we consider and weigh our evidence (what position does the evidence we have support and why?), seek out new evidence (how can we test our view?), formulate new theories, and so on. We may also evaluate our theories on various practical or normative grounds: one theory may be simpler than another; one theory may involve a racist presupposition or lead to morally problematic conclusions.

Of course, there are many difficult issues about the evaluation and revision of our theories: In what does our evidence consist? Exactly what role do (or should) pragmatic and normative considerations have in our evaluation of our beliefs? These are the subject matter of epistemology and the philosophy of science. We cannot address these issues here; I will take it that we have a reasonably good working grasp of the kinds of activities that we engage in in the course of theorising, and that there is wide agreement about a range of core cases, even if there is disagreement about some peripheral cases and about the correct theoretical description of the cases and our activities.

When Cappelen says that "it's important to make sure our words have as good meanings as possible", and "we should try to find good meanings", he does not simply have these theoretical activities in mind. Cappelen is aiming to defend a claim that he thinks some will reject, or at least find surprising. When Cappelen is suggesting that we need to "make sure our words have as good meanings as possible" and "try to find good meanings", he is suggesting some novel activity, something over and above assessing our beliefs in light of evidence and the like. Otherwise, he would merely be advocating that we go on doing what everyone already agrees that we do.

In short, Cappelen should be understood as endorsing the following claim:

Distinctness Conceptual engineering—the process of assessing concepts and word meanings—is something distinct from theorising. It may involve such activities as seeking out and weighing evidence, but it must include something that goes beyond this.

In the terminology above, Cappelen is aiming to defend *ambitious* (rather than anodyne) conceptual engineering.

With this in mind, let's turn our attention back to the Master Argument. Given Distinctness, (3) must be read in something like the following way:

3+Distinctness   When we speak, think, and theorise, there is an additional activity (over and above theorising and the familiar kinds of speaking and thinking that contribute to theorising) that it's important to engage in: we have to make sure our words have as good meanings as possible.

I deny that there is any such further activity. When we are engaging in definitional disputes, we evaluate our theories and our beliefs; we try to determine which are true and false, which are supported by the evidence, which are right and which are wrong. Once we have done that, there is just nothing further to do—no further way to assess meanings.

Similar remarks apply to (4) and (5): if "trying to find good meanings for core philosophical terms" and "assess[ing] and ameliorat[ing] the meanings of central terms" are understood as engaging in some further activity, additional to theorising, that is apt to resolve definitional disputes, then (4) and (5) are false.

Why do I think these things? They follow from a wide range of plausible metasemantic views, including the view to be defended in this book. In order to illustrate this, I will first turn my attention to a familiar metasemantic story that shares some features with my preferred form of temporal externalism: the Ramsey-Carnap-Lewis (RCL) view of theoretical terms. To be clear, I do not myself endorse the RCL view. I am appealing to the view here for two reasons: first, it is easy to show that if the RCL view is correct, then Distinctness is false, and second, the feature of RCL in virtue of which it is incompatible with Distinctness is shared by the temporal externalist account of definitional disputes that this book goes on to defend.

2. Ramsey-Carnap-Lewis Metasemantics

In his classic "How to Define Theoretical Terms" (1970b), David Lewis described how theories can be seen as determining the meaning of the theoretical terms they contain. Lewis's proposal is meant to apply to terms that are "introduced by a given theory T at a given stage in the history of science" (1970b, 428)—this is what Lewis means by "theoretical terms". Lewis's view is inspired by earlier work by Rudolf Carnap and Frank Ramsey, and the view is sometimes called the Ramsey-Carnap-Lewis view (RCL).

I introduced above a technical sense of the word "theory", according to which a theory encompasses everything we believe and accept. It would be possible to develop a view on which all of our attitudes play a role in determining meaning. (This would be a *holist* view; see Chapter 10, Section 7 for more discussion.) This was not Lewis's proposal; he claimed that only the core elements of a theory—what he called *platitudes*—play a role in determining meaning (Lewis, 1972). With this in mind, consider the following set of platitudes:[1]

Platitudes 1 Midi-chlorians are a species of sentient and microscopic organisms that inhabit the cells of every life form. The Force is an all-encompassing energy field. Midi-chlorians create the Force.

Most of the vocabulary of this set of platitudes is familiar—"sentient", "microscopic", etc.—and we will take it that the meanings of these familiar expressions are not determined by this theory. The expressions that are unique to this theory are "midi-chlorians" and "the Force"; let's suppose that those terms are introduced by the platitudes in such a way that that Lewis's metasemantic proposal should be understood as applying to them.

A key insight of RCL is that the meanings of various terms are interrelated. One might attempt to define "midi-chlorian" as "the species of sentient and microscopic organisms that inhabit the cells of every life form, which create the all-encompassing energy field known as the Force"; but that would only work if one had already defined "the Force". RCL shows how to work around this issue. First, one replaces all of the theoretical terms with variables:

(6) x_1 are a species of sentient and microscopic organisms that inhabit the cells of every life form. x_2 is an all-encompassing energy field. x_1 creates x_2.

Second, one binds the variables with existential quantifiers:

(7) There is a unique x_1 and a unique x_2 such that: (x_1 are a species of sentient and microscopic organisms that inhabit the cells of every life form) and (x_2 is an all-encompassing energy field) and (x_1 creates x_2).

The result is a sentence with much the same significance as the original theory, but which contains no theoretical terms. And this sentence can be used to define the terms of the original theory:

(8) *The Force* = the unique x_2 such that there is a unique x_1 such that: (x_1 are a species of sentient and microscopic organisms that inhabit the cells of every life form) and (x_2 is an all-encompassing energy field) and (x_1 creates x_2);

---

[1] Adapted from https://starwars.fandom.com/wiki/Midi-chlorian.

or, if nothing uniquely satisfies the description, then "The Force" denotes nothing.

Crucially, Lewis's idea isn't to give a method that we might choose to use to stipulatively define theoretical terms. He thinks that the meaning of theoretical terms just is given by the platitudes in which they appear. He therefore sees the RCL method as descriptive—as providing a way of stating explicitly the meanings that such terms already have.

Let's suppose that this is right. Then it might seem that theoretical terms are ripe for ambitious conceptual engineering. For if RCL is right, then theoretical terms will be implicated in a range of claims stemming from the platitudes; for example, sentences like "If the Force exists, then the Force is all-pervasive". And we might worry about this consequence. For example, we might advocate a view on which "The Force exists and is merely widespread (not all-pervasive)" is true; but such a view would be ruled out by definition given (8).

Given RCL, a successful defence of "The Force exists and is merely widespread (not all-pervasive)" will involve changing the meaning of "The Force". For example, we might abandon (8) in favour of:

(9) The Force = the unique x_2 such that there is a unique x_1 such that: (x_1 are a species of sentient and microscopic organisms that inhabit the cells of every life form) and (x_2 is a widespread energy field) and (x_1 creates x_2); or, if nothing uniquely satisfies the description, then "The Force" denotes nothing.

But given RCL, to adopt (9) would be to abandon *Platitudes 1* in favour of *Platitudes 2*:

Platitudes 2 Midi-chlorians are a species of sentient and microscopic organisms that inhabit the cells of every life form. The Force is a widespread energy field. Midi-chlorians create the Force.

Of course, we might debate which of these sets of platitudes is to be preferred: for example, we might look to the evidence. But this is a matter of theorising. The attempt to do conceptual engineering just resulted in further theoretical activity. This violates Distinctness: there is no activity here over and above theorising. When we try to propose a new meaning or concept, there is nothing for us to do but to evaluate the competing theories in familiar ways. If there is conceptual engineering here, it is anodyne.

Is there some other way we could assess or improve the meanings of our theoretical terms, given RCL? It's hard to see what it could be. Given RCL, differences in meaning are determined by differences in theory. It is not as though we could have the right theory, but the words in which the theory is couched have the wrong meanings. Once we get the theory right, the meanings will take care of themselves.

Therefore, if RCL is true, then *3+Distinctness* is false. Given RCL, there is only theorising; there is no independent activity of conceptual engineering (for theoretical terms).

3. The Appropriateness of Meaning to Theory

What is the source of the conflict between RCL and ambitious conceptual engineering?

Much of Cappelen's own discussion is focused on objections that rely on the idea that we cannot control the meanings of our words. As Cappelen observes, externalist metasemantics—the view that meaning is determined in part by facts about our environment, potentially at least outside of our control—poses a challenge to the view that we can attempt to change what we mean and be very certain of our prospects of success. Cappelen (2018, 75) has several lines of response to this worry; among other things, he points out that we often engage in normative theorising about matters we cannot control. (I might, for example, judge that we must greatly reduce carbon emissions, without having any clear idea about how to bring it about that we greatly reduce carbon emissions.) In these cases, our normative conclusions are of independent interest; why not too our normative conclusions about concepts? In short, Cappelen maintains that assessing our words and concepts would be of interest even if we cannot improve them.

I think that Cappelen is correct about this: we are often interested in normatively evaluating things that are or may be outside our control, and there is nothing obviously problematic about this. So control is not the issue. Rather, the issue derived from Distinctness. To a first approximation, the issue is that given RCL, there is nothing to do but theorise. To imagine a different concept just is to imagine a different theory; to compare concepts just is to compare theories. This is so because of two features of RCL. First, according to RCL, *what one means is determined by one's theory*. Second, according to RCL, *what one means fits with one's theory*, so that there is no possibility that one would have the "wrong" meaning for a theory: meanings are determined by theory in a way that is perfectly suited to the theory. Of course, one might have a bad theory; and bad theories will produce problematic meanings—in particular, the theoretical terms of a false theory will fail to refer. But the only way to remedy this is to change or replace the theory.

Let's consider these two features of RCL in more detail. Call the first feature *Determination of Meaning by Theory*.

Determination of Meaning by Theory To use a word with a particular meaning just is to accept a certain theory. There can be no difference in meaning without a difference in theory—in one's beliefs, judgements, or acceptances.

Determination of Meaning by Theory is not in itself sufficient to motivate an argument against ambitious conceptual engineering. This is because Determination of Meaning by Theory does not say exactly how meaning is determined. In principle, it might be that one's otherwise apparently reasonable theory determines really problematic meanings; for example, we can imagine a (bizarre and implausible) metasemantic view according to which accepting Platitudes 1 makes it the case that "the Force" is correctly applied to all and only red things. If that were the case, then someone might look for a theory that does not have this undesirable result (and this might count as a kind of conceptual engineering, independent of theorising as it is ordinarily conceived). So Determination of Meaning by Theory alone does not make ambitious conceptual engineering impossible.

But RCL does not result in bizarre determinations of meaning. It determines meanings that are appropriate to our theories—meanings that make sense, that are (at least roughly) the sorts of meanings that we would expect. I want to suggest that a metasemantic theory will make trouble for the possibility of ambitious conceptual engineering if it obeys Appropriateness:

Appropriateness Meaning is determined in a way appropriate to the theory.

It is hard to give a more substantive characterisation of what it takes for a way of determining meaning to be appropriate. We do not want to insist that the meanings are determined in such a way as to guarantee that the theory is true; some theories are false. To a first approximation, we want meanings to be such as to make the theory true when it ought to be true. Given Appropriateness, a theory cannot end up with meanings that are "wrong", that don't fit with its claims. Different theorists might disagree about how to fill in the details; I take the intuitive idea to be clear enough to work with.

Any theory that includes Appropriateness will produce arguments to the effect that conceptual engineering, construed as an activity distinct from theorising, is impossible. The argument will proceed as follows. Suppose meaning is determined by theory, and suppose one is dissatisfied with some aspect of one's vocabulary or conceptual apparatus. Then either this dissatisfaction is due to a problem with the theory (e.g., it is false), or it is due to inappropriateness; although there is nothing wrong with the theory, the words that compose or are used to express it have meanings that are inappropriate. The latter case is ruled out by Appropriateness. But in the former case, the right response is to modify or replace the theory; nothing over and above theorising, and hence no ambitious conceptual engineering.[2]

4. RCL and TE

I don't myself think that RCL is correct. In order to complete the case against ambitious conceptual engineering, I need to show that the temporal externalist metasemantic view to be defended in Part II of this book can be used to develop an a version of the argument from Appropriateness in the previous section. Doing this will require anticipating some of the discussion to come. Although the discussion in this section is self-standing, readers may wish to return to it after having read Chapter 6.

The crucial difference between RCL and the variety of temporal externalism defended here is that RCL maintains that the meaning-determination relation is synchronic: what one means at any time is determined by the theory that one accepts at that very time. Temporal externalism maintains that the meaning-determination is diachronic: what one means at a given time is determined by the theory that one accepts at a later time.

It would be possible to develop diachronic views that violate Appropriateness. For example, Lewis discusses a possible combination of RCL and a Kripke-style causal theory of meaning:

> According to this position, we may be unable to discover the meanings of theoretical terms at a given time just by looking into the minds of the most competent language-users at that time. We will need to look at the past episodes of theory-proposing in which those terms were first introduced into their language. The working physicist is the expert on electrons; but the historian of physics knows more than he about the meaning of "electron", and hence about which things could truly have been called electrons if the facts had been different.
> (Lewis, 1970b, 446)

---

[2] There is one further moving part that could in principle offer the ambitious conceptual engineer some comfort. We noted that Lewis does not think that it is entire theories that determine meaning; a part of the theory, the platitudes, do that work. In principle, theorists might share a theory but disagree about which elements of that theory are, or should be, platitudes. And in principle, the ambitious conceptual engineer might consider the effects of considering different parts of a theory to be the platitudes. I set this possibility aside for two reasons: first, it is not clear that we are in control of which parts of the theory are platitudes, and even though Cappelen is right that we can normatively assess or evaluate things outside of our control, many ambitious conceptual engineers do want to implement their proposals; and second, it is not clear why anyone would want to change the platitudes while keeping the content of the theory exactly the same. (Plausibly, this is part of what is at issue in Richard's (2020) discussion of Haslanger (2012): Richard asks in effect what is gained by convincing someone that a particular claim is a platitude (in the sense at issue here) or an element of a definition, in contrast to merely convincing them that the claim is true.)

A naive version of this view would violate Appropriateness (with respect to our best current physics): J. J. Thompson's initial theory of the electron contained many elements that we now regard as false; hence applying the procedure described above would produce a description that nothing satisfies; hence the most straightforward version of the view predicts that "electron" as we use it now fails to refer, and thus much of physics consists of false or meaningless claims.[3]

Temporal externalism is a diachronic view; it differs from the Kripke-style view in that it looks to the future rather than the past. This difference makes a difference: the version of the view defended here does not violate Appropriateness in most cases. For example, consider again the dispute about conceptual art: I say, "So-called 'conceptual art' is not really art", and you disagree. If we mean the same thing by "art", then there is no way of making both of our theories true. But this does not entail that we violate Appropriateness; Appropriateness says only that we need to make theories true *when they ought to be true*—and as long as we are disputing (not agreeing that our dispute is merely verbal), no party to the debate thinks that both of our theories are true. All parties to the debate agree that we should look to vindicate only one of them; we disagree only about which one should be vindicated.

The temporal externalist maintains that if we arrive at the view that so-called "conceptual art" is indeed art, that goes towards making it the case that the word "art" is correctly applied to conceptual art; and likewise if we arrive at the view that so-called "conceptual art" is not really art, that goes towards making it the case that "art" is not correctly applied to conceptual art. In either case, all parties to the dispute will regard the meaning of "art" as appropriate to the theory that they have arrived at. That is, the version of TE that I defend will support the idea that meanings will be determined by the theories that we arrive at at the end of a debate and appropriate to those theories.

Of course, in cases where we change our view, TE may make our meanings inappropriate to theories that we hold at earlier times. For example, if on Tuesday I think that so-called "conceptual art" isn't really art, but on Wednesday I become convinced that conceptual art is in fact art (and this conviction is settled and suitably shared by my linguistic community), then the meaning of "art" is inappropriate to the theory I held on Tuesday. But it certainly does not follow from this that I ought to be engaging in some activity distinct from theorising to fix the problem. On the contrary: the inappropriateness of the meaning of "art" to my Tuesday theory is created because I adopted a new theory. And adopting the new theory solves the problem. To imagine different meanings for the word

---

[3] Lewis attempts to avoid this consequence by letting the view be that theoretical terms refer to the "components of the nearest near-realization" (1970b, 446) of the theory. It isn't clear to me that this will yield a view that preserves Appropriateness, but in any case the details are irrelevant to our primary concerns.

"art" just is to imagine different theories of art; to evaluate the different meanings just is to evaluate different theories. There is no distinctive activity of conceptual engineering. 3+Distinctness is false, and Cappelen's master argument fails.

5. Are There Cases of Ambitious Conceptual Engineering?

This concludes our discussion of Cappelen's master argument. But Cappelen has another argumentative strategy that is worth considering independently: he points to various examples of philosophical projects as examples of (presumably ambitious) conceptual engineering projects. Among his cases are Haslanger's (2012) revisionary or "ameliorative" theorising about race and gender; Clark and Chalmers's (1998) discussion of the "extended mind" view (that one can count as believing propositions even when one's access to those propositions is mediated by external devices, such as a notebook); compatibilist views of free will; and naturalist views of value (such as that defended in Railton, 1989) that require abandoning common-sense judgements about what is valuable.

These examples have several notable features: in some cases, the proponents of various views in the debate describe themselves as assessing and improving words, concepts, or meanings; in some cases, the views advanced are highly revisionary; and in some cases, the views are motivated by normative or pragmatic considerations. I will consider each of these features in turn, and argue that none of them motivate Distinctiveness.

Self-Description
Cappelen points to the following passage, in which Clark and Chalmers respond to an objection to their "extended mind" view:

> We do not intend to debate what is standard usage; our broader point is that the notion of belief ought to be used so that Otto qualifies as having the belief in question. In all important respects, Otto's case is similar to a standard case of (non-occurrent) belief ... By using the "belief" notion in a wider way, it picks out something more akin to a natural kind. The notion becomes deeper and more unified, and is more useful in explanation.
> (Clark and Chalmers, 1998, 14, quoted in Cappelen, 2018, 10–11)

Cappelen's suggestion is that we should take seriously the idea that what Clark and Chalmers are doing is something over and above comparing theories: they are considering and weighing different possible meanings for the word "belief".

Do examples of this kind pose a challenge to the argument we are considering (on the supposition that some theory that obeys Appropriateness is true)? No. A first point is that even if it were true that some theorists think that they are engaging in a distinctive activity of conceptual engineering, it does not follow that they are in fact doing so. (Consider the traditional problem of squaring the circle—i.e., constructing a square with the same area as a given circle using compass and straightedge. It can be proved that the task is impossible, but that has not stopped many people from spending years in the attempt. Likewise the assessment of meaning: the claim is not that no one could possibly think that they were engaged in a distinctive activity of assessing meanings—that is an obvious falsehood—but rather that if anyone thinks that they are doing this, they are either just theorising or are confusedly attempting the impossible.)

In fact, on closer inspection, it does not appear that Clark and Chalmers really think that they are engaging in some distinctive activity of conceptual engineering. They are in the first instance comparing two theories: one on which a person can believe some bit of information even if their only access to that information is via some device external to their bodies, and another on which this is not the case. And their claim is that the former theory is to be preferred to the latter.

The quoted passage is answering an objection: in effect that even if it were true that the former theory is in most respects better, the result would be problematic because the meaning of the word "belief" is such that it simply cannot be correctly applied to the relation between individuals and information that is only available to them via some external device. *But note that the objection amounts to a straightforward denial of Appropriateness*: the objector is in effect saying that the meaning of "belief" is inappropriate to Clark and Chalmers's theory. If Appropriateness is true, then the objection is a non-starter: if Clark and Chalmers can convince us to adopt the theory, then the meaning of "belief" will suit the theory we adopt.

One reading of the quoted passage, then, would see it as offering a response to a theorist who denies Appropriateness. Such a theorist might think that Clark and Chalmers's view is false in virtue of the meaning of "belief". The response to such a theorist is to suggest that there is an alternative way of understanding the view—a metalinguistic way, the way of ambitious conceptual engineering. Read thus, the example is no threat to the argument developed in this chapter; it is directed at someone who denies a premise of that argument.

Plausibly, many theorists who present themselves as engaging in ambitious conceptual engineering are implicitly denying Appropriateness. I would argue that such theorists are labouring under a false metasemantic theory.

Revision

A second feature shared by most of the projects discussed by Cappelen is that they involve revision of some deeply held parts of our theories, including parts that one might antecedently have held to be analytic or matters of definition. But it is crucial to the temporal externalist view to be developed in Part II that such claims—even claims that one attempts to make matters of stipulation—can be revised in the course of theorising (see Chapter 10, Section 3). So, examples that involve revising deeply held parts of our theories do not provide evidence for a distinctive activity.

Appeal to Normative Considerations

A third feature of many of the cases discussed as examples of ambitious conceptual engineering is that they appeal to practical and normative considerations as reasons to adopt one view or another. For example, one proposal that is often discussed in this context is Haslanger's (2012) claim that we ought to adopt views of gender and race because those views would facilitate certain political ends. But there are many familiar cases in which normative considerations play various roles in our theorising. For example, feminist epistemologists and philosophers of science have argued that normative considerations play an important role in shaping (among other things) the cognitive values we want our theories to exhibit (e.g., Longino, 1994) and the kinds of questions and hypotheses we consider (e.g., Anderson, 2004). Taking these cases seriously may make us reconsider various aspects of our theoretical practice. But there is no novel, distinctive activity here.

More generally, there are a range of ways in which normative or pragmatic considerations might be relevant to inquiry that are a matter of evidence gathering and theory choice. First, normative and pragmatic considerations provide norms of theory choice. Just as we might have reason to prefer one theory to another because it is simpler—and simplicity is arguably a pragmatic matter—we might have reason to prefer one theory to another because it is morally better. Second, normative considerations might provide evidence that bears on the theoretical questions we are interested in. For example, it is quite possible to maintain that moral and even practical considerations bear on questions of the definition of art or of gender. Third, normative considerations might provide higher-order evidence. For example, if we were convinced that our views on some question were shaped by a society that is biased in some respect, that would give us reason to revisit those views, since it would give us reason to think that bias might have shaped the evidence available to us or our interpretation of that evidence.

As long as normative and practical considerations play one of these roles, there is no evidence for a novel or distinctive practice. But we have already seen that very many normative and pragmatic considerations that do not fall into one of these categories do not settle definitional disputes: they seem irrelevant, like the wrong kind of reasons (see Chapter 2, Section 3). So, there is independent reason to doubt that examining contributions to definitional disputes that appeal to normative considerations will reveal a distinctive, worthwhile activity: any such appeals are likely to be a matter of norms of theory choice or (possibly higher-order) evidence, or to fail to advance the debate.

6. Conclusion

This chapter has argued that any metasemantic theory that respects a plausible constraint—Appropriateness—will render ambitious conceptual engineering impossible. We began by contrasting ambitious conceptual engineering with another view—anodyne conceptual engineering—on which we assess and improve representational devices, but doing so is not a distinct activity.

My own view is that there is no reason to reject anodyne conceptual engineering. After all, our minds are representational devices, and (at least on one popular view) our beliefs and concepts are mental representations. Re-combining our concepts so as to replace true beliefs with false ones—or, for example, racist beliefs with anti-racist ones, and so on—constitutes an improvement in these representational devices, and so is, in the anodyne sense, conceptual engineering. But improvements of this kind need not involve meaning change. And there is no further distinctive activity to be found.

4
Why Are Paradoxes Hard?
On the Explanatory Inefficacy of Inconsistent Concepts

Chapter 3 discussed the view that conceptual engineering is a novel methodology for addressing definitional disputes. We have rejected this view. But what motivates the search for a novel methodology in the first place? Why not just take something like Conservatism about Practice for granted? Why would we be tempted to give it up?

One motivation for revisionism about practice comes from a diagnosis of why certain disputes seem interminable and intractable. In some cases, recognisably similar problems and arguments arise again and again despite our best efforts to stamp them out. It appears to many that little or no progress has been made on these problems despite (in some cases) thousands of years of effort. Relatedly, some philosophers have expressed the sense that many philosophical disputes seem "pointless" (Chalmers, 2011). It is natural for those who are drawn to a view of this kind to try to find something to do that is not just carrying on the old disputes in the old ways; they may well be motivated to methodological revision.

One prominent diagnosis of the apparent intractability of certain disputes (such as disputes about the correct resolution of paradoxes) appeals to the idea that those disputes involve *inconsistent concepts* or *inconsistent words* (Eklund, 2002, 2007; Scharp, 2013a,b; Burgess, 2006; Burgess and Burgess, 2011; Patterson, 2009).[1] (Proponents of these views disagree about exactly what it is for a concept or a word to be inconsistent, and we discuss various possibilities below.) In itself, the claim that a particular word or concept is inconsistent does not provide a solution to paradoxes or an account of which side of a dispute is correct. Instead, it is concerned to explain why we are attracted to the reasoning in the first place, and why the paradox is so hard to resolve satisfactorily.

The idea of inconsistent words and concepts is the target of this chapter. I argue that the claim that "true" or the concept of truth is inconsistent can play no important role in making sense of our engagement with paradox; on many versions of the view, the proposed explanation presupposes the very disposition

---

[1] Tarski (1933) is often taken to be the progenitor of this kind of view, though see Collins (2015) for discussion. Chihara (1979) is the inspiration for much of the contemporary literature.

that it is supposed to explain (Section 1), while other versions simply fail to explain the phenomenon (Section 2). I end by considering discussions of other hard problems, such as finding a cure for the common cold or a proof for Fermat's Last Theorem; I find a pattern of explanation of why problems are hard—such problems tend to be big, under-resourced, and evaluating potential solutions requires significant education—and argue that it fits the case of paradox well (Section 3). I conclude on this basis that our difficulties in resolving paradoxes are probably not distinctive; paradoxes are hard, but their hardness is not qualitatively different than the hardness of problems in other fields. They therefore do not motivate abandoning Conservatism about Practice.

1. Truth and Inconsistent Concepts

We know that sentences like (10) are trouble:

(10) (10) is not true.

The reasoning is, of course, familiar, but it will ease discussion to present it fairly explicitly. Suppose:

(A) (10) is true.

Now "(10)" is just a name for the sentence "(10) is not true". So (A) is equivalent to:

(B) "(10) is not true" is true.

But the following schema seems extremely plausible:

(T) $\ulcorner \phi \urcorner$ is true if and only if ϕ.

(Just consider examples: if the sentence "Snow is white" is true, then snow is white.) But by (T) and (B), we can infer:

(C) (10) is not true.

So we have reasoned from the supposition that (10) is true to the conclusion that (10) is not true. But that looks like an obvious contradiction; so our supposition must be wrong: (10) can't be true. But by similar reasoning, we can reason from the supposition that (10) is not true to the conclusion that (10) is true! So (10) can't be not true either. But it looks like (10) has to be either true or not; and since neither option seems acceptable, we have a paradox.

What is a paradox? Sainsbury gives the following account: "an apparently unacceptable conclusion derived by apparently acceptable reasoning from apparently acceptable premises" (2009, 1), and something like this thought is widely accepted. Of course, as Sainsbury goes on to point out, paradoxes so conceived "come in degrees, depending on how well appearance camouflages reality" (2009, 1). Some apparently acceptable premises can be revealed to be unacceptable given only a little thought. (Sainsbury mentions Russell's story of the barber who shaves all and only those who do not shave themselves; though the claim that there could be such a barber is apparently acceptable at a superficial glance, it doesn't take much to reach the conclusion that such a barber is in fact impossible.) But in other cases—the Liar prominent among them—we feel stuck: no resolution to the paradox seems acceptable despite our best efforts.[2] Let's call this phenomenon *hardness*:

The Hardness of Paradox   A problem is *hard* to the extent that no solution to it seems acceptable, even after much reflection, study, and debate. Paradoxes such as the Liar are characteristically hard.

So what is going on in these hard paradoxes? Why are they hard? Why do we get stuck? Sainsbury claimed that the premises that lead to the unacceptable conclusion are "apparently acceptable"; but it might be suggested that (at least in the hard cases), the premises are more than acceptable: they are extremely appealing, even compelling. We feel drawn to them, disposed to accept them. When a claim persistently attracts us in this way (so that we are persistently disposed to believe it), let's say that it exerts *pull*.[3]

Some have supposed that the fact that the premises of paradoxical reasoning exert pull constitutes an explanation of why the paradoxes are so hard:[4]

---

[2] One might very reasonably be reminded of ideas associated with Wittgenstein: paradoxes involve a kind of perplexity or puzzlement, where one isn't sure what to do, doesn't "know one's way about" (Wittgenstein, 1953, §121), caught (like the fly in the fly-bottle (Wittgenstein, 1953, §309)) in a pattern of reasoning from which one does not know how to escape; regardless of one's views of Wittgenstein's ideas about philosophy, there is something right in this as a description of the phenomenology of grappling with these issues.

[3] I adopt this terminology from Eklund (2002); it's too apt to resist. But where Eklund builds into the notion of pull the idea that our attraction to the premises is a result of linguistic or conceptual competence (2002, 252–253), I do not assume this: as I use the term, any proposition that we are persistently disposed to believe exerts pull, regardless of the aetiology of the disposition.

[4] This is most explicit in Eklund and Burgess, but also plays a role in the thinking of Chihara, Scharp, and Patterson.

The Pull Hypothesis Paradoxes are hard because we are persistently disposed to accept premises that are jointly inconsistent—that is, because jointly inconsistent premises exert pull.

The Pull Hypothesis suggests a further question: why are we disposed to accept the premises of the inconsistent reasoning? For example, why are we disposed to accept the problematic instances of (T)?

Several prominent attempts to answer these questions appeal (in somewhat different ways) to the idea that certain words or concepts—notably including the word "true" and the concept of truth—are inconsistent. Following Eklund, let's focus our attention on words. (Much the same view could be developed in terms of concepts, and for our purposes nothing much turns on whether we think that words or concepts are inconsistent; we will therefore follow other authors in speaking of *inconsistent concepts* in some of what follows.) Now one way in which a word might be inconsistent is if there is some object to which it is correctly applied and from which application is correctly withheld; for example, one way in which "true" might be inconsistent is if (10) is both true and not true. Views of this kind certainly have proponents in the literature (Priest, 2006); but the proponents of inconsistent words and concepts on which we will focus want to resist the view that we ought to endorse inconsistent claims. Instead, they want to propose a way in which a word or concept might be inconsistent that allows users of the word to be consistent.

In what follows, I consider several variations on this view, beginning with Eklund's own account, according to which pull is explained by facts about what is required in order to be competent with words like "true". I will argue that Eklund's view fails to explain the pull of paradox because the explanation it proposes is circular: it presupposes exactly what it is meant to explain.

1.1 The Competence View

On Eklund's view, competence with the word "true" requires that one be disposed to accept the premises of the paradoxical reasoning—premises like the relevant instances of (T). Someone who feels no attraction to the reasoning is thereby manifesting a lack of semantic competence (Eklund, 2002, 252). Of course, Eklund does not maintain that one must actually accept the premises of the reasoning (still less its conclusion); one can feel attraction to a given claim without succumbing to the claim's charms. So using an inconsistent word does not commit one to believing contradictions. Eklund even thinks that "true" is perfectly meaningful, and that many utterances using "true" are correct. ("That 'true' is meaningful and that some sentences are true are, as it is sometimes put, Moorean facts"

(2007, 571).) So at least for ordinary purposes the inconsistency of "true" is not a defect that necessitates replacement with something consistent.

Eklund's core claims, then, are:

1. Competence with the word "true" requires one to be disposed to accept instances of (T); and
2. (1) explains our stubborn attraction to the relevant instances of (T), even in the face of their apparent inconsistency, and hence the hardness of the Liar paradox.

To make these claims stick, Eklund needs an account of linguistic competence. His discussion focuses on the conceptual role theory, according to which to be competent with a word just is to be disposed to form certain beliefs and make certain inferences associated with that word. Conceptual role theorists have traditionally held that the relevant dispositions must be dispositions to believe truths and make truth-preserving inferences. But Eklund suggests that this is inessential: conceptual role theorists could hold that the dispositions in which competence consists could be dispositions to assert or believe falsehoods, or to make inferences that are not truth-preserving; for example, competence with "true" might require dispositions to accept every instance of (T), even though acting on these dispositions would lead to inconsistency.

1.2 The Circularity Objection

This proposal may seem to be a compelling explanation of our attraction to the paradoxical reasoning. In fact, however, it is a mere relabelling of the problem. What we wanted to explain was why we are disposed to accept the premises of the paradoxical reasoning. And the proposed explanation was: we are attracted to the premises because we are competent with the word "true". But on the described view, to be competent just is to have these dispositions; the dispositions are constitutive of competence. And that means that competence cannot explain why we have the dispositions. Given the conceptual role theory, to ask why we have the dispositions is just to ask why we are competent; and obviously *because we are competent* is no answer to this question.

In short, the problem with Eklund's suggestion is this: given the Pull Hypothesis, explaining why paradoxes are hard requires explaining the pull of premises of the paradoxical reasoning. This means that our explanatory task is the following:

Explanatory Task In order to explain why paradoxes are hard, we must explain our disposition to accept jointly inconsistent claims.

Eklund's strategy for carrying out this task is by defending the following claim:

Explanatory Strategy   We are disposed to accept jointly inconsistent claims because we are competent with inconsistent words implicated in those claims.

And his account of what it is for a word to be inconsistent is this:

Inconsistent Words   Inconsistent words are words competence with which consists (at least in part) in dispositions to accept jointly inconsistent claims.

Explanatory Strategy has it that we are disposed to accept jointly inconsistent claims because we are competent with certain words. *Inconsistent Words* has it that this competence consists in precisely the disposition to accept jointly inconsistent claims that it was supposed to explain. Spelled out explicitly, the putative explanation is clearly circular. It seems clear that we can still ask: but *why* do we have the dispositions? And it seems equally clear that we have made no real progress in providing an answer to this question.

2. Responses and Alternatives

This concludes the exposition of the basic objection to the attempted explanation of the hardness of paradox in terms of inconsistent words or concepts. In my view, even without further elaboration, the objection is compelling: once the structure of the proposed explanation is made explicit, it is clear that the explanation is problematically circular.

Still, I have found that for some people, the feeling may persist that appeals to inconsistent concepts reveal *something* explanatory. In order to dispel this feeling, I want to consider several possible responses to the circularity objection:

1. *Avoiding Circularity* It has not been established that the proposed explanation is *circular*, because it could be that the inconsistent claims alluded to in *Explanatory Task* and *Explanatory Strategy* are distinct from the inconsistent claims alluded to in *Inconsistent Words*.
2. *Clarifying the Explanation* If *Explanatory Strategy* is understood as an attempt at a causal explanation—an explanation of the form *As cause Bs*—then the resulting explanatory structure would indeed be circular. But it should not be so understood; the kind of explanation at issue here is not a causal one. (Perhaps it alludes to causation in some way, but should not be understood as simply claiming that competence with inconsistent words causes the disposition to accept the problematic claims.) Exactly how to respond to this line of thought will depend on what kind of explanation

is held to be at issue; I consider three possibilities, based on apparently similar cases in other areas of philosophy: (a) *Constitutive explanation*; (b) *Selectional explanation*; (c) *Programme explanation*.

3. *Against the Conceptual Role Account of Competence* The account is circular if we adopt Eklund's conceptual role account of competence with inconsistent words (sketched in *Inconsistent Words*). But there are alternative accounts on which the reasoning is not circular. I draw three such accounts from the literature: (a) *The Fregean account* (discussed by Eklund); (b) *The Chomskian account* (defended as an account of inconsistent concepts by Alexis Burgess and Douglas Patterson); and (c) *The Interpretative account* (defended by Kevin Scharp).

2.1 Can the Circularity Be Avoided?

Is it so clear that Eklund's view is *circular*? The view requires that we explain our disposition to believe certain inconsistent claims—the premises of the paradoxical reasoning (e.g., the relevant instances of (T)). And it also requires that competence with inconsistent words involves the disposition to accept inconsistent claims. But it does not require that the premises implicated in the paradoxical reasoning are precisely the principles that conceptual or linguistic competence requires one to be disposed to accept. For example, perhaps conceptual competence requires one to accept something distinct from the relevant instances of (T), which entails those instances.[5] If this were the case, then one could non-circularly explain our attraction to instances of (T) by appealing to our attraction to instances of some (T′).

I concede that the proposed structure is not strictly speaking circular, but two points should be made. First, the proposed explanation is extremely shallow: until we have an explanation of why we are disposed to accept (T′), we have advanced little in understanding why we are disposed to accept (T). Second, even if we have given a non-circular explanation of why one particular paradox is hard—the paradox that involves reasoning from instances of (T) to a contradiction—there is another paradox—the one that involves reasoning from the relevant instances of (T′), to (T), to a contradiction—which (presumably) will be just as hard, and the hardness of which we have not explained.

I therefore conclude that the circularity objection stands. But the next line of objection requires much more discussion.

---

[5] Thanks to Simon Hewitt for raising this possibility.

2.2 Clarifying the Explanation

The structure of Eklund's proposed explanation is something like this:

(11) (Disposition to accept inconsistent claims) explains (possession of an inconsistent word) explains (disposition to accept inconsistent claims)

That looks circular. But there are superficially similar cases in which it is reasonable to think that something genuinely explanatory is going on. For example, it is plausible that in some sense the fact that John is unmarried can play a role in partly explaining the fact that he is a bachelor. True, the fact that John is unmarried is not a causal antecedent of the fact that John is a bachelor. If we want to give a causal explanation of John's bachelorhood, we will have to allude to other kinds of facts—facts about his character and interests, or his history of romantic attachments. The fact that John is unmarried is something like a metaphysical basis or ground of the fact that he is a bachelor; to provide it is to provide a partial *constitutive explanation* of the fact that John is a bachelor. But, it also plausible that the fact that John is a bachelor can play a role in an explanation of the fact that he is unmarried. For example, it may be his bachelor lifestyle that repels potential spouses (and this looks like a causal explanation of his unmarried status).

In short, although the following structure exhibits the appearance of circularity, both of the explanations seem genuine:

(12) (The fact that John is unmarried) explains (the fact that John is a bachelor) explains (the fact that John is unmarried)

Is there a genuine circularity here, and if so, why is it unproblematic? In order to clarify discussion, let's break (12) into two parts:

(13) a. The fact that John is unmarried (*explanans 1*) constitutively explains the fact that John is a bachelor (*explanandum 1*)
b. the fact that John is a bachelor (*explanans 2*) causally explains the fact that John is unmarried (*explanandum 2*)

Our brief discussion of the case suggests two reasons to think that the proposed explanation is not genuinely circular. First, *explanandum 1 is not explanans 2*. Although we have described both using the expression 'the fact that John is a bachelor', we are using this expression to pick out different phenomena in the two cases. Explanans 2—what causally explains John's remaining unmarried—

is his lifestyle (a lifestyle characterised by (let's suppose) messiness, late-night parties, and financial irresponsibility.) But it is quite clear that the fact that John has this lifestyle is *not* constitutively explained by his being unmarried. What is constitutively explained by his being unmarried is just that he is a bachelor (full stop)—and stereotypes aside, it is possible for bachelors to have different lifestyles. In short, the explanations in (13) would be more clearly and accurately stated as follows:

(14)   a. The fact that John is unmarried (*explanans 1*) constitutively explains the fact that John is a bachelor (full stop) (*explanandum 1*)

b. the fact that John is messy, prone to late-night parties, and financially irresponsible (*explanans 2*) causally explains the fact that John is unmarried (*explanandum 2*)

And the explanations in (14) do not look circular.

Still, one might worry that the circularity has not entirely been avoided. After all, isn't it plausible that the fact that John is a bachelor plays a role in causally explaining John's lifestyle? (If he were married, his spouse would make him clean up his act.)

But there is a second reason to think that the explanation proffered in (13) and (14) are not circular: *explanans 1 is not explanandum 2*. It is plausible that (at least in this kind of case) a cause must precede its effect. So even if we can make the case that the fact that John is a bachelor causally explains the fact that John is unmarried, it must be the fact that John is a bachelor at some time t causally explains the fact that John is unmarried at a later time $t+1$. On the other hand, the constitutive explanation in question is simultaneous—the fact that John is unmarried at t constitutively explains the fact that John is a bachelor at t. With this in mind, the explanation proffered by (13) can be more clearly and accurately stated as follows:

(15)   a. The fact that John is unmarried at t (*explanans 1*) constitutively explains the fact that John is a bachelor at t (*explanandum 1*)

b. the fact that John is a bachelor at t (*explanans 2*) causally explains the fact that John is unmarried at $t+1$ (*explanandum 2*)

And again, this doesn't look circular.

Causal and Constitutive Explanation

Let's return to the Eklund-style explanation of our attraction to paradoxical reasoning. Following the example above, we can break the explanation into two parts:

(16) a. Disposition to accept inconsistent claims (*explanans 1*) explains possession of an inconsistent word (*explanandum 1*)

b. possession of an inconsistent word (*explanans 2*) explains disposition to accept inconsistent claims (*explanandum 2*)

The first thing that should be clarified is the kinds of explanation at issue. I take (16a) to be offering a constitutive explanation—in effect, it is just a statement of Eklund's definition of inconsistent words. And I take it that (16b) is not offering a constitutive explanation. The most natural suggestion is that (16b) is offering a causal explanation; I will consider this first before turning to alternative suggestions.

Following the discussion of bachelors above, we might observe that there are grounds for thinking that *explanans 1 is not explanandum 2*. As in the case of John's bachelorhood, taking into account that a cause must precede its effect, we should say: supposing that the fact that I have a disposition to accept certain claims at a time t constitutively explains my possession of an inconsistent concept at t, then my possession of an inconsistent concept at t can at most causally explain the fact that I have a disposition to accept certain claims at $t + 1$. We will therefore arrive at the following explanatory structure:

(17) a. Disposition to accept inconsistent claims at t constitutively explains possession of an inconsistent word at t

b. possession of an inconsistent word at t causally explains disposition to accept inconsistent claims at $t + 1$

Now I am happy to concede that the explanatory claims in (17) are non-circular. In fact, I think that (18) is true:

(18) Disposition to accept inconsistent claims at t causally explains disposition to accept inconsistent claims at $t + 1$

The truth of (18) is grounded in the apparent fact that once dispositions of this kind are acquired, they tend to persist; so one can (partially) explain the presence of a disposition at a later time by appealing to the presence of that disposition at an earlier time.

But neither (17) nor (18) really offers the explanation we want. In effect, we can explain why we have the disposition at one time by appealing to the fact that we have it at earlier times (and that nothing has made it go away); but what we wanted to know is how we acquired the disposition in the first place. If t_0 is the earliest time at which we have the disposition, we can explain why we have it at later times by appealing to the fact that we had it at t_0; but we need some other kind of explanation of why we have the disposition at t_0. For that, we need some other explanation, and we have as yet no clear idea what that could be.

Programme Explanation
So the idea that explanans 1 is not explanandum 2 does not put us in a position to provide a non-circular explanation of why we have the disposition to accept the premises of paradoxical reasoning in the first place. Does the idea that explanandum 1 is not explanans 2 help? Recall our discussion of John's bachelorhood; there the key idea was that the expression "the fact that John is a bachelor" could be used to call to mind certain facts about John's lifestyle, and that it was these facts that causally explain John's unmarried state. Can something similar be made plausible in the case of (16)?

In the case of John's bachelorhood, it was fairly clear what facts were doing the real causal work, and I don't see a similarly clear possibility here. (Just what causally relevant fact is called to mind by the expression "the fact that I possess an inconsistent concept"?) And without a concrete suggestion in mind, the proposal is difficult to evaluate. Still, it might be illuminating to contrast the discussion here with an issue familiar in the philosophy of mind. Our mental states causally explain our actions—for example, my desire to drink beer might cause me to go to the pub. But mental properties are not fundamental; I have the property of desiring beer in virtue of having some complex of more basic (e.g., neurobiological) properties. And well-known arguments suggest that non-fundamental properties are screened off or excluded from causal relevance (e.g., Kim, 1998). How then can mental properties be relevant to the causal explanation of actions?

One line of response—a line closely related to the suggestion that explanans 1 is not explanandum 2—is that, although it is not strictly speaking true that my having the property of desiring beer causes my actions, the property of desiring beer is systematically related to lower-level properties that cause my actions. Frank Jackson and Philip Pettit describe the idea in the following terms:

> The realization of the property ensures—it would have been enough to have made it suitably probable—that a crucial productive property is realized and, in the circumstances, that the event, under a certain description, occurs. The property-instance does not figure in the productive process leading to the event but it more or less ensures that a property-instance which is required for that process does figure. A useful metaphor for describing the role of the property is to say that its realization programs for the appearance of the productive property and, under a certain description, for the event produced. (Jackson and Pettit, 1990, 114)

Jackson and Pettit call an explanation of this kind a *programme explanation*. A programme explanation offers a causal explanation (so to speak) indirectly; to say that A programme explains B is not to say that A causes B, but rather that the presence of A ensures that there is some C that causes B.

It isn't too much of a stretch to see the kind of explanation going on in the case of John's bachelorhood. The fact that John is a bachelor itself does not figure in the productive process leading to John's future unmarried state. In this case, it doesn't even "more or less ensure" that something else causes John to remain unmarried. But (given popular stereotypes about bachelors) it makes it reasonably likely that John leads a lifestyle that causes John to remain unmarried; and in that (somewhat weakened) sense, we can think of it as a kind of programme explanation.

Jackson and Pettit also appeal to programme explanations in explaining the causal relevance of dispositional properties. They think that there is a risk that dispositional properties will be causally excluded by their categorical grounds, in much the way that high-level psychological properties risk being excluded by low-level physical properties. But they maintain that one can explain (e.g.) a certain glass's breaking by appealing to its fragility even if one maintains that only categorical properties are really causally efficacious, because something's being fragile ensures that it will have some categorical property or other that will cause it to break in the relevant circumstance.

Can something similar be said about (16b)? Competence with an inconsistent word, on Eklund's view, is or involves having a dispositional property—the property of being disposed to accept certain claims. If Jackson and Pettit are right, we can appeal to this property in programme explanations. For example, we might explain the fact that a certain person in fact believes instances of schema (T) by appeal to the fact that they are disposed to accept them; and what such an explanation would amount to is the claim that there is some categorical property or other that explains why they accept them. But we need to observe two things about this explanation. First, even if this is a kind of explanation, it is quite superficial; it is saying little more than that there must be some feature that explains why we believe the instances of (T) when we do. (One might reasonably reminded of the idea that laudanum causes sleepiness because it possesses dormitive virtue; this might count as a kind of programme explanation, but few would regard it as illuminating.)

Second, we need to be particularly attentive to the explanandum. The fact that one has a disposition to ϕ may help explain the fact that one ϕs—or so, following Jackson and Pettit, we are allowing. So the fact that one is disposed to believe a certain claim might help explain why one believes it. But what we were aiming to explain is not why we in fact believe the instances of (T)—that in itself would not explain why paradoxes are hard, because it would not explain why we cannot simply revise our beliefs—but rather why the instances of (T) are so attractive, why they have pull, why we are disposed to believe them. The problem we are focused on is that attempting to explain pull by appeal to inconsistent words or inconsistent concepts is in effect attempting to explain our disposition to believe them by appealing to our disposition to believe them. And it is not clear how appealing to programme explanation could possibly help; it is not clear how the fact that one has a disposition to ϕ (at a particular time) could explain the fact that one has a disposition to ϕ (at that time).

Selectional Explanation
I therefore see little prospect of understanding the proposed explanation of Pull and Hardness in terms of inconsistent concepts by appealing to programme explanation. But these reflections suggest one further way of understanding claims like (16b) on which they result in no problematic circularity. We are interested in paradox. But remember Sainsbury's account of paradox: "an apparently unacceptable conclusion derived by apparently acceptable reasoning from apparently acceptable premises" (2009, 1) (where it is understood that apparent acceptability comes in degrees, so that in the case of genuine, truly hard, paradoxes, the premises will continue to appear acceptable even after much investigation). Now nothing just appears acceptable simpliciter; to appear acceptable is to appear acceptable to someone. This suggests an implicit relativisation to a thinker or to a community, at a time: what appears acceptable to me now might not appear acceptable to you now or to me tomorrow. Correspondingly, what is a paradox for me now may not be a paradox for me tomorrow.

One way of construing the notion of an "apparently acceptable premise" (for x, at t) is as a premise that x is disposed to accept at t. So understood, Sainsbury's definition will entail that the premises of paradoxes exert pull. Some puzzles that may have been (for a long or short period of time) paradoxes for us in the past (such as Russell's barber) are paradoxes no longer. Their premises have ceased to exert pull on us. Those patterns of reasoning that are genuine, truly hard, paradoxes for us now will have withstood much investigation; they are the ones whose premises continue to exert pull.

It is a familiar idea from biology that selectional pressures can explain various facts about populations of organisms: we can explain why polar bears are white by appealing to the fact that having that colour contributed to survival and reproductive success in their environment. The suggestion we are considering is that paradoxes are selected for persistent pull: a pattern of reasoning retains its status as a paradox for us only so long as its premises retain their pull; hence as we work to resolve paradoxes, only those problems that continue to exert pull despite our best efforts to resolve them remain.

I think that this is a genuine, non-circular explanation of something. What has just been defended is the following claim:

(19) The fact that those patterns of reasoning that are paradoxes exert pull is explained by the fact that only those patterns of reasoning that continue to exert pull retain their status as paradoxes.

But this does not address the problem with which we began. We started out with the Liar paradox, and we wondered: why do the instances of (T) exert pull on us—that is, on particular individuals? And plausible arguments show that (at least in this kind of case) selectional explanations cannot explain why individuals have the features they do.

It may seem paradoxical that selection can explain why all paradoxes exert pull, but not why I feel the pull of particular claim. But consider the following example (due to Elliott Sober):

> Imagine that entrance to a school classroom is governed by an admission test; to get in, a student must read at the third grade level. Suppose that Sam, Aaron, Marisa, and Alexander pass the test and so are admitted, whereas other students do not pass, and so are excluded. The selection process explains why the room contains only individuals with trait F, rather than containing other individuals who lack F. However, it does not explain why Sam has trait F (rather than not-F), nor why Aaron does, and so on. A developmental story would have to be told about Sam to explain why he has F; his earlier experience and mental endowment would do the explaining. Selection explains the composition of the classroom, not the reading abilities of individual students. (Sober, 1995, 384)

Sober's claim that selection never explains the features of individuals is controversial; but putative counterexamples in the philosophy of biology always involve reproduction over generations. (For example, suppose Sam has feature F because all humans of his parents' generation have F; since the latter fact can be explained by selection, perhaps Sam's having F can be explained by selection too (Neander, 1988, 1995; Matthen, 1999).) But these cases are irrelevant to the putative explanation of paradox that we are considering. (Paradoxes do not mate.) And that case seems quite similar to Sober's classroom: even if selectional facts explain why all paradoxes exert pull, they do not explain why I feel disposed to accept some particular paradoxical claim. What is called for is (as Sober says) "a developmental story"—a story about me or my development that explains how I came by that disposition—and this is something that the inconsistent word/inconsistent concept theorist does not provide.

2.3 Against the Conceptual Role Account of Competence

I conclude that appeal to inconsistent concepts, where inconsistency is understood along the lines that Eklund suggests, cannot offer an explanation of pull, and hence cannot explain the hardness of paradox. One diagnosis of its failure would point to the conceptual role account of competence that Eklund offers. The idea is that Eklund is right to think that our competence with inconsistent words explains our attraction to paradoxical reasoning. So we may retain Explanatory Strategy.

What got us into trouble was the view of what competence with inconsistent words consists in. By replacing Eklund's view of competence—the view exemplified by Inconsistent Words—we can arrive at an explanation of pull that avoids circularity.

But with what should we replace Eklund's view? In what follows, I consider the three alternatives I am aware of in the literature: one discussed briefly by Eklund himself, one developed by Douglas Patterson and Alexis Burgess, and one developed by Kevin Scharp. I will show that each of them either fails to escape the charge of circularity, or fails to explain pull for other reasons.

The Fregean Account

Eklund mentions an alternative: "Fregean accounts of meaning", according to which expressions are associated with descriptive senses that determine their contribution to truth-conditional content. A theory of this kind will only be able to explain the phenomenon if it is associated with a theory of competence. Perhaps the obvious theory would have it that to be competent with an expression ϕ, where ϕ is associated with descriptive sense D, is to be disposed to believe that ϕ is the D (or that ϕs are Ds, or something of that kind). But this is just an instance of Eklund's original conceptual role theoretic proposal, and seems to offer no additional resources for non-circularly explaining the dispositions in which the hardness of paradox is supposed to consist.

The Chomskian Account

What Eklund would need to make the explanation work is a view of semantic competence on which competence with a word is prior to, and in no way constituted by, the relevant dispositions. Only then would we have the prospect of a non-circular explanation.

Two closely related approaches in the literature—those of Alexis Burgess and Douglas Patterson—may be construed as having the right structure. Burgess claims that "the rules governing the appropriate use of the truth predicate are inconsistent" (2006). The idea that meaning is a matter of rules is, of course, at the centre of a mass of difficult philosophical problems (Kripke, 1982), and Burgess would avoid the kinds of circularity that make Eklund's view problematic only if he has an account of how words like "true" get associated rules like (T) that does not depend on the fact that we are disposed to accept the instances of (T). But a hint as to an alternative can be found in Burgess and Burgess's remark that "Meaning can be given by rules [...] for there can be no objection to positing rules in semantics, given that linguists have been freely positing them in syntax and phonology ever since the downfall of behaviourism" (2011, 101). Patterson agrees; on his view, the idea that the hardness of paradox can be explained by appeal to the kind of psychological states postulated by syntacticians in the Chomskian tradition. Chomskian linguists maintain that linguistic competence is a matter of having a certain sort of mental representation of the *grammar* of one's language. But such representations aren't ordinary instances of belief or knowledge; they are not, for example, introspectively accessible in the way prototypical beliefs are. So Chomsky (1986) postulates a cognitive relation—*cognising*—which one bears to the grammar of one's language. Patterson's claim is that we also cognise a semantic theory that includes or entails the premises of paradoxical reasoning, such as (T) or its instances.

This view has the right structure to resist the objections to Eklund from the previous section. But even if we grant that this is the right way to understand meaning and linguistic competence, the problem with this suggestion is that it does not really explain the phenomenon of pull. The pull of paradoxical reasoning is *persistent*: even once we see the problem, we don't see our way out. Our grasp of meaning is not generally like this; we are generally much more flexible in updating our usage of words in the face of evidence. Someone may use the word "fortnight" as though it applied to a period of exactly ten days, and it makes sense to suppose that her attraction to claims like "A fortnight is ten days" could be explained by the fact that she cognises a claim to the effect that "fortnight" means *period of ten days*. But this attraction would be fleeting when she is confronted with testimony from other speakers. Once she discovers that "fortnight" is typically used to pick out periods of 14 days, the attraction of the claim that a fortnight is ten days would evaporate completely. So in general, if our understanding of linguistic meaning is a matter of what we cognise, what we cognise must be flexible: it changes in response to evidence. And likewise, if our understanding of meaning is a matter of commitment to rules, this commitment must be flexible. But this just means that appeals to what we cognise and to our commitments cannot explain pull: the phenomenon of pull is precisely that our attraction to problematic claims like the instances of (T) is inflexible and not easily abandoned.

The Interpretation Account
Kevin Scharp (2013a) develops a somewhat different view of inconsistent concepts. On Scharp's view, words and concepts are associated with *constitutive principles*. Constitutive principles guide interpretation: a principle is constitutive for a word if and only if someone's failure to accept that principle is an "interpretative red flag": prima facie reason to think that they are misunderstanding the word or using it with a different meaning. For example, if someone seems not to accept that all bachelors are married (for example, because she says "Some bachelors are married") that is a prima facie reason to think that she is not using the word "bachelor" with its ordinary meaning (and hence is not using the sentence to express the claim that some bachelors are married), or that she misunderstands or is incompetent with the word "bachelor". But (Scharp claims) it is possible that this prima facie reason is ultimately outweighed by other considerations, so that we may judge in the end that we are speaking to someone with an idiosyncratic

view about bachelorhood or marriage rather than someone with an idiosyncratic way of speaking or a linguistic misunderstanding.

Scharp claims that a word is inconsistent if and only if its constitutive principles are inconsistent. And he maintains that the hardness of paradox is explained by the inconsistency of the words involved in the paradoxical reasoning. For example, the constitutive principles for "true" include all instances of the (T), and this fact helps explain why the Liar paradox is hard. In detail, Scharp's explanation is the following: a thinker who takes all of the instances of the (T) to be constitutive for "true" will feel "compelled to either accept the instances of the [(T)] or treat herself as incompetent with 'true'" (2013a, 56). To the extent that she is unwilling to regard herself as incompetent, then, she will feel compelled to accept the instances of (T). More generally, Scharp's idea is that constitutive principles will exhibit pull because thinkers will tend to feel that if they reject the principles, then they are subject to a linguistic or conceptual misunderstanding, and hence are linguistically or conceptually incompetent.

To my mind, this is a surprising claim; it does not seem to capture the phenomenology of grappling with paradox. (It is not as though I consider rejecting certain instances of (T), find the thought plausible and attractive, think that the paradox is satisfactorily solved, and then reject the solution on the grounds that I may be becoming incompetent; that line of reasoning strikes me as bizarre.) But one would not want to rest too much on the phenomenology—in many cases, our reasoning processes are opaque to us—and in any case, there are two stronger objections to Scharp's view. First, even if we grant that words are associated with principles that aid in interpretation, it is hardly clear that we apply these principles to ourselves in the same way we apply them to others. A theorist may regard herself as perfectly linguistically and conceptually competent, while at the same time recognising that her own view is idiosyncratic in that she denies principles that others—perhaps everyone else!—take to be crucial matters of definition. Such principles may be constitutive in that they play a crucial role in interpreting others, while playing no role in the theorist's self-interpretation, and hence posing no threat to her self-conception as competent.

Here is an example: in a well-known paper, Tyler Burge (1986) imagines a theorist who maintains that sofas are not pieces of furniture made for sitting. The theorist maintains that sofas are in fact religious artefacts, and (though she admits that some sofas have been sat upon) maintains that most sofas would not support a person's weight, and that typical remarks about the nature and function of sofas, as well as apparent memories of sitting on sofas, are the products of a delusion. (Burge supposes further that the theorist is willing to subject the theory to reasonable empirical tests.) Let's add to Burge's story that it is a part of the theory that everyone else in the community is in the grip of the delusion: the theorist takes it that she is the only one who knows the true nature of sofas. In these circumstances, the theorist would reasonably treat claims like "Sofas are furniture" as constitutive in roughly Scharp's sense: if another speaker rejects these claims, she would take that to be prima facie evidence that that speaker fails to understand "sofa" or is using the word differently. But it would be very odd for her to hold herself to the same standard; her view is just that she knows things that others do not. She would feel no pressure to regard herself as incompetent: that her own views are idiosyncratic, and that she must therefore be interpreted in a different way, is part and parcel of her theory.

This phenomenon is particularly salient in the case of thought about paradox. A dialetheist (who maintains that some claims are simultaneously both true and false) might reasonably take herself to be linguistically and conceptually competent despite believing that her view is widely or universally rejected among the folk. If a stranger (outside the context of academic philosophy) announces that some claim is both true and false, the dialetheist may reason: either this person has adopted my view, or he is not competent with the concepts of truth and falsity. But (alas!) very few people have adopted my view; so it is by far more likely that this person is not conceptually competent. The dialetheist may nonetheless continue to find the Liar puzzling—she has arrived at a solution which does the best that can be done with a difficult problem, but she continues to feel the pull of the principles she rejects—despite having no doubts about her own competence.

In short, rejecting principles one takes to be constitutive (in that they play an essential role in interpreting others) is perfectly compatible with regarding oneself as conceptually competent. Since Scharp's explanation presupposes that rejecting principles one takes to be constitutive as putting pressure on one's own competence, his explanation fails.

The second objection to Scharp's proposal stems from how it predicts we ought to respond to paradox. Suppose that we are grappling with the Liar: we consider various solutions and the arguments that can be mustered in their favour, but find none satisfactory. We are stuck: we do not know what to do next. Scharp's suggestion (2013a, 56) is that we should simply revise the way we interpret ourselves and others: we must either give up on the idea that some of the principles which we took to be constitutive are in fact constitutive, or we must adopt a policy of interpreting people as linguistically and conceptually competent—possessing the concept in question and using the word with its ordinary meaning—even when they do not accept many of the concept's constitutive principles. But this suggestion simply flies in the face of the facts. Making these changes just does not make the Liar any easier—or so I submit. We may very generously allow others to make all sorts of mistakes while possessing the concept of truth, understanding the word "true", and despite this find the paradox extremely difficult and puzzling.[6]

---

[6] There is another thread in Scharp's thinking about constitutive principles. In addition to the claim the constitutive principles are those principles that guide interpretation in the way we have described, Scharp thinks that constitutive principles are epistemically significant. Scharp's proposal relies on the

3. Towards an Explanation of Hardness

How then should Hardness be explained? Many problems in biology, medicine, mathematics, and other fields are hard. My strategy for addressing the hardness of paradoxes like the Liar will be to consider what makes these problems hard, and to argue that the same factors apply in the case of paradox. Whereas proponents of inconsistent words and concepts tend to think that there is something distinctive about paradox—paradoxes are qualitatively different than problems in other areas. I reject this. In my view, paradoxes are hard, but there is no reason to think that paradoxes are distinctively hard:

Non-Distinctiveness The correct explanation of the hardness of paradox is qualitatively similar to the correct explanation of the hardness of problems in other domains that are generally regarded as hard. We do not need distinctive explanatory resources to explain the hardness of paradox.

Consider the attempt to find a cure (or vaccine) for the common cold. Until quite recently, researchers were generally pessimistic about the prospects for a cure; all extant ideas seemed hopeless, and they were at a collective loss as to what to try next ("the ultimate prevention of the common cold seems to remain a distant aim" (Heikkinen and Järvinen, 2003)).[7] The problem is partially one of scale: many different viruses can cause cold symptoms, and the most common of these, rhinovirus, has more than 100 strains. This makes the problem difficult because it is time-consuming to research the wide variety of causes of cold symptoms and difficult to produce a single remedy that counters all of them. This problem is exacerbated by a lack of resources. Curing the common cold is a hard problem, but if sufficient resources were devoted to it, there is reason to believe that progress could be made. But (for good reason) research funding has tended to be devoted to more serious conditions.

There are even better analogues in other areas of research. *Scientific American* interviewed mathematicians about why Fermat's Last Theorem was so difficult to prove (Scientific American, 2017). Until recently, the problem of finding such a

---

notion of *entitlement*, which is (roughly) the status a proposition has just in case it is epistemically appropriate to believe it even in the absence of evidence. But Scharp rejects the idea that it is always epistemically appropriate to believe constitutive principles; in some cases—particularly in cases where the constitutive principles are inconsistent and one realises this—the right thing to do is to reject one or more of the constitutive principles. So he maintains that if one possesses a concept, one is *quasi-entitled* to the constitutive principles for that concept, where quasi-entitlement means that one would be entitled provided one had no countervailing evidence (2013a, 47). As far as I can tell, Scharp does not intend this idea to play a role in explaining pull (and rightly so: it's hard to see how it could play any such role). I therefore set it aside.

[7] See Heikkinen and Järvinen (2003) and Wat (2004) for discussion. For a popular presentation, including discussion of the history, see Davison (2017).

proof seemed likely to be insoluble; mathematicians had no clear idea about how to approach it, and it is very easy for the novice to become frustrated at the failure of her first approaches. Why was it so hard? The responses focus on appeals to scale ("Fermat's Last Theorem is a very sweeping, general statement: for *no* exponent n greater than 2 is there a solution to the Fermat equation. It is much easier to attack the problem for a specific exponent.") and to sociological factors which resulted in a dearth of resources devoted to the problem (until recently the problem looked isolated from the issues that mathematicians found most interesting, hence few mathematicians were motivated to focus on it). And there is one further factor worthy of comment: "The theorem itself is very easy to state and so may seem deceptively simple; you do not need to know a lot of mathematics to understand the problem. It turns out, however, that to the best of our knowledge, you do need to know a lot of mathematics in order to solve it." Mastery of the tools required by Wiles's proof of the Theorem requires many years of study; it is not surprising that the task would look unachievable to those with limited background. (The same is true of the common cold. We all get them, and it's easy to appreciate what a cure would be like; but only a virologist is in a position to appreciate the details of potential solutions to the problem.)

In short, the hardness of many other hard problems is partially explained by the fact that the problems are big (sweeping, general, with many cases to consider). Big problems can be tackled with big resources; but the problems we regard as hard tend to be under-resourced, and this makes the sociological and economic factors that explain this under-resourcing relevant to the causal explanation of why we have not solved the problem and continue to find it hard. And this under-resourcing is exacerbated by the fact that being in a position to understand the possible solutions to hard problems requires a great deal of education.

The same factors are at work in the Liar paradox. It is big: just as Fermat's Last Theorem is a "sweeping, general statement", (T) is a sweeping general schema: it covers every declarative sentence, no matter its syntax or subject matter. It is unsurprising that it is hard to come up with a way of restricting it that accommodates every case.

There is a second sense in which the problem is big. The literature on the Liar, and the range of novel approaches to it, are vast. The *Stanford Encyclopedia of Philosophy* entry on the Liar (Beall et al., 2017) lists six "families" of solutions, several of which have between three and five sub-headings, each of which discusses many views that differ in detail. Attempted solutions have appealed to a wide range of logical techniques and tools, as well as to ideas from the philosophy of language and the philosophy of mind. Given the proliferation of different approaches since Tarski and Kripke and the flexibility and power of the resources of contemporary logic, there is little doubt that this is only scratching the surface. Sifting and evaluating these responses requires no little dedication, time, and expertise.

But many hands make light work: if governments prioritised research on the Liar, spending vast sums training logicians and philosophers of language, who is to say what might not be accomplished? It has not been so (for good reasons). And just as Fermat's Last Theorem seemed peripheral to the primary interests of most mathematicians, contemporary work on paradox seems peripheral to the primary interests of most philosophers—abstract, technical, of little relevance to other areas of philosophy—so that few among us are motivated to work seriously on the Liar.

And few of us are even equipped to do so. In introducing the notion of hardness, I described the phenomenology of grappling with paradox: one feels trapped, like no solution is adequate, one does not know what to try next. This phenomenology is very salient when one encounters a paradox for the first time. (You can just see it in good undergraduates introduced to the Liar.) It is less clear whether the phenomenology is still experienced by veteran thinkers who know the literature around a paradox, have seen all the moves, and perhaps even want to defend a particular view. Grappling with a paradox like the Liar—learning the logic, the philosophy of language, the metaphysics, and so on necessary to see the space of candidate solutions—requires a great deal of education, and the majority of those who have the relevant education seem not to find the problem as hopeless as the proponents of inconsistent words and concepts seem to think.

Perhaps the hardness of paradox is qualitatively different than the hardness of other hard problems. But I do not think the case that it is has been made. I therefore am inclined to think that the hardness of paradox can be at least partly explained in the same way as the hardness of problems in other fields: Non-Distinctiveness is true.

4. Conclusion

I have rejected the attempt to explain the hardness of the Liar in terms of inconsistent concepts, and have sketched in its place a view on which the hardness of the Liar is explained in the same way as the hardness of other hard problems: it is a big problem, which requires deep education to engage with in a serious way, and which has not had vast resources thrown at it.

I do not claim that this explanation is complete; and I would agree that pull has a role to play in explaining the hardness of the Liar. But even if this is so, an explanation of pull will most likely appeal to the same kinds of facts that explain our other beliefs and dispositions: for example, perhaps our attraction to the instances of (T) is partly the result of some innate "core cognition" (as are many of our deep and recalcitrant beliefs and dispositions (Carey, 2009)), and partly inculcated or reinforced through education. There is no reason to expect a distinctive explanation of pull.

This conclusion has significance beyond the literature on the Liar. The idea that the concept of knowledge is inconsistent has been defended as a way of explaining the pull of sceptical reasoning (Schiffer, 1996; Spicer, 2008); and I would raise similar objections to other attempts to give a diagnosis of the hardness of philosophical problems that make them qualitatively distinct from other hard problems (such as McGinn's (1991) well-known claim that facts about our cognitive make-up make the mind-body problem intractable).

We began this chapter with the idea that some problems are intractable or pointless. But—although it's clear that some problems are hard—it isn't clear that we should grant that progress is impossible without methodological revision. There has been a great deal of progress on many popular definitional disputes; for example, if issues about whether marriage is possible between people of different religions, or after divorce, or between people of the same sex, are not settled once and for all, it's at least clear which way the wind is blowing. And the same is true in academic philosophy; as Daniel Stoljar (2017) convincingly argues, many philosophical issues have been settled—and the fact that we can still appreciate the considerations that settled them suggests that debate about them was worthwhile and unconfused. I therefore think that we should be aiming to make sense of our practice rather than attempting drastic revision; that is to say, the seeming intractability of paradox gives no reason to abandon Conservatism about Practice.

Making progress on paradoxes like the Liar is very hard. But in his preface to *Words and Things*, Ernest Gellner's scathing polemic against ordinary language philosophy (of the sort pursued by Malcolm, discussed in Chapter 1), Bertrand Russell objects to the idea that ease of progress is a good thing:

> When I was a boy, I had a clock with a pendulum which could be lifted off. I found that the clock went very much faster without the pendulum. [. . .] The linguistic philosophy, which cares only about language, and not about the world, is like the boy who preferred the clock without the pendulum because, although it no longer told the time, it went more easily than before and at a more exhilarating pace.
> (Russell, in Gellner, 1959, 15)[8]

Learning about the world—whether it be the world of medicine or of mathematics or of philosophy—is hard. The true story is likely to be complicated, as is the story of the obstacles that stand in the way of appreciating it.

---

[8] Russell is similarly quoted in the epigraph to *Words and Things*: "The later Wittgenstein [. . .] seems to have grown tired of serious thinking and to have invented a doctrine which would make such an activity unnecessary. I do not for one moment believe that the doctrine which has these lazy consequences is true."

PART II
TEMPORAL EXTERNALISM

5
Definition: What and When

In Chapter 1, I introduced three key themes of the view of definitional disputes defended in this book. Part I defended two of these themes—Meaning Sameness and Conservatism about Practice. I now turn my attention to the third theme:

Temporal Externalism Facts about what happens at later times can play a role in determining the meaning of our words (and the contents of our mental states) at earlier times. In particular, definitional disputes can play a role in determining meaning, even though they do not involve change of meaning.

My overall argumentative strategy in this chapter and the next is to show that a view incorporating Temporal Externalism offers the best explanation of how we can engage in definitional disputes compatibly with Meaning Sameness and Conservatism about Practice. In order to do this, it will be necessary to develop an account of definition, and in particular of the kind of definition that is at issue in definitional disputes.

Developing that account is the task of Chapter 6. This chapter lays the groundwork for that account by developing some traditional distinctions between various types of definition: descriptive and stipulative, nominal and real (Section 2). I motivate these distinctions by considering a puzzle (Section 1). Everyone agrees that we should sometimes begin a piece of writing or a conversation by defining our terms. Put roughly, the puzzle is this: why doesn't stipulatively defining our terms in this way resolve definitional disputes? A natural suggestion is that such stipulative definitions at most determine the meanings of words as we will go on to use them for the purposes of this conversation, and since our disputes are not merely about such limited-term claims about meaning, stipulations do not resolve the dispute. Although the suggestion is right, this chapter shows that it is not sufficient to explain our definitional disputes (Section 3). We also need to provide a metasemantics that explains how we could mean the same thing despite our very different views; and traditional (externalist) metasemantic theories won't work in the cases at issue. I conclude in Section 4 by discussing Tyler Burge's theory of normative meaning-giving characterisations; I argue that it does not (and is not designed to) do the metasemantic work required.

1. Definitions: Beginning or End?

Everyone agrees that sometimes we are talking past each other, misunderstanding each other. And everyone should agree that taking some steps to prevent this kind of misunderstanding is worthwhile. A natural suggestion is that we can do this if we begin our discussion by defining our terms; if I had begun by stipulating: "By 'art', I mean the product of a particular cultural tradition", then we would not have been confused.[1] The lesson of this line of thought is nicely summarised by Hobbes, who sees failure to begin inquiry with definitions as a major cause of confusion:

Hobbes's Advice "The first cause of Absurd conclusions I ascribe to the want of Method; in that they begin not their Ratiocination from Definitions." (Hobbes, 1996, ch. 5, p. 34)[2]

Again, everyone should agree that taking Hobbes's advice is often a good idea. (Taking it may involve a modest methodological revisionism, but (*pace* Hobbes) it is broadly consistent with our current way of conducting debates; we do it sometimes, and it's the kind of thing that we often tell our students to do.) But once we have taken Hobbes's advice and defined our terms, shouldn't that settle the issue? After all, if I say "By 'art', I mean the product of a particular cultural tradition and conceptual art is part of that tradition; therefore, conceptual art is art", am I not speaking truly? What room could there be for further debate?

It seems clear that mere stipulation of this kind does not settle the debate about art. As Frank Jackson says about a related case:

> If I say that what *I* mean—never mind what others mean—by a free action is one such that the agent would have done otherwise if he or she had chosen to, then the existence of free actions so conceived will be secured, and so will the compatibility of free action with determinism. [...] I have turned interesting philosophical debates into easy exercises in deductions from stipulative definitions together with accepted facts.   (1998, 31)

---

[1] For a canonical twentieth-century statement of this view, see Ogden and Richards (1946, 130ff.). Chalmers (2011) is a prominent recent proponent of a closely related view.

[2] Ogden and Richards (1946, 109) quote this passage as an epigraph to their chapter on definition, and I'm following them in presenting Hobbes's advice as relevant to issues about verbal disputes; but in fact Hobbes's main worry is not that his opponents are talking past him but that they are making no sense at all: "And therefore if a man should talk to me of a *round Quadrangle*; or *accidents of Bread in Cheese*; or *Immateriall Substances*; or of *A free Subject*; *A free-will*; or any *Free*, but free from being hindred by opposition, I should not say he were in an Errour, but that his words were without meaning; that is to say, Absurd" (1996, 34). As far as I can see, Hobbes does not register the possibility that someone who asserts "There are round quadrangles" is not using the word "quadrangle" to mean *quadrangle*. (Charitable interpretation does not seem to have been at the forefront of his concerns.) We will consider Hobbes's advice but will set aside his own way of motivating it. (I'm grateful to Alex Douglas and James Harris for discussion of this point.)

Jackson is presupposing that the philosophical debate is interesting and valuable. Taking Hobbes's advice may help remove a confusion, but taking it to settle definitional dispute ruins something good.

Hobbes-style stipulation does not resolve definitional disputes; having the disputes is still worthwhile. If we come to agree on a definition, that will be as a result of having had the dispute. This suggests a picture of the role of definition very different than Hobbes's—a picture one can find in Kant:

Kant's Advice "in philosophy the definition [...] must conclude rather than begin the work." (Kant, 1997, A731/B759, p. 639)

This seems correctly to describe a philosophical practice, familiar since Plato: Socratic dialogues typically consist largely in (usually unsuccessful) attempts to find definitions. Socrates asks "What is virtue?" or "What is courage?", and proceeds to discuss, criticise, and modify his interlocutors' initial attempts to answer these questions. A definition, if it were found at all, would be what is arrived at in the end of such a discussion rather than what is laid out in the beginning.

2. The Puzzle

Kant's advice suggests that stipulation does not suffice to resolve definitional disputes. But why not? After all, can't stipulations give us definitions? Here is an attempt to regiment the puzzle:

1. Disputes about the definition of art are resolved if the parties to the dispute come to know certain true answers to the question, "What is art?"—i.e., there are certain claims of the form, "Art is the N," which are such that if the parties of the dispute came to know them, the dispute would be resolved.
2. If one makes a stipulation to the effect that by "art", one will mean *the N*, then one can truly say, "Art is the N", and one will know what one says thereby.
3. Stipulations do not resolve disputes about the definition of art.

(1) and (2) appear to entail that stipulations can resolve disputes about the definition of art, which is inconsistent with (3). I find Kant's advice (and Jackson's remarks) persuasive, and so I do not want to give up (3). Something must be wrong with (1) or (2).

Let's set aside a couple of initial worries about the puzzle. First, not just any claim of the form "Art is the N" will settle the debate. We might agree that art is John's favourite hobby; but that would not settle a definitional dispute. But this is consistent with (1): (1) says only that some claims of this form will settle the issue, not that every claim will. (We return to the issue of which such claims can settle the issue below.)

Second, (2) might be found objectionable on the grounds that, even if stipulation puts one in a position to utter sentences that express truths, it does not necessarily thereby put one in a position to know those truths. For example, Keith Donnellan imagined the following scenario: "I close my eyes and say (pointing), 'I will call the color of that "Murple."' I do not know what I am pointing to, if anything," and concludes, "were I to use assertively the sentence 'Murple is the color of that' with eyes open, I would express a truth, but with eyes closed I do not believe I would know the truth of what I would have asserted" (2012, 172). Donnellan's judgement about the case is plausible, but it is hard to see how to motivate the idea that something similar is going on in the "art" case, since there need be no analogous ignorance.

The remainder of this chapter will develop one line of response to the puzzle, and will argue that it is insufficient. This line of response begins with the thought that Hobbes's advice and Kant's advice are really about different kinds of things: there is one kind of definition that we can stipulate in the beginning of an argument, another that we can only arrive at by investigation (at the end of a debate). And this suggests that there will be no sound argument from (1) and (2) to something inconsistent with (3); the truths that we can know by stipulation are not the kind of thing that can resolve definitional disputes.

At least two variations on this kind of response can be drawn from the literature. In order to consider them explicitly, we need to introduce two distinctions between kinds of definitions: the distinction between *nominal* and *real* definitions, and the distinction between *stipulative* and *descriptive* definitions.

2.1 Nominal and Real Definition

Roughly, a definition of a *word* is something that gives the meaning of the word. But (at least according to a notable philosophical tradition) there is another possibility: we can define *things* as well as words. To a first approximation, the definition of a thing says what the thing is.

Let's call definitions of words *nominal definitions*, and definitions of things *real definitions*.[3] Different authors give different accounts of the nature of real definition. According to Aristotle, a real definition "is an account that signifies the essence" (Aristotle, 1995, *Topics* 1.5, p. 73), and Gideon Rosen defends a sophisticated development of this view (on which ϕ is the real definition of F just in case it is a necessary truth, grounded in the nature of F, that when a thing is F it is F if and only if, and because, it is ϕ (2015, 199–200)). Others adopt a less theoretically loaded construal:

---

[3] The terminology is Locke's (1894, III.iii.15, p. 26) (though Locke speaks of nominal and real *essences* rather than definitions).

A real definition of something, X say, would identify a set of properties such that each and every X has all the properties that make up the set and only Xs have that set of properties. A real definition specifies a group of properties each of which is *necessary* for something's being an X and which, taken as a group, are also *sufficient* for something's being an X. In other words, a definition of X characterises what all Xs and only Xs have in common.   (Davies, 2005, p. 227)

An attempt to resolve this dispute would take us well beyond the scope of this chapter, and the discussion to follow will be neutral between the various accounts.

It would be natural to present the distinction between nominal and real definitions as a matter of *what is being defined*—in traditional terminology, the *definiendum*. But the distinction between nominal and real definition is not just a matter of whether the definiendum is a word or not. After all, words (like other things) will have essences or necessary and sufficient features. So words will have real definitions.[4] The crucial feature of nominal definitions is not just that the definiendum is a word. It is also that the *definiens*—the expression that defines the definiendum—does so by *giving its meaning*. Entities that have no meaning do not have a nominal definition.[5]

2.2 Description and Stipulation

We have now seen two kinds of definition—nominal and real. We said that nominal definitions give the meaning of a representation. But what exactly does that amount to? There seem to be at least two senses in which this might be done.

First, one might take an extant representation and describe its meaning. This is, at least to a first approximation, what dictionaries try to do, and there are several strategies for doing it. First, one can give a synonym. For example, a dictionary might contain entries like:

---

[4] On one way of individuating words, words have their meanings essentially, so that giving a real definition of a word will require giving its meaning (see Fine 1994, 13). Thought of in this way, giving the real definition of a word will require giving a nominal definition.

[5] In addition to nominal and real definition, many authors speak as if there were a third possibility: defining *concepts*. Claims of this kind can be hard to interpret because of the variety of views about concepts in the literature. (Margolis and Laurence, 2007, is an influential presentation of the issues in this area.) According to some writers, concepts are representations. On a natural development of this kind of view, concepts will be particular physical entities—brain states, perhaps—that are meaningful in that they have features such as truth and falsity. If this is what concepts are, then concepts can be given nominal definitions in the same way as words: they are representations, with meanings, and their meanings can be stated. To state them is to give a nominal definition. (They can, presumably, also be given real definitions.)

On another view, concepts are not themselves representations; they are rather what is represented: universals, or something of the sort. On this way of understanding what concepts are, concepts do not have nominal definitions; they will only have real definitions.

So understood in one way, concepts have nominal definitions; understood in another, they have real definitions. It is hard to see that putting the problem in terms of concepts presents an interesting alternative. I will therefore continue to discuss nominal and real definitions; definitions of concepts should fall under one or the other of these headings.

bachelor: unmarried man.
furze: gorse.
big: large.

But this is hardly the only kind of entry one might find in a dictionary. For example, the *Oxford English Dictionary* gives the following as the main entry for "the": "Definite article (determiner). Referring to an individual item (or items). Marking an item as having been mentioned before or as already known, or as contextually particularized" (*Oxford English Dictionary*, 2021). This describes the meaning of "the", but is about as far from a synonym as it could be.

Definitions of this second kind—descriptions of a word's meaning that do not rely on synonyms—will not meet some putative requirements on definitions—for example, that definiens and definiendum be intersubstitutable in sentences without change of meaning. I propose nonetheless to count them as definitions. This is clearly consonant with one ordinary use of "definition"; my grounds for relying on this use are that it will bear fruit in what follows.[6]

An objection to regarding the OED's entry for "the" as a definition might be that it fails to specify the meaning *fully* or *completely*. One might get enough from the definition to begin using "the", but the definition hardly tells us everything about the meaning of "the".

Let's concede that the OED entry is not a *complete* definition of "the". Nonetheless, if a nominal definition is something that gives the meaning of a word, the OED entry is at least a step in the right direction; it tells us something about the meaning, even if not everything. Giving the meaning of a word is something that can be done completely or partially. So we should allow for the possibility of *partial* nominal definitions. (And presumably the same is true of real definitions: we should admit that we can give a partial description of a thing's essence, or a partial set of necessary and sufficient conditions.)

The second sense in which one might give the meaning of a representation is by stipulation—what Quine called "legislative definition". Stipulation is typically conceived of as endowing a new word with meaning.[7] (One could think of it as *giving a representation its meaning* rather than *giving the meaning of a representation*.) Successful stipulation plays a metasemantic role.

Descriptive nominal definitions can be given in multiple ways—by giving a synonym for a word, or by describing the way it can be used. It seems clear that a word could be stipulatively introduced in either of these ways. (For example, we could introduce a definite article by stipulation using the OED definition of

---

[6] Fine (1994, 13) claims that in giving a nominal definition, not just any specification of a meaning will do; one must give the essence of the meaning. (Hence nominal definitions involve real definitions of meanings.) We are flouting this supposed requirement; a definition can do the work we need even if they pick out meanings in some other way.

[7] Or, if we are individuating words in such a way that they do not have their meanings essentially, stipulation can give a word a new meaning.

"the".) So one traditional conception of stipulation, on which "A definition is a declaration that a certain newly-introduced symbol or combination of symbols is to mean the same as a certain other combination of symbols of which the meaning is already known" (Whitehead and Russell, 1963, 11) does not cover every case. We can introduce a word by stipulation even if there is no extant synonym for it, as long as we can describe what it is supposed to do.

The distinction between stipulative and descriptive definition is clearest with respect to nominal definitions. The usual notion of real definition is descriptive. It is an interesting question whether there can be stipulative real definitions: i.e., whether there are entities that can be introduced—brought into being, or given an essence—by stipulation. (See Juhl, 2009, for discussion.) But even if this is possible (say, for mathematical abstracta), it seems clearly not to be what is going on in the kinds of disagreement about definition that are our focus. Our debate about art does not bring any relevant entity into existence; the phenomena each of us take to be art already exist before our discussion begins.[8] I therefore set stipulative real definition aside.

3. Hobbes's Advice: Evaluation

With these distinctions in mind, let's return to the puzzle. The puzzle is that stipulation can put us in a position to knowledgeably make claims of the form "Art is the N", which in some sense give a definition; but this knowledge does not seem to resolve disputes about the definition of art. And the suggested resolution we are considering is that what we need to resolve disputes about the definition of art is a different kind of definition than what we can get by stipulation.

When we make stipulations, we are giving stipulative nominal definitions. If the definitions we need to resolve definitional disputes are a different type, they must be either descriptive nominal definitions, or (descriptive) real definitions.[9] Let's consider each option in turn.

---

[8] Perhaps this is not entirely obvious on every definition of art; for example, Kathleen Stock's "radical stipulativist" view maintains that what makes it the case that a particular object is a work of art is (at least in part) the fact that users of the concept of art recognise it as art (Stock, 2003). *Perhaps* a version of this view could be developed on which our debate about art results in something like a stipulation of a real definition. It is pretty clear that this would be an unusual case, and I therefore set it aside.

[9] It is perhaps worth noting that there is no consensus on (and surprisingly little explicit discussion of) the question of what kind of definition is at issue in the literature on the definition of art. Some take the debate to be about nominal definitions; Kendall Walton writes that most participants in the debate take "the question to be asking for a definition of the word 'art,' although it does not have to be understood this way" (2007, 148), while others seem primarily interested in how human mental representations work (Dean, 2003). Stephen Davies's entry in *The Routledge Companion to Aesthetics* (2005) presupposes that what is at issue is real definition. But Kathleen Stock's entry in Wiley-Blackwell's *A Companion to Aesthetics* (2009), of which Davies is one of the editors, is entitled "the definition of 'art' ", strongly suggesting that the word is at issue.

3.1 Descriptive Nominal Definitions

The idea that definitional disputes are about descriptive nominal definitions may seem surprising; after all, the methodology of philosophical argument seems to have little in common with descriptive lexicography. But since the days of ordinary language philosophers like Malcolm, the view that much philosophy is a matter of descriptive nominal definition has had defenders, none more notable in the contemporary literature than Frank Jackson. Jackson sees philosophical claims (of the sort he calls "serious metaphysics") as answering questions about whether "matters described in one vocabulary are made true by matters described in another" (1998, 41). For example, are psychological states just brain states, or are psychological states something distinct? (Or are there, perhaps, only brain states, and no psychological states at all?) On Jackson's way of thinking, this boils down to the relationship between matters described using words like "pain" and matters described using (say) neuroscientific vocabulary.

How do we answer these questions? Jackson's proposal is that we do it by analysing what we mean by the word "pain".[10] We consider possible cases (described without using the word "pain") and make judgements about what would count as "pain" in those situations. By considering a wide variety of such cases, we can draw a general conclusion about the sort of situations in which "pain" applies and does not apply, and this will amount to a description of the meaning (i.e., a definition) of "pain".

Does Jackson's view make good sense of our dispute about art? Jackson's view has considerable appeal in cases where the discussion is guided by examples: for example, disputes that are based on giving, and revising one's theories on the basis of, counterexamples. But our dispute about art is not like this. You are aware that I will regard *Fountain* and *Shoot* as works of art, and also that they do not count as works of art on your view of what art is. You do not accept that they are *counterexamples* to your view, and I do not propose them as such. They are cases that we disagree about; cases that are in dispute.

Now the fact that there are cases in dispute already puts Jackson in a difficult position. If we (clear-headedly, after suitable reflection) disagree about the cases, by Jackson's lights we mean different things by "art". Jackson writes about a related case:

> I have occasionally come across people who resolutely resist the Gettier cases. Sometimes it has seemed right to accuse them of confusion—they haven't properly understood the cases, or they haven't seen the key similarities to other cases

---

[10] Jackson speaks of *conceptual* analysis, but is clear that "our subject is really the elucidation of the possible situations covered by the *words* we use to ask our questions" (1998, 33). And Jackson is clear that what we are seeking is descriptive rather than stipulative (1998, 31).

where they accept that subjects do not know, or the key differences from cases they accept as cases of knowledge—but sometimes it is clear that they are not confused; what we then learn from the stand-off is simply that they use the word "knowlege" to cover different cases from most of us. In these cases it is, it seems to me, misguided to accuse them of error (unless they go on to say that their concept of knowledge is ours).   (1998, 32)

But if that's right, it is hard to make sense of the fact that we are advancing *arguments* for and against our positions.[11] When I claim that art can be intended to be disturbing, I am *trying to get you to change your mind*. And in most normal disputes of this kind, the disputants *do* regard each other as wrong, as making a mistake. *Contra* Jackson, it is hardly obvious that this is "misguided": trying to get someone to change his or her mind about a case is something we do all the time in debates of this kind. (Consider debates about gender or marriage; here the parties to the debate differ precisely about how to classify certain key cases, aim to change each other's minds, and regard members of the other camp as being in error.)

Of course, there are other, related issues that it still might make sense to dispute. For example, we might be interested in whether your usage of "art", or mine, or neither, captures typical or ordinary usage—as Jackson says, the folk theory. But if this is what we are interested in, again, our appeal to arguments makes no sense: the claim that *Fountain* is commonly regarded as art is obviously true; and if it is doubted the doubt should be settled by surveys or studies of linguistic corpora rather than by arguments of the kind we are considering.

There are also special circumstances in which it might make sense to argue, to change someone's mind about a case, even given Jackson's conception of what the debate is about. For example, it seems to many at first glance that one can imagine possible situations in which someone feels nothing despite being in exactly the physical state I am in when I feel pain. If that's right, then there will be no good description in physical terminology of the meaning of "pain"; the application of "pain" in some possible situations floats free from physics (and neuroscience). But some philosophers have argued that there is in fact a difficult-to-discern incoherence in the idea that a physical duplicate of a person who feels pain could fail to feel pain (Shoemaker, 2003; Tye, 2006). On their view, although it may *seem* that "pain" is not correctly applied to certain possible cases, this is not in fact the case; and we may need to give arguments to draw out the incoherence.

But again, our dispute about art is quite different. I do not think there is anything incoherent about your usage of "art", and I need not think that close attention to the cases will make you change your mind about them. (I may try to point out

---

[11] Of course, Jackson might be right in particular cases; sometimes, we really are talking past each other. We discuss such cases further in Chapter 6, Section 3 and in 9, Section 4. The point here is just that we can disagree about cases even when we aren't talking past each other.

features of the cases that you may not have noticed; but I might also accept that you have examined the cases closely, and no further attention of this kind will make any difference.) I just think you are wrong: wrong about the cases, wrong about art. What I am trying to do is to convince you of this. I am trying to get you to change your mind, both about the cases and about the nature of art. It is hard to see how this makes sense if what it at issue is descriptive nominal definition.

3.2 Real Definitions

So a Jackson-style view on which we are seeking nominal definitions cannot be the whole story—not, at least, if we want to respect Conservatism about Practice, to make good sense of our arguments. The alternative seems to be that we are seeking *real definitions*.

If we take our utterances at anything like face value, then it is clear that this is part of the story. Suppose, for example, that our debate ends when I say "So you see, to be art is just to be a part of a particular cultural tradition", and you say, "Yes, I see that now. *Fountain* and *Shoot* are indeed works of art." Now even if part of the point of what I said is to convince you of something about the word "art", it is hard to avoid the conclusion that I am also making a claim about art (not "art"); in a very obvious sense I am not talking about words but about an extra-linguistic phenomenon.[12] In the terminology introduced in Chapter 2, it's very plausible that getting you to accept a view about that extra-linguistic phenomenon is my first aim. And if that's so, then I am advancing (and you are accepting) a real definition.[13]

Of course, our debate may not resolve with us reaching agreement; debates about matters such as the definition of art are notoriously long-lived, and it is unlikely that any little discussion between us is going to resolve the matter.[14] But it seems clear that in engaging in such a debate, we are aiming at some goal; we are trying to achieve something, even if we are unlikely to do so. At least in many cases, the outcome we are trying to achieve is (perhaps among other things) a real definition.

The interesting question is whether that can be the end of the story. I want to argue that the view that what we are aiming at, and (in the good case) achieving, is a real (and not a nominal) definition leaves important facts about our debate unexplained (and apparently inexplicable). You began the debate with the view

---

[12] See Williamson (2007, ch. 2) for a detailed defence of this claim.
[13] Proponents of any conception of real definition are likely to accept this: if one thinks that real definitions describe essences, one is likely to see such a description (or at least a partial one) in my assertion; and clearly I am giving at least a partial real definition if real definitions are merely a matter of necessary and sufficient conditions.
[14] We return to the seeming intractability of such disputes in Chapter 10, Section 9. See also the discussion of hardness in Chapter 4.

that to be art is to be created to be beautiful; I began the debate with the view that to be art is to be a part of a certain cultural practice. We are each gesturing at a genuine phenomenon; there really are objects that are created to be beautiful, and there really is a relevant cultural practice. What's more, we both ought to agree that each of these phenomena really exist. If I were to stipulate that "schmart" is to pick out the products of such and such cultural practice, and then claim that to be a work of schmart is to be the product of that cultural practice, you should agree that I have succeeded in producing a correct real definition of schmart (as well as a correct nominal definition of "schmart"); and likewise if you stipulate that "flart" is to pick out objects created to be beautiful and claim that to be a work of flart is to be created to be beautiful, I should agree that you have produced a correct real definition.

So it seems that making sense of our dispute on the hypothesis that we are concerned with real definition requires the assumption that we are both using "art" to pick out the same phenomenon; only then does it make sense for us to argue about the nature of this phenomenon. Given the conception of semantics and of meaning that we are working with, this amounts to the claim that we must be using "art" with the same meaning.[15]

But now we face a difficult question: how could this be the case? The question is pressing precisely because our views of what art is, and our views of whether individual works are works of art, differ so substantially. As Kendall Walton describes the debate:

> It is not at all clear that these words—"What is art?"—express anything like a single question, to which competing answers are given, or whether philosophers proposing answers are even engaged in the same debate. Introductory textbooks and encyclopedia articles commonly recount a rather bizarre historical sequence of proposed answers [...] The story goes something like this—with variations, of course: The Greeks defined 'art' in terms of mimesis (representation, imitation), it is said. Then followed formalist definitions, and definitions in terms of expression, and of communication; after that came claims that what makes art art is its institutional status or its historical role, or its place in a symbol system with certain syntactic and semantic properties, or an interpretive theory.

---

[15] A referee suggests that in order to establish a claim of this kind, we would need to defend a general theory of when two uses of words (potentially by different people, at different times) have the same meaning. I disagree. What the argument above shows is that any theory that respects Conservatism about Practice requires participants in typical definitional disputes to use their words with the same meaning. Since Conservatism about Practice is independently motivated, this argument provides at least prima facie evidence that any adequate theory of sameness of meaning must yield this result. I sketch a general account of meaning sameness in Chapter 7, Section 5; but the discussion here is independent of that account.

The sheer variety of proposed definitions should give us pause. One cannot help wondering whether there is any sense in which they are attempts to capture the same concept or clarify the same cultural practices, or address the same issue.

(2007, p. 148)

I just argued that making sense of our dispute requires treating us as using the word "art" with the same meaning. But what Walton is pointing out is that the fact that we use the word differently—applying it to different cases, offering very different definitions—creates pressure to treat each of us as using the word "art" with a different meaning. This raises a question: our practice of engaging in definitional disputes makes sense only if we mean the same thing by our words. But how is it possible that we mean the same given our deeply divergent views? How can we be talking about the same things when we have such different ideas about how our words are correctly applied?

Answering these questions will require giving an account of what makes it the case that we each mean what we do—a metasemantic theory. The remainder of this section develops two desiderata that an adequate theory ought to meet. (In Chapter 6, Section 5 we show how the temporal externalist theory meets them.)

What we are now claiming is that any metasemantic theory that makes sense of definitional disputes must predict that it is possible for two thinkers with very different views about a word and the phenomenon it refers to, including views about matters of definition and about whether a given word is correctly applied to particular cases, to use that word with the same meaning.

Metasemantic Desideratum I Provide a theory of how words come to have the meanings that they do according to which we can mean the same thing despite very different views about the phenomenon, and very different views and dispositions about how our words ought to be applied.

Taken on its own, this desideratum is not so difficult to meet; a wide range of familiar externalist views—views on which what we mean is determined in part by factors outside of us—meet it. After all, on views of this kind, our beliefs play at most a limited role in determining what we mean; it is therefore reasonable to expect that they will predict that people with different beliefs can mean the same thing. But familiar views of this kind fail for other reasons in a wide range of cases of definitional dispute.

There are two reasons that we cannot simply appeal to familiar metasemantic accounts.

First, many such accounts cannot be applied in the cases at hand. Call this *the Inapplicability Objection*. For example, some externalist views rely on the idea that there are *natural kinds*, which we can talk about even if we are ignorant of their nature. On this style of view we can use the word "water" in such a way that is correctly applied to all and only samples of H_2O, even if we do not know that water is H_2O, because H_2O is a chemical kind. But art is not a natural kind, and there is no clear sense in which *objects created with certain aesthetic intentions* is more natural than *objects that are part of a particular cultural tradition*.

Similarly, some externalist views rely on the idea that the meanings of our words are determined by the nature of the phenomena that we causally interact with. For example, a view of this kind might have it that "water" refers to H_2O because H_2O is the substance causally associated with our use of "water". But no view of this kind is likely to settle our dispute about art: most of the objects casually associated with our use of "art" have both of the features at issue (they were created with the relevant aesthetic intentions and are the products of the relevant historical tradition), and although there are some objects that have only one (e.g., Duchamp's *Fountain* and Burden's *Shoot*), we disagree about whether those objects are art.

Our relations to objectively special properties or kinds (such as H_2O) might play an important role in determining meaning in some cases. But in cases of definitional dispute, there typically are no objectively special or natural properties or kinds (there are multiple properties and kinds, none of which stands out from the others as uniquely special or natural) and no single kind to which we bear a privileged relation (we bear roughly the same relations to multiple kinds). So metasemantic views that appeal to objectively special properties or kinds and our relations to them get no grip.

Other kinds of externalist view appeal to the views of experts. On this style of view, laypeople can use a word like "elm" to refer to elms, even if they have limited information or false views about what elms are, because the meaning of "elm" is determined by experts, who do not suffer such ignorance and error. But this view, too, is inapplicable in many of the cases we are interested in, since many definitional disputes are disputes *among experts* whose views are mutually incompatible and hence cannot all determine meaning.

The second reason why we cannot simply appeal to familiar externalist views is closely related to the arguments against metalinguistic negotiation and the idea that definitional disputes are verbal in Chapter 2. Consider, for example, a version of Kripke's (1980) causal view of meaning (on which the meaning of a term is fixed by an initial stipulation and inherited by later users in virtue of their causal relations to this initial use, so that the judgements and dispositions of later users play no meaning-fixing role), applied to words like "art". Such a view would easily predict that we mean the same thing; this will be so as long as we are each causally connected to the same initial stipulation.

My objection to this view is that it predicts that the kind of consideration that would settle the issue between us is evidence about the origin of our "art"-using practice. But, although evidence about the origin of our practice might bear on the debate in various ways, it seems clear that it would not in itself settle the issue. For example, suppose that I produce evidence that, many hundreds of years ago, the word "art" or some ancestor was introduced by stipulation, using just the definition I favour. Would you back down? I think not; it would be very reasonable for you to continue to argue your case. Considerations about the origin of the word just don't seem especially relevant to our dispute. So, the Kripke-inspired view predicts that considerations about the origin of a word which carry little if any force ought to decide the issue. We may regiment the argument as follows:

The Argument from Spurious Evidence

Premise 1 If meaning is determined in the way the Kripke-inspired view suggests, then considerations about the historical origin of the practice of using a word would settle definitional disputes.

Premise 2 In many cases, considerations about the historical origin of the practice of using a word do not settle definitional disputes.

Conclusion Therefore, in many cases, meaning is not determined in the way the Kripke-inspired view suggests.

Of course, no one has seriously defended a Kripke-style view about words like "art"; and the argument presented here is not intended to refute the claim that the history of a word plays some role in determining what we mean in many cases. (Nor is the argument intended to refute the claim that Kripke in fact defended, that the history of a proper name plays a very important role in determining its reference.) But the Argument from Spurious Evidence generalises to a range of other possible views. For example, suppose we were to be able to show that being a part of a particular cultural tradition is a natural kind. That might not be entirely irrelevant to the debate. But it also need not settle the matter. (You might simply insist that that is irrelevant, and that art is not a natural kind.)

A view that avoids the Inapplicability Objection and the Argument from Spurious Evidence would need to meet the following desideratum:

Metasemantic Desideratum II Provide a theory of how words come to have the meanings that they do, which is applicable in cases of definitional dispute, and which does not make false predictions about which claims are evidence or relevant to settling the debate.

4. Burge on Normative Meaning-Giving Characterisations

There is one externalist view in the literature which may seem to avoid the objections developed in the previous section: the view of Burge (1986). Since Burge's view is specifically designed to account for definitional disputes, I will present it in some detail before rejecting it on the grounds that, despite initial appearances, it fails to meet the desiderata.

Burge develops a notion of *normative meaning-giving characterisations*: "statements about *what Xs are* that purport to give basic, 'essential', and necessarily true information about *Xs*", which also "set a norm for conventional linguistic understanding" (1986, 703). It will be useful to distinguish three elements of his view of the matter.

First, Burge provides a theory of how we arrive at normative meaning-giving characterisations. On his view, we arrive at normative meaning-giving characterisations through a process of *dialectic*, which typically involves competent speakers reflecting on "archetypical applications" of the word ("perceptually backed, indexically mediated applications (or imagined projections from these) to 'normal' or 'good' examples" (1986, 703)). A correct normative meaning-giving characterisation must be consistent with these archetypical applications, and must also be broadly in keeping with the characterisations that competent speakers give prior to dialectic (1986, 703–704). Given that these constraints are met, the correct normative meaning-giving characterisation is what is reached at the end of dialectic: "The conventional linguistic meaning of a term has been correctly specified when [...] the most competent speakers have reached equilibrium on a characterization" (1986, 704). In short:

Burge Principle 1   Normative meaning-giving characterisations:
- BP1.i are arrived at via a process of dialectic between competent speakers;
- BP1.ii are arrived at via reflection on archetypical applications, and must be consistent with these applications; and
- BP1.iii are achieved when a dialectic between competent speakers reaches equilibrium.

This account of how we arrive at meaning-giving characterisations relies on the notion of a *competent speaker*; this is the second element in Burge's theory. The most competent speakers are those who are able to convince others of their views (1986, 702); this will typically involve the application of substantive reasons and evidence, and not merely practical reasoning about how to use words (1986, 703). As a result, "In the course of the dialectic, we *stand corrected*. We recognize ourselves as convicted of *mistakes*, not merely infelicitous strategies for communication" (1986, 704). Relatedly, even though meaning-giving characterisations aim to describe meaning, they are typically pursued by "attempting to arrive at factually correct characterisations of empirically accessible entities" (1986, 705). Despite this, the most competent speakers may also rely on arational factors such as "the attractiveness of the style of speech, the power or status of the speaker, or the impressionability of the hearer" (1986, 704). In short:

Burge Principle 2 Competent speakers:
- BP2.i are those who are able to persuade others;
- BP2.ii appeal to substantive reasons (rather than merely practical reasons about how to use words) in the course of dialectic around meaning-giving characterisations;
- BP2.iii in the course of typical discussion about definition, aim to characterise the entities under discussion; and
- BP2.iv may also rely on arational factors for their ability to convince.

Finally, Burge draws a distinction between the *correctness* of a normative meaning-giving characterisation (as a characterisation of meaning), and its *truth* (or, to borrow the language quoted above, its status as a factually correct characterisation of empirically accessible entities). Normative meaning-giving characterisations capture what we mean by an expression to the extent that they produce *synonyms*, where two expressions are understood as synonymous just in case "the most competent speakers would use the two relevant expressions interchangeably" (1986, 701). Correctness in this sense is what we arrive at when competent speakers reach equilibrium. But such interchangeability does not guarantee that the normative meaning-giving characterisation correctly describes the entities at issue in the archetypical applications. As Burge puts it, "there is no transcendental guarantee that people cannot agree in making mistakes. The authority of the 'most competent' rests on an ability to turn back challenges. But usually there is no method for demonstrating that every possible relevant challenge has been answered" (1986, 706).

Burge Principle 3 Normative meaning-giving characterisations are
- BP3.i correct characterisations of meaning when competent speakers use them interchangeably with the expression being defined; and
- BP3.ii true when they correctly describe the entities picked out in archetypical applications.

Burge's view captures many of the data points about definitional disputes that we have already seen, as well as some that we will go on to develop in the next chapter. Definitional disputes are a process of dialectic between competent speakers aiming to arrive at a characterisation of some relevant entities (i.e., a real definition) that also captures linguistic meaning (i.e., a nominal definition) (BP1.i, BP2.iii). Definitions are arrived at in the end of inquiry (BP1.i). Participants in definitional disputes give substantive reasons, not merely the kinds of practical reasons that bear on how to speak (BP2.ii). On my view, these are all genuine and important features of definitional disputes.

Moreover, Burge's view may appear to satisfy the Metasemantic Desiderata we have just developed. It appears to satisfy Metasemantic Desideratum I since it is possible (at least prior to dialectic reaching equilibrium) that competent speakers disagree about what characterisations are correct even if they use the word with the same meaning, as long as they are in agreement about the archetypical applications; one of Burge's main concerns is to argue that this picture allows competent speakers to doubt and to contest synonymies. And there may appear to be no serious threat of inapplicability or spurious evidence. But I want to raise two considerations that, in my view, show that this appearance is not sustained; in fact, Burge's view does not satisfy either desideratum.

The first consideration is this. Burge emphasises the role of archetypical applications; on his view, any correct meaning-giving characterisation must be consistent with the archetypical applications (BP1.ii). The cases of definitional dispute that he discusses are ones in which everyone agrees about the core cases in which the term applies but disagrees about how to characterise those cases. (For example, the most famous case from Burge (1986) is one in which a person agrees with other competent speakers, e.g., that *this* is a sofa and *that* is a sofa, but argues that sofas are "works of art or religious artifacts" rather than "furnishings to be sat on" (1986, 707).) But many cases of definitional dispute are not like this. In many cases, the status of certain examples, which would previously have been regarded as "normal" or "good" or are so regarded by many speakers, is precisely what is at issue. Consider, for example, the Bush administration's attempt to argue that waterboarding is not torture on the grounds that an act is torture only if it inflicts pain "of an intensity akin to that which accompanies serious physical injury such as death or organ failure" (Bybee, 2002, 46), and that waterboarding does not inflict this level of pain. Surely the majority of competent speakers, if they were be in a situation in which they could make a "perceptually backed, indexically mediated" application of "torture" to cases of waterboarding would do so—would affirm, "That is torture". The Bush administration's aim was precisely to contest whether those archetypical applications were correct. Or consider philosophical debate about free action; many positions about free will would require radical revisions to our judgements about core cases of free action. For example, incompatibilist views could easily commit us to the claim that no actual actions are free.

Of course, I am not suggesting that incompatibilist views are true. (Still less Bush-/Bybee-style views of torture.) My point is only that in a wide range of cases, archetypical applications are up for debate; they are no more sacred than general principles, claims about synonymy, or other claims.[16] At a minimum, then, Burge has not satisfied Metasemantic Desideratum I in many key cases: he

---

[16] As far as I can see, acknowledging that there can be disagreement about archetypical applications is compatible with respecting Burge's view that there could be no "objective, empirical meaning" without some terms being correctly applied in perceptual cases (Burge, 1986, 705; Burge, 1977).

gives no metasemantic story about cases in which there is disagreement about the archetypical applications.

Arguably, Burge also fails to satisfy Metasemantic Desideratum II, since his position would validate a kind of paradigm case argument—any view that rules that archetypical applications are incorrect must be mistaken—and such an argument would be spurious, providing no real evidence against the views it targets. But I won't press this point, since it might be suggested that Burge's claim about archetypical applications is inessential to his position. Perhaps BP1.ii could simply be dropped.

The resulting view would not be subject to the kind of objection that we have just discussed. But it would still not provide an account that satisfies our Metasemantic Desiderata. Consider Burge's distinction between the correctness of a meaning-giving characterisation as a characterisation of meaning and its truth. Burge gives clear criteria for a characterisation's being correct: it is correct just in case competent speakers have reached an equilibrium on it—i.e., at least roughly, they have agreed on it as the conclusion of their dialectic (BP1.iii)—and competent speakers use the characterisation interchangeably with the definiendum (BP3.ii). But a characterisation can be correct in this sense even if it is not true. Burge might hold, for example, that if competent speakers reach the conclusion that "art" refers to the products of a certain cultural tradition, then that is a correct characterisation of the meaning of "art"; but it is possible nonetheless that "art" refers to the products of certain aesthetic intentions (and hence that that meaning-giving characterisation is false).

A metasemantic theory in our sense would be a theory that explains, at least partially and in some cases, how sentences come to have the truth conditions they do. But Burge is not giving (and does not aim to give) a theory of this kind. He is giving a theory of correctness; but a meaning-giving characterisation that is correct in the relevant sense might fail to capture the definiendum's contribution to truth conditions. So Burge's theory is not a metasemantic theory in our sense. And so Burge has not tried to provide a theory that satisfies our Metasemantic Desiderata. His view is interesting and suggestive but incomplete, since it does not explain how our words can mean the same (in the sense of having the same semantics) despite our very different views.

5. Conclusion

We began this chapter with a puzzle. The following three claims are each plausible, but mutually inconsistent:

1. Disputes about the definition of art are resolved if the parties to the dispute come to know certain true answers to the question, "What is art?"—i.e., there

are certain claims of the form, "Art is the N", which are such that if the parties of the dispute came to know them, the dispute would be resolved.
2. If one makes a stipulation to the effect that by "art", one will mean *the N*, then one can truly say, "Art is the N", and one will know what one says thereby.
3. Stipulations do not resolve disputes about the definition of art.

One aim of this chapter was to evaluate an initial line of response to this argument. The response is that the appearance of inconsistency relies on an equivocation: stipulation provides stipulative nominal definitions, but what resolves definitional disputes is something else (descriptive nominal or real definitions). But the response is problematic. What resolves definitional disputes cannot be descriptive nominal definitions—the best version of this view, Jackson's, cannot explain disputes that involve certain kinds of disagreement about cases. And the idea that what resolves definitional disputes is real definitions is at best incomplete; it requires a metasemantic theory that makes it possible for speakers to mean the same despite deep disagreement in view, but does not also generate spurious evidence. The next chapter aims to develop such a theory.

6
Stipulation Reconsidered: Temporal Externalism

This chapter addresses the puzzle about stipulation posed in the previous chapter. We argued there that stipulations do not seem to resolve definitional disputes; if this is right, the following two claims are inconsistent:

1. Disputes about the definition of art are resolved if the parties to the dispute come to know certain true answers to the question, "What is art?"—i.e., there are certain claims of the form, "Art is the N", which are such that if the parties of the dispute came to know them, the dispute would be resolved.
2. If one makes a stipulation to the effect that by "art", one will mean *the N*, then one can truly say, "Art is the N", and one will know what one says thereby.

This chapter will show how (2) can sensibly be rejected by developing an account of how—and when—stipulation determines meaning (Section 1 and Section 3), and an accompanying account of a kind of definition: covert implicit definition (Section 2). Sections 4 and 5 defend the idea that the temporal externalist account of meaning determination developed in Sections 2 and 3 offers the best explanation of definitional disputes. In Section 6, I argue that the account is not committed to objectionable claims about analyticity. The chapter concludes with an appendix that gives a detailed account of an example definitional dispute.

1. Stipulation Reconsidered

Resolving the puzzle will require reconsidering the notion of stipulation. Here are three features commonly associated with stipulation:

Meaning-Determining Role Stipulations play a meaning-determining role. When we stipulate, we make it the case that a word has a certain meaning.

Introductory Role A stipulation comes before a word is used (with a particular meaning); it introduces that use of the word. (If we are individuating words in such a way that a word has its meaning essentially, then we can put the point by saying that stipulations introduce new words.)

Infallibility Stipulations are infallible. A speaker's stipulation that x, as they use it, is to mean m makes it the case that x means m.[1]

Call the conjunction of these three features *the traditional conception of stipulation*.

Infallibility has a consequence relevant to our focus on making sense of arguments and definitional disputes. If definitions are infallible, it makes no sense to argue for or against them, to try to adduce evidence for or against them, and so on. As the Port Royal Logic has it: "The definition of names cannot be contested... for we cannot deny that a man has given to a sound the signification which he says he has given to it" (quoted in Robinson, 1954, p. 64). If we agree that someone has made a stipulation, we must agree that the word as they use it does mean what the stipulation says it means.

Quine raises a doubt about this consequence of *Infallibility*. He claims that, in practice, stipulations can be questioned, argued against, and rejected:

> Suppose a scientist introduces a new term, for a certain substance or force. He introduces it by an act either of legislative definition or of legislative postulation. Progressing, he evolves hypotheses regarding further traits of the named substance or force. Suppose now that some such eventual hypothesis, well attested, identifies this substance or force with one named by a complex term built up of other portions of his scientific vocabulary. We all know that this new identity will figure in the ensuing developments quite on a par with the identity which first came of the act of legislative definition [...] Revisions, in the course of further progress, can touch any of these affirmations equally. (1966, 124)

As an example of the kind of scenario Quine seems to have in mind, suppose that the word "atom" was introduced by stipulation in the following way: "An *atom* is a particle that is mereologically simple—i.e., not composed of other particles." After much research, we take ourselves to have discovered the atoms, and the use of "atom" to pick out particular kinds of particles becomes established. But further research reveals that the particles in question are in fact composed of other particles. Then we seem to be committed to the truth of the following three sentences:

1. Atoms are mereologically simple.
2. X, Y, and Z are atoms.
3. X, Y, and Z are not mereologically simple.

---

[1] The proponent of Infallibility may want to make exceptions for cases in which a stipulation fails because it is inconsistent (for example, Prior's, 1960, stipulative introduction of "tonk"). But this complication is not relevant to the concerns of this chapter.

Quine's point is that it makes sense to give up (1), even though (1) was a consequence of the stipulation by which we introduced the term "atom".

So far, the point is unexceptionable; as a matter of historical fact, "atom" was introduced with something like the described stipulation, and (1) was given up.[2] But the proponent of *Infallibility* has a response. Of course, we can "give up" a stipulation; for example I might begin a course of investigation by stipulating that "atom" is to pick out mereological simples, but later stipulate that "atom" is to pick out the kind of particle that X, Y, and Z are instances of (whether mereologically simple or not). My second stipulation *changes the meaning* of "atom". As Robinson puts the point:

> A stipulative definition stipulates that, whatever the word may mean in other communications or even in earlier parts of this communication, it is for the rest of this communication to be taken as having no meaning whatever except the one now stipulated. Any previous meanings are thereby abolished for the remainder of this communication. (Robinson, 1954, p. 60)

And (the response goes) this is the case in Quine's examples too. Even if we are not explicitly replacing one stipulation with another—for example, we don't say anything like "I hereby stipulate that 'atom' will henceforth have a new meaning"—we are doing so in effect. Our initial stipulation governed the meaning of "atom" until we gave it up, at which point the meaning changed and some other claim came to govern it.

Perhaps this is the right way of understanding some cases of rejection of stipulation. But we have good grounds to resist the claim that every such case must be understood in this way; it simply does not constitute a charitable description of how many debates of this sort proceed.[3] In particular, it makes nonsense of most of our retrospective evaluations of our previous claims. For consider: why did we reject (1)? The answer suggested by the understanding of stipulation that we are now investigating is that, although (1) is true given the meaning of "atom" as we have used it up to now, we now find that there are practical benefits to using "atom" with a different meaning on which (1) is not true. This suggests that the correct description of what is going on when we give up (1) is something like:

(20) We used to say "Atoms are mereological simples", and the belief that we thereby expressed was true. Now we say, "Atoms are not mereological

---

[2] This description of the case is idealised. In actuality, the word "atom" has become ambiguous: it is possible in some situations to use that word to talk about mereological simples (for example, in discussions of the history of philosophy). This complication would not substantially affect the discussion to follow, since in the context of physical theorising the stipulation was abandoned. Thanks to Roy Sorenson for discussion of this point.

[3] The argument in the next two paragraphs is inspired by Burge (1979).

simples", and the belief that we thereby express is also true. The meaning of "atom" changed, so there is no conflict between what we said and believed then, and what we say and believe now.

If that is right, then the case is not correctly described in this way:

(21) We used to say "Atoms are mereological simples", because we thought that atoms were mereological simples. But we were wrong. It turns out that atoms are not mereological simples.

But of course, (21) is a perfectly ordinary description, the kind of judgement that most people—including philosophers, well versed in the ways of use and mention—would very naturally make in this sort of case. Why? Are we so confused about what is going on here that we cannot tell that we've changed the meaning of "atom"? So confused that we mis-attribute error to our past selves, and conflict between our past and present beliefs?

It hardly seems charitable to force an interpretation on our words that makes us so confused.[4] This is not to say that confusion is impossible; of course, I do not want to argue that we are infallible with respect to what we used to mean, or to whether what we said before was true or false. We can forget, get confused, make mistakes—that is possible. But in the described case, failure of memory is not at issue, and we do not seem confused. This kind of retrospective evaluation is very natural, the kind of thing that seemingly reasonable people do all the time.

The problem with the response to Quine that we are considering (and more generally with the traditional conception of stipulation) is that it requires that rejection of an initial stipulation constitutes a change of meaning, but the correctness of our retrospective evaluations seems to require that no meaning change has taken place. Very similar issues arise even in cases where no explicit initial stipulation is made, if we change our views about the kind of deep truths about a subject matter that we would have taken to be matters of definition; then too, we will retrospectively evaluate our past views as having been mistaken, and it is hard to make sense of this if change in view brings with it change in meaning.

I have focused the discussion on *disputes*, which involve more than one thinker. In those cases, I have argued, we should not typically interpret speakers as using words with different meanings or as changing what they mean over the course of the conversation. What we are suggesting now is that we should treat a single thinker changing their mind about definitional matters over time in much the same way: such a change should not typically be understood as a change of

---

[4] See Ebbs (2002) for related discussion; Ebbs argues that Davidson's principle of charity is inconsistent with our practices of interpreting and learning from those who have different views.

meaning. Therefore, we should reject the traditional conception of stipulation and look for another understanding of what is going on.

It is worth pausing here to clarify exactly what explanatory work we are looking for metasemantics to do. Giving an account of definitional disputes (or changes in belief across inquiry) involves psychological explanation: we appeal to claims about what was said, what we came to believe on that basis, which beliefs we thereby came to reject, and so on. And what we have just argued is that the best such account will involve Meaning Sameness—that is, it is difficult to see how to give plausible psychological explanations of this kind, if meanings and concepts are changing. But traditional and plausible views about what makes it the case that we mean what we do—views such as the traditional conception of stipulation— predict that meanings do change. What we need is a metasemantic view to replace these: a view that would explain what makes it the case that we mean what we do, but which also respects Meaning Sameness.

Before we move on entirely, there is one further lesson to be drawn from the flawed response to Quine.

2. Covert Implicit Definition

The response to Quine adds to the traditional conception of stipulation a further claim: that the stipulations that fix the meaning of a term need not be obvious. We can stipulatively fix the meaning even if we do not say anything along the lines of "I hereby stipulate that...." or "By 'atom' let us henceforth mean...". Nor do we need to make our claim with a special, stipulative intention (though we may do so). We may in effect stipulate simply by saying, "Huh! So X, Y, and Z are atoms, and some atoms are composite after all. (What a surprise!)". A claim that looks to be ordinary, just like any other, can do the meaning-determining work of a stipulation.

How does this kind of stipulation work? Consider by way of contrast the view of stipulative definition in *Principia Mathematica* (quoted above): "A definition is a declaration that a certain newly-introduced symbol or combination of symbols is to mean the same as a certain other combination of symbols of which the meaning is already known". This kind of stipulation takes for granted an extant fact about meaning—say, that the phrase *xyz* means *m*. The meaning-determining function of the stipulation is to make it the case that some other word—*w*, say—means the same as *xyz*, and hence that *w* means *m*.

Now there are other ways we might exploit extant meanings in our stipulations. We have seen one already: we can stipulatively introduce a new term by describing the meaning we want it to have. For example, suppose that we were to introduce "the" by stipulation, using the OED definition. This exploits the fact that the words used in the definition mean what they do. But rather than making it the case that "the" means what these words mean, we use the words to indicate a certain role for "the" to play; at least roughly, the stipulation makes it the case that "the" takes on whatever meaning it has to in order to play that role.

What the proponent of the response to Quine is suggesting is not quite this. But there is another familiar way to stipulatively introduce a word by exploiting extant meanings of other words: the method of implicit definition. One implicitly defines a word when one stipulates that a certain sentence involving that word is to be true. For example, one might introduce a word like "atom" by explicitly stipulating "Let 'atom' refer to mereologically simple particles"; but one could achieve the same effect by stipulating that the sentence "An atom is a mereologically simple particle" be true. Given the extant meaning of "is a mereologically simple particle", this fixes the meaning of "atom"; since the sentence is true only if "atom" refers to mereologically simple particles, stipulating that the sentence is true makes it the case that "atom" refers to mereologically simple particles.

The objection to Quine relies on the idea of implicit definitions, and (perhaps more surprisingly) on the idea that implicit definitions can come in the course of debate without being explicitly acknowledged or announced. We simply make a certain assertion—"X, Y, and Z are atoms"—and that assertion takes on a meaning-determining role. So we can make an implicit definition (as it were) explicitly by announcing "I hereby stipulate that the sentence 'X, Y, and Z are atoms' is true". But we can also make an implicit definition *covertly*, simply by asserting "X, Y, and Z are atoms." (We may not even be aware that this is what we are doing.) Of course, this will not be a *complete* definition, but we have already acknowledged that both descriptive and stipulative definitions can be partial.

We have upheld Quine's view against the objection because we rejected the objector's defence of *Infallibility*. But the objection is right to endorse the possibility of covert implicit definitions—implicit definitions that play a meaning-determining role despite not being announced as definitions, despite looking just like any other assertion. This notion will play an important role in the concluding sections of this chapter.

3. Distinguishing Two Roles

Quine's point motivates rejecting *Infallibility*. In order to say more about what happens when we give up a claim that we had once attempted to stipulate, we need to draw a further distinction between two roles stipulation has been thought to play.

It is, of course, quite true that a stipulation can *introduce a word*. In order to do this, the stipulation needs to give us enough information to begin using the word. Aside, perhaps, from exceptional cases, this will require telling us something about the meaning. But Quine's examples show that it need not infallibly settle the meaning once and for all. It just needs to give us something to go on, a place to begin. Call stipulations that play this role *introductory* stipulations.

A stipulation can also *determine the meaning of a word*, making it the case that the word means what it does. Call stipulations that play this role *meaning-fixing* stipulations.

The traditional conception of stipulation assumes that all and only introductory stipulations are meaning-fixing. But this assumption should be rejected. If the argument of the previous section is successful, the Quinean observation that introductory stipulations can be given up shows that introductory stipulations need not be meaning-fixing. One stipulation can introduce a word, while a second stipulation can fix its meaning.

This is not to say that no introductory stipulations are meaning-fixing. An introductory stipulation is an *attempt* to fix the meaning, and it might succeed. But it also might not. Or it might succeed in some respects (making it the case that "atom" picks out particles) but not in others (making it the case that "atom" picks out mereological simples); it might be a *partial* meaning-fixing stipulative definition without being a complete one.

So introductory stipulations need not be meaning-fixing. But when introductory stipulations do not fix meaning, what does? We should be open to the idea that there are different factors at work in different cases (see the discussion of partial metasemantic theories in Chapter 1, Section 5, and also the discussion in Chapter 10, Sections 5 and 9). But in the case where we are disputing about a definition and we reach a resolution—I convince you, or you convince me, or we come to agree on some compromise—we have a natural alternative. The definition that we arrive at in the end of our discussion is available to play a meaning-determining role. If I conclude my argument by reaffirming my view:

(22)   Therefore, to be art is to be the product of a certain cultural tradition,

and you are convinced (and tell me so), then (at least *ceteris paribus*) my utterance is a covert implicit definition that fixes the meaning of "art". But the meaning of "art" does not change: the definition fixes the meaning of the word *as we used it all along*.

The suggested way of understanding definitional disputes, as well as definition-changing inquiry like the Quinean atom case, is that there no change of meaning (Meaning Sameness) because the conclusions we arrive at in the end of our dispute or inquiry are covert implicit definitions that determine what our words meant all along. The view is a version of temporal externalism, since it entails that things that happen at later times (the end of our dispute) determines what we meant at earlier times.

4. The Argument from Charity

Since the previous sections have developed a key argument for temporal externalism, it will be worth pausing to make that argument explicit. Over the course of an inquiry, we may make a series of claims:

Initial Views "Art must be intended to be beautiful"; "Atoms are mereological simples".

Considered Views "Art is the product of a cultural tradition and need not be intended to be beautiful"; "Some atoms are not mereological simples".

Retrospective Reports "I used to think that art had to be created with a certain intention, but now I see that that isn't so: some works of art are intended to shock"; "My initial view was that atoms such as X, Y, and Z were mereological simples. But that was wrong. Now I see that X, Y, and Z have parts; some atoms are not mereologically simple".

No plausible view can make all of these claims true. In particular, although *Initial Views* and *Considered Views* might both be true if the meaning of key words such as "art" and "atom" change, we have now seen multiple reasons to think that they do not change. First, the metalinguistic views discussed in Chapter 2, which would predict such a change, are explanatorily inadequate. Second, views on which the meaning of "art" or "atom" change to make *Initial Views* and *Considered Views* true will make *Retrospective Reports* false. *Retrospective Reports* attribute error to initial views; if I say, "I used to think that art had to be created with a certain intention, but now I see that that view is false", the correctness of the report is incompatible with the correctness of the initial view I am reporting on.

So we must give up one of these claims. In my view, we should in typical cases look for an account of the cases that lets us give up *Initial Views*, while making *Considered Views* and *Retrospective Reports* true. My strategy for defending this claim has two steps: first, I will argue that (in typical cases) we should not abandon *Retrospective Reports*; then, I will argue that (in typical cases) it is more charitable to give up *Initial Views* than *Considered Views*.

It is important that our retrospective reports are, at least in general, true. The practice of being able to evaluate our past views, to assess our evidence and our reasons, is crucial to rational inquiry. If our evaluations and assessments are systematically in error, we are systematically confused about how we arrived at our views, and about the evidence against other positions and for our own. For example, when I say, "I used to think that art had to be created with beauty-related intention, but now I see that that isn't so: some works of art are intended to shock", I am reporting not only on my change in view but also on my reasons, my evidence.

I came to believe that some works of art are intended to shock, and concluded on that basis that my view of art is wrong.

It is crucial when I am assessing the strength of my present position that I be able to assess my reasons for it (and against alternatives) in this way. I want to know: why do I believe that art is not a matter of aesthetic intentions? Why do I believe that art is a matter of historical traditions? Well, what I think is that I got a certain bit of evidence—that some artworks are intended to be shocking—that told against my initial view, and (presumably in conjunction with other evidence) in favour of my considered view. Suppose I am wrong about that. Then why do I believe what I do? What evidence, what reason do I have? Do I have any reason at all? How confident should I be? I would have no idea how to begin to answer these questions. And although in many ordinary cases it may not be important to remember how we arrived at a view, or to be able to marshal our evidence (Harman, 1986), typical definitional disputes are not like this. In many cases of this kind, we are precisely trying to evaluate what evidence we have for and against various claims—and in many such cases, it seems that we can, that we do know what our evidence is and what brought us to our present view.

It might be replied that giving up the literal truth of our retrospective reports would not be as bad as I am suggesting, since there is a way of pragmatically reinterpreting our retrospective reports so that they are reporting something true. For example, proponents of views on which there is meaning change might suggest that we should reinterpret claims like, "I used to think that art had to be created with a certain intention, but now I see that that isn't so: some works of art are intended to shock" in something like the following way: "I used to think that we should use the word 'art' in such a way that the sentence 'Art must be created with a certain intention' is true, but now I see that this isn't so; we should use the word 'art' in such a way that the sentence 'Some works of art are intended to shock' comes out true."

I have two lines of response to this suggestion. First, although there may be cases in which the utterance of a sentence like "I used to think that art had to be created with a certain intention, but now I see that that isn't so: some works of art are intended to shock" might be understood in the way suggested (for example, in virtue of the kind of Gricean mechanisms discussed in Chapter 1, Section 4), many relevant cases do not involve the utterance of sentences at all. We are concerned with dispute, but also with inquiry involving *a single person's* change of view over time. In some cases, we are not speaking at all, but just thinking to ourselves, trying to come to a conclusion or evaluate some new thought. It is far from clear that there is a way of developing the pragmatic reinterpretation strategy that would save us from error and irrationality in this kind of case.

Second, even if this kind of strategy could establish that our retrospective reports in some sense convey something true, what they thereby convey would not play an appropriate rational role. For example, perhaps I read the diaries of various artists and discover that the works I find shocking are badly executed attempts to create something beautiful. What should I do then? It would be natural for me to revisit my reasoning: it seems to me as though I had reasoned from the premise that some works of art are intended to be shocking; now it is unclear to me that this premise is true, and correspondingly unclear what support, if any, I have for the conclusion. If I in fact reasoned from the premise that we ought to use the word "art" in such a way that the sentence "Some works of art are intended to be shocking" comes out true, it is much less clear what I ought to do. (It is not clear that my new evidence (the artists' diaries) bears on this metalinguistic claim at all.) So reinterpreting our retrospective reports in this way is likely to make our responses to new evidence confused and irrational.

I conclude that we should not give up *Retrospective Reports*. Our options, then, are to give up *Initial Views* or to give up *Considered Views*. There are a range of cases, and in some, it is reasonable to maintain the truth of someone's initial views at the expense of their considered views (see Chapter 10, Section 8 for further discussion). However, suppose that the inquiry was in general well conducted; the participants responded rationally to evidence and changed their views in ways we recognise as reasonable. In that case, we should certainly not insist on the truth of their initial views. To systematically maintain *Initial Views* over *Considered Views* is to block inquiry, to convict anyone who responds reasonably to evidence of error. That seems at best an extremely uncharitable interpretation of the cases.

It may seem surprising that it is charitable to attribute error. But keep in mind the situation: we are considering cases in which a person's view has changed, and is believed by them to have changed. In these cases, the attribution of error at some stage of the inquiry is inevitable. The question is: *which* claim is false? And my contention is that, at least in many cases, it is most charitable to maintain that the initial view is false (even if that view was the result of an attempt to stipulate what we mean).

We may summarise the argument so far in the following way:

The Argument from Charity

Premise 1   In some cases of inquiry or dispute about matters of definition, at least one of our initial views, our considered views, and our retrospective reports must be false.

Premise 2   If our retrospective reports are false, then we are not in a good position to assess the reasons and evidence for our views.

Premise 3   At least in many cases, we are in a good position to assess the reasons and evidence for our views.

Conclusion 1   Our retrospective reports are typically true. (From Premise 2 and Premise 3.)

Conclusion 2 Therefore, in the cases at issue, either our initial views or our considered views must be false. (From Premise 1 and Conclusion 1.)

Premise 4 In typical cases of well-conducted inquiry (including inquiry that involves dispute), it would be grossly uncharitable to insist that our initial views are true and our considered views are false.

Conclusion 3 Therefore, in typical cases of well-conducted inquiry, we should prefer an account that makes our considered views true and our initial views false. (From Premise 4 and Conclusion 2.)

So, we need a view that makes it the case that our initial view is false and our considered view is true. In the previous chapter, we considered externalist views that might do this. But we showed there that the features appealed to in such accounts—naturalness, causal history, expert opinion, and so on—either don't seem applicable to cases of definitional disputes with which we are concerned or generate spurious evidence.

But now that we have separated the meaning-fixing role of stipulation from the introductory role, we can see another clear possibility. If our considered views are a covert implicit definition which does not occur at the beginning of the practice of using a word but plays a role in determining the meaning of a word across the whole practice, then our considered views are true and our initial views are false. So the temporal externalist account of covert implicit definition developed above meets the criterion described in Conclusion 3; since no other view does, we should accept the temporal externalist account.

The argument can be understood as an inference to the best explanation. Such arguments are always in principle vulnerable to the formulation of alternative explanations, and if another view could preserve our considered judgements and retrospective reports, while avoiding the Inapplicability Objection and the Argument from Spurious Evidence, it would be worthy of serious consideration. As far as I know, there is no alternative view that meets these criteria. I therefore conclude that there are good reasons to believe the temporal externalist account I have developed. In order to further substantiate the account, I will now return to the metasemantic desiderata developed in Chapter 5.

5. The Metasemantic Desiderata

Chapter 5 presented two desiderata for a metasemantic theory relevant to the understanding of definitional disputes:

Metasemantic Desideratum I Provide a theory of how words come to have the meanings that they do according to which we can mean the same thing despite very different views about the phenomenon, and very different views and dispositions about how our words ought to be applied.

Metasemantic Desideratum II Provide a theory of how words come to have the meanings that they do, which is applicable in cases of definitional dispute, and which does not make false predictions about which claims are evidence or relevant to settling the debate.

It is clear how the view meets Metasemantic Desideratum I: the definition that we arrive at in the end of a dispute fixes what all parties to the dispute meant all along, regardless of what they believed at earlier times.

In order to draw out how the view satisfies Metasemantic Desideratum II, it is worth considering how we motivated the desideratum. In Chapter 5, we considered a Kripke-inspired view according to which the meaning of "art" is determined by an initial baptism which introduces the word. The problem with the Kripke-inspired view is that it predicts that the facts in place *at the beginning of our debate* make it the case that at most one of us is right, and if one of us is right, determine which it is. This means that in order to find out who is right, it makes sense to investigate those facts; in effect, the Kripkean predicts that there is a strange and surprising source of evidence or reasons that would settle the matter.

The temporal externalist view that we have reached in this chapter—the view that the conclusion we reach at the end of the debate can act as a stipulation that determines what we meant all along—has a very different shape. On this view, the facts that determine who is right—the meaning-determining stipulation—are not in place until the end of the debate, and there is no way to investigate them besides *having* the debate.[5] As we conduct the debate, we will form and retain some beliefs and reject others for various reasons—the reasons we and our interlocutors provide in the course of the debate. There is no comparable strange and surprising way the debate might be resolved.[6]

Over the course of a dispute or an inquiry, we will be considering and weighing the evidence for and against different positions. This evidence will not typically bear directly on how we ought to use words. Instead, it will typically bear directly on the phenomena we are investigating. We come to a view about these phenomena—in many typical cases, about their real definitions. In so doing, we determine what our words mean and meant all along.

So our temporal externalist view does not produce spurious evidence, and therefore satisfies Metasemantic Desideratum II. But it might be objected that

---

[5] Please hold tricky questions about determinism and the open future until Chapter 7!
[6] What if by clairvoyance or time-travel we can discover the outcome of the debate? The temporal externalist account predicts that this information would be relevant to our debate. But this is not surprising or strange, at least in the case where we know that a debate is well conducted: everyone should agree that if we know that as a result of a well-conducted debate we will conclude that p, that knowledge is a piece of higher-order evidence that supports p.

there is still a problem. In a typical definitional dispute, the participants will be open to changing their minds, if they encounter persuasive evidence. The temporal externalist view predicts that this means that in a typical definitional dispute, participants will be open to the idea that their view, which they take to capture the definition of the words they are using as well as the definition of the phenomenon at issue, might be false. But this makes the debate puzzling: how can we defend a view, when we would acknowledge that we might be wrong?

It strikes me as simply a matter of fact, independent of temporal externalism, that we might be wrong when we engage in such debates. If the right response to this fact is to reduce our confidence, then we ought to reduce our confidence regardless of our metasemantic views. And there is no reason to think that temporal externalism produces incorrect predictions about how confident we ought to be, or how we ought to defend our judgements. Consider an analogy: I make a promise: say, to meet you at noon. I might or might not go on to keep that promise: it is a contingent matter. If I don't keep the promise, I have (in a sense) done something wrong; but that wrong might be excusable if my failure to keep the promise was caused by factors I couldn't have foreseen. It is reasonable for me to make the promise just in case I am confident that I will be able to keep it, and my confidence is justified.

I want to say something similar about definitional disputes. If you and I are arguing about art, it might come to pass that you win the argument and it might come to pass that I win. That is a contingent matter. At least to a first approximation, if I win, then you were wrong; your seeming evidence and arguments fail, or at least are not decisive. And if you win, I am wrong, and my arguments fail. In each case, one of us has made a mistake; we are not entirely blameless. But it is nonetheless reasonable for each of us to make the judgements we do, and to defend our respective positions, to the extent that we are justifiably confident that our evidence and arguments are convincing. So, each of us should be confident in our judgement to the extent that we take ourselves to have convincing evidence, and we ought to be confident when our view of our own evidence is justified. This strikes me as exactly the right result.

It is a consequence of this that we cannot be certain that our views about definition are correct. (In many cases, we cannot even be confident.) Our judgements about definitional claims are always in principle subject to further reflection and possible revision.

It is also possible that neither of us convinces the other. Two different kinds of scenarios are worth considering. First, it may be that something prevents us from continuing the dispute: we lose interest, run out of time, the world ends before we reach a resolution. In that case, the view we have just described—that the conclusion we reach is a covert implicit definition, that determines what we meant all along—makes no prediction. The temporal externalist might predict that, in this case, it is indeterminate what we mean; or, at least in some cases, the temporal externalist might claim that some other factor steps in to determine meaning. (See Chapter 10, Section 9 for further discussion.) Second, it may be that we decide that we have been talking past each other: what I mean is one thing, what you mean is another, and our dispute is confused. In the spirit of Conservatism about Practice, we have stressed that it is important to make sense of our disputes where possible; but in the case where *the participants in the disputes themselves decide that the dispute makes no sense*, it seems important to vindicate this judgement too. Therefore, in this kind of case, we should predict that the judgements at the end of dispute define what each party meant (and hence that they meant different things), thus making it the case that the parties were talking past each other all along.

6. Analyticity

It is past time to address a worry about the account. We are dealing in definitions (even if covert ones); and we are also letting a kind of example drawn from Quine drive the discussion. But Quineans might be worried about accepting the idea of covert implicit definition. Does this not commit one to the existence of an analytic/synthetic distinction?

Even those with significant Quinean sympathies, sceptical of traditional views about analyticity, might find something appealing in the notion of a covert implicit definition, understood in a temporal externalist way, especially once the possibility of partial definition is on the table. There is a sense in which covert implicit definitions are analytic. But the proponent of temporal externalist covert implicit definition need not accept the problematic idea that analytic sentences are true in virtue of meaning, if this is understood to mean something like "in some appropriate sense, it owes its truth-value completely to its meaning, and not at all to 'the facts' " (Boghossian, 1997a, 334). For example, it is entirely consistent with temporal externalism that sentences express propositions that exist and have their truth values independently of any human psychological or linguistic activity. What the temporal externalist is providing is a mechanism that explains why a particular representation expresses a certain proposition rather than some other proposition or no proposition at all. It does not explain why the proposition exists or has the truth value it has—except in the special case where the proposition is about language, or about some phenomenon that depends on language. A covert implicit definition to the effect that "Art is the product of so-and-so cultural tradition" is true will make it the case that the sentence "Art is the product of so-and-so cultural tradition" expresses a particular proposition (the proposition that is true just in case art—that is, the product of so-and-so cultural tradition—is the product of so-and-so cultural tradition). It plays no role in making it the case that that proposition is true.

Nor does the temporal externalist need to accept the idea that analytic sentences will be accepted by everyone who understands a word (or related epistemic claims, such as that the proposition expressed by such a sentence is known or knowable a priori). On the contrary: the view is specifically designed to handle cases in which a sentence turns out to be analytic for a word, even if at some times during that word's usage speakers firmly reject it (for example, because they take themselves to have stipulated a different, incompatible meaning for the word). Moreover, because covert implicit definitions express ordinary propositions, disputes can involve giving reasons and evidence in the ordinary way. The appendix to this chapter develops an example in detail.

There is a final reason why opponents of analyticity need not worry about temporal externalist covert implicit definition. Although we have presented the case as though a single assertion defines "atom", it would also be possible to defend a more holistic view on which a range of claims, even all of the "atom"-involving sentences that one asserts or accepts, are partial implicit definitions. (One traditional holist view would have it that all of the "atom"-involving sentences that one accepts at a given time determine the meaning of "atom" as one uses it at that time. The possibility we are now contemplating is that sentences that one accepts at a later time might determine the meaning of "atom" as one uses it at an earlier time. But that is independent of the question of whether some particular "atom"-involving sentence or sentences are meaning-determining, or whether all "atom"-involving sentences are meaning-determining. See Chapter 10, Section 7 for further discussion.)

7. Conclusion

Chapter 5 developed a puzzle: why can't we resolve definitional disputes by stipulation? The answer defended here is that attempted stipulations can fail to determine meaning, and so fail to put us in a position to know definitional truths (nominal or real). In order to understand definitional disputes, we need a metasemantic theory on which meanings don't differ between speakers with different views (setting aside cases where the speakers themselves conclude that their dispute was merely verbal) and don't change over the course of a conversation. I have suggested that we can provide such a theory by giving an account of the definitions that we arrive at in the end of a dispute.

These definitions are stipulative and nominal (in that they play a meaning-fixing, but not an introductory, role). To that extent, they are about how we should talk (and so, more generally, what we should do). But they are (typically covert) implicit definitions. And to that extent, they are about matters of fact—hence they are also typically real definitions. Our dispute about the definition of art is indeed about art—that is why our arguments make sense—but its resolution also plays a role in fixing the meaning of "art".

We say the things we do because we think that they are true and helpful to our interlocutors—not typically because we want to make it the case that our words take on a certain meaning. We advance the arguments we do because we take them to provide reasons to believe the claims we take to be true. It's not the case that our claims are always true, but that coincides with our considered judgement about the cases, and in cases where our considered judgement is that our claims were true, we are (at least typically) right. Nor is it the case that our arguments always support our claims, but again that coincides with our considered judgements. Our retrospective reports are usually correct, as are our evaluations of what we and others said and thought, because there is (in typical cases) neither change of meaning nor difference in meaning between speakers. And this is possible, despite our (interpersonal and intrapersonal across time) differences in view, because what we mean is determined by a common factor—our judgements at the end of the dispute—which (unlike certain other externalist views) generates no spurious ways our dispute might be resolved.

APPENDIX A

A Case Study

Sometimes when I have presented this material, I have been asked for a detailed case study that demonstrates how the temporal externalist would understand what is going on in a definitional dispute. This appendix is an attempt to give a detailed description of definitional dispute in temporal externalist terms.

Let's suppose that Barack and Michelle are discussing free will. At the beginning of the debate, Barack takes a naive view of free will; his position that there is nothing more to free will than being able to do what you want. So he says:

Barack (1)   As long as I can do what I want, I have free will.

Michelle disagrees. She thinks that free will requires the ability to do otherwise. So she decides to raise an objection to Barack's view:

Michelle (2)   That's not true! If you were addicted to a drug, then you would desire to take the drug; but if you did take the drug, that action would not be free.

While Barack is pondering this objection, Michelle decides to press her point home by offering a defence of her own view:

Michelle (3)   Look, if you're right, then we can be free even if our actions are determined by the laws of nature and the facts about the distant past. But if our actions are determined by the laws of nature and the distant past, then we would have power over our actions only if we have power over the laws of nature or the distant past. Which of course we don't. Your view can't be right: doing what you want to do isn't enough for free will. You also have to have the ability to do otherwise.

Now Barack has a response to this ready:

Barack (4)   I don't accept the idea that freedom requires the ability to do otherwise. After all, if I were locked in a room absorbed in something I enjoy, I might never even try to leave; and in that case, I'm staying freely, even though I couldn't do otherwise than stay. And for this reason, I also reject the idea that I don't have power over my actions if those actions are determined: even if I lack the power to do otherwise, my actions are in my control—after all, they come from my own desires!

And Barack also has come up with a response to Michelle's initial objection:

Barack (5)   But I take your point: the drug addict isn't free. So I was wrong to think that there is nothing more to freedom than the ability to do what you want. Real freedom requires not only doing what you want but also having the desires that you want. The problem with the drug addict is that he doesn't want to want the drug.[7]

Michelle finds this plausible. After thinking a while, she concludes:

Michelle (6)   Ok, I was thinking that free will requires the ability to do otherwise. But now I see that isn't true. I'm convinced: free will is just the ability to do what you want, and to want what you want.

Barack and Michelle have come to an agreement; let's assume that the agreement lasts (so that neither Barack nor Michelle changes their minds) and that the view they have arrived at is shared within the community. The temporal externalist will therefore take it that the expression "free will" is defined by something like the final sentence that Michelle utters—"free will is just the ability to do what you want, and to want what you want"—throughout the conversation. In short, the temporal externalist will defend the following hypothesis:

TE Hypothesis   In virtue of the fact that Barack and Michelle have come to agree on the truth of the sentence "Free will is just the ability to do what you want, and to want what you want", the meaning of the expression "free will" through their conversation is such that it is true to say of someone that they "have free will" just in case they can do what they want, and want what they want.

1. Constraints on an Account of the Dispute

Now what I want to suggest is that this hypothesis puts us in a position to offer a plausible account of each utterance in the debate. The account is designed to meet three constraints. First, following Grice, we recognise that conversation is a kind of action, and that people act as they do for reasons. A plausible description of what is going on ought to put us in a position to say why the speaker said what they did: what were they hoping to accomplish, and why was that utterance a reasonable way to attempt to accomplish it? (It is this

---

[7] Michelle's and Barack's arguments are, of course, inspired by classic positions in the philosophical literature on free will: van Inwagen (1975) and Frankfurt (1969, 1971).

constraint that the Wrong Kinds of Reasons Argument and the Argument Argument suggest that the metalinguistic negotiation view cannot meet.)

The second constraint is that Barack and Michelle are sensitive to plausible norms governing their conversation. The conversation is a sincere one; neither Barack nor Michelle are lying or attempting to mislead. They are trying to communicate something they take to be true, and that they take themselves to be justified in believing. In so doing, they are trying to obey something like the following norms of assertion:

Truth Norm   Assert that p only if it is true that p.
Knowledge Norm   Assert that p only if you know that p.

Saying that they are trying to obey these norms does not beg the question against accounts which (like the metalinguistic negotiation account) would attempt to give a pragmatic reinterpretation of their speech; a person can speak sincerely even if what they are communicating is distinct from the literal meaning of the sentences they utter. For example, when Romeo says "Juliet is the sun", he is speaking sincerely, and aims to communicate something that he takes to be true and that he takes himself to know. But our temporal externalist account does not rely on any such pragmatic reinterpretation: we will take Barack's and Michelle's speech acts at face value. When Barack says, "As long as I can do what I want, I have free will", he is asserting the semantic content of that sentence: that as long as he can do what he wants, he has free will.

Of course, the claim that they are trying to obey these norms does not entail that everything they say is true; like any of us, sometimes they may make mistakes. But if we become aware that we have said something false in this kind of discussion, we typically do something that shows that we regard ourselves as bound by the norm: for example, we might apologise, or we might retract what we said.

Let's say that in a conversation in which a given norm is not intentionally violated, and in which when someone becomes aware that they have inadvertently violated a norm, they do something (such as retracting their assertion) that shows continued commitment to the norm, the norm is *disobeyed* but not *disregarded*. In my view, it is unproblematic if a view predicts that norms are sometimes disobeyed; it is simply a fact that they are sometimes disobeyed. It would be much worse if a view predicts that such norms are routinely disregarded. But, to anticipate the discussion below, the temporal externalist will predict that in well-conducted discussions (such as the debate between Barack and Michelle about free will) norms are disobeyed but not disregarded.

The third constraint is that an account of the dispute should respect the speaker's informed and considered views. I suggested above that in cases where a speaker changes her mind, no account can make true everything a speaker says. In particular, at least one of the following must be false:

1. The speaker's initial view (e.g., "As long as I can do what I want, I have free will", or "Doing what you want to do isn't enough for free will. You also have to have the ability to do otherwise".).
2. The speaker's retrospective reports (e.g., "I was wrong to think that there is nothing more to freedom than the ability to do what you want", or "I was thinking that free will requires the ability to do otherwise. But now I see that isn't true".).
3. The speaker's considered view (e.g., "Real freedom requires not only doing what you want, but also having the desires that you want", or "Free will is just the ability to do what you want, and to want what you want".).

If the retrospective reports are true, then the speakers use "free will" (and related expressions like "freedom") with the same meaning across the debate. But if that's so, then their considered views are inconsistent with their initial views. Something has to give. I suggest that, at least in cases of a well conducted inquiry, where speakers are responding to arguments and evidence appropriately, it is most reasonable to prefer the views that the speaker holds at the end of the debate: her considered view, and also her considered view of the course of the dispute as presented in her retrospective reports. The alternative seems highly uncharitable: surely we ought not to hold the speaker to her initial view, and to ignore the epistemic progress she has made in the course of considering the evidence and arguments.

In the remainder of this appendix, I will argue that the TE Hypothesis puts us in a good position to explain how each contribution to Barack and Michelle's conversation meets these constraints. I will consider each statement in turn with respect to the first two constraints, and will return to the third constraint once we have reached the end of the dialogue.

2. Analysis of the Dispute

Begin with Barack (1). It is not hard to see why Barack might say something like this: he wants to discuss the issue, and his utterance serves to introduce it; and he wants both he and Michelle to come to have true beliefs on the matter, and his utterance serves to communicate what he takes to be the truth to Michelle. But it is a consequence of the TE Hypothesis about the meaning of "free will" that what he says is false: he says that free will requires only the ability to do what one wants, but given how the discussion develops, it turns out that it is a definitional truth that free will requires something else as well. Still, he is not deliberately saying something false; he is sincerely expressing a belief that (let's suppose) it is reasonable for him to hold at the time.

Moreover, he goes on (in Barack (5)) to retract his assertion. This retraction is important for two reasons. First, it reflects Barack's own considered judgement about Barack (1); the fact that Barack himself comes to take this assertion to be false suggests that it is reasonable if our metasemantics also rules it false. Second, it shows that, although Barack is inadvertently disobeying the Truth Norm, he is not disregarding it.

It might be suggested that what Barack is saying in Barack (1) is incoherent in a way that ought to be obvious to him. (After all, he is asserting something that is false by definition.) But a wide range of externalist views will predict that speakers can reasonably hold views that someone who fully grasped the definition of crucial words might regard as obviously false. Consider, for example, Burge's (1979) famous cases, such as the case of the patient who believes that arthritis can occur in the thigh. The belief is obviously false to anyone who fully understands the definition of arthritis; but its falsehood is not obvious to the patient. So if there is a problem here, it is a problem for a wide range of externalist views.[8]

Now consider Michelle's reply (Michelle (2)). Supposing that Michelle, too, wants herself and Barack to hold true beliefs on the matter, then her reply makes sense in the conversation; Michelle believes that Barack's view is not true, and is giving (what she takes to be) evidence for this belief by proposing a counterexample to Barack. Further, as with Barack, Michelle is sincerely expressing a belief that (we may suppose) it is reasonable for her to hold; and

---

[8] For further discussion of externalism and self-knowledge of what we think and mean, see Chapter 7, Section 4.

although she is inadvertently violating the Truth Norm, she goes on to show her respect for those norms by retracting her assertion.

Michelle (3) proposes a positive argument for Michelle's view of free will. The argument appears to be a reasonable one; the premises are claims that many people find plausible, and it looks like the premises entail the conclusion. Of course, there are further interesting and difficult questions about exactly why people find those claims plausible, and whether they are justified in doing so. In the end, Barack and Michelle agree that Michelle's argument is mistaken; still, the mistake is a subtle one, and putting forward the argument was a reasonable means to her ends. (Given that she is putting forth what is widely regarded as one of the strongest arguments against compatibilism, it is hard to see what better means to her ends she might have adopted.) Moreover, again no norm is disregarded: Michelle (6) retracts the crucial claim.

At this point, the temporal externalist account has it that Michelle has given an argument for the negation of Barack's view. Barack can see that there is pressure on his position from the argument, and that he needs to resolve that pressure somehow; and contesting a premise of the argument is a natural way to do this. Barack's response (Barack (4)) is in effect to make the case that a premise of Michelle's argument is false. Again, this is a reasonable response. What's more, the premise that he is contesting is very closely related to Michelle's view of free will; in contesting it, he is in effect also mounting an objection to that view.

Up until this point, no one has conceded anything or changed their mind about the nature of free will: Barack has not given any indication that he is willing to give up his naive compatibilism, and Michelle has not hinted that she is going to change her mind that free will requires the ability to do otherwise. Two issues remain outstanding: Michelle's challenge (in Michelle (2)) that Barack's view predicts incorrectly that the drug addict has free will, and Barack's argument (in Barack (4)) that free will does not require the ability to do otherwise.

Barack's next move is to address the issue of the addict. He does this by modifying his position. He admits that his initial view about free will was wrong (an admission that the temporal externalist can take at face value, and can accept as true), and proposes a new view. According to the new view, the unwilling addict is not free; this accords with Barack and Michelle's judgement about the case, and so removes the challenge raised by Michelle (2).

There remain interesting questions about whether, and if so why and how, Barack is justified in accepting this new view. We have not developed the case in enough detail to be really sure about what evidence he has, or how whatever arguments he used to motivate his old view might bear on the new view. But this kind of modification of one's view in response to seeming counterexamples (or "Chisholming") is common in philosophy, and it doesn't seem to raise any particular problem for the temporal externalist.

Finally, Michelle (6) concedes—a reasonable thing to do given her aims, once she is convinced that her earlier view is false. She does so by saying that her earlier view was false (an assertion that the temporal externalist can take at face value as expressing a literal truth) and, in so doing, retracts her earlier assertion, thus ensuring that the Truth Norm is not disregarded.

I take the discussion so far to have established that our first two constraints are met: each contribution to the discussion makes a reasonable contribution to a recognisable aim, and although the speakers sometimes assert falsehoods, they do not disregard any norms. Let's turn our attention to the third constraint: have we vindicated the speaker's considered views?

At the end of the debate, Michelle and Barack agree that Barack (1) was false, and temporal externalism vindicates this judgement: Barack is asserting that free will requires only the ability to do what one wants, but this is not the case given what "free will" means on the TE Hypothesis. They agree that Michelle (2) was a good objection to Barack (1), and temporal externalism vindicates this judgement as well: when Michelle said that the addict's actions were not free, she was saying something true (since the addict does not want what he wants to want, and that is required on the view of freedom at which they arrive).

Barack and Michelle come to agree that the argument presented in Michelle (3), despite its initial plausibility, is ultimately unsuccessful. Michelle (3) suggests that if one's actions are determined by some factor, then one has power over one's actions only if one has power over that factor. Given the TE Hypothesis and the view of free will at which Barack and Michelle arrive, there are two diagnoses of what has gone wrong in this argument. It might be that the claim about power is false; one can have power over one's actions even if those actions are determined by factors over which one has no power. (This seems to be what Barack suggests in Barack (4).) Alternatively, it would also be consistent with the TE Hypothesis to maintain that the claim about power is true, but the kind of power in question is not required for free will. In either case, their considered judgement that the argument in Michelle (3) fails is vindicated.

Barack and Michelle agree that Barack (4) is a good objection to Michelle's position, and temporal externalism vindicates this judgement: Barack's claim that the person locked in a room is acting freely is true on the view of freedom at which they arrive. And of course, they agree that the view that Barack arrives at in Barack (5) is correct; and this claim is precisely TE Hypothesis: the core of the TE view of the case.

I therefore conclude that the TE Hypothesis offers a reasonable interpretation of each stage in the debate: it vindicates Barack and Michelle's considered judgement, and it provides an independently plausible account of what was said and why. I know of no other metasemantic view that can do the same (even in concert with a strategy for pragmatically reinterpreting utterances as a matter of metalinguistic negotiation).

7
The Metaphysics and Epistemology of Backwards Determination

A central claim of Chapter 6 was that claims we arrive at in the end of a discussion or debate can be definitions—real definitions, but also stipulative nominal definitions, the kind that play a metasemantic role. These definitions fix the meanings of words *as we used them all along*; for example, if we conclude that art is the product of a certain cultural tradition, that judgement makes it the case that "art" as we always used it picks out the products of that tradition. This is Temporal Externalism (TE): the view that facts about later times can fix meaning at earlier times.

The view raises various metaphysical questions; addressing these is the aim of the first two sections of this chapter. How can the future make a difference to the past (Section 1)? How does the view relate to questions about the metaphysics of time (Section 2)? Moreover, because the view is a variety of externalism, it faces familiar challenges that have been raised to externalist views. One such challenge relates to mental causation (Section 3) (How can our mental states be causally efficacious if their content is determined by factors outside us?) Another relates to self-knowledge (Section 4). (How can we know what we think or mean if what we think and mean is determined in part by external factors?) I suggest that temporal externalists can answer standard versions of these objections in much the same way as other externalists.

TE emphasises cases in which meaning does not change. But in some cases, we want to say that meaning has changed over time, such that past or future uses have a different meaning and do not directly bear on what we mean now. In the final section of this chapter (Section 5), I develop resources to address cases in which meaning changes, especially when such changes occur gradually.

1. Can the Future Determine the Past?

(TE) is a claim about what "fixes" meaning. But what is it for one thing to fix another? The basic idea is that some truths are more basic than others, and that the less basic truths depend on the more basic truths. Consider an example from David Lewis: "Imagine a grid of a million tiny spots—pixels—each of which can be made light or dark. When some are light and some are dark, they form a picture, replete with interesting gestalt properties" (1999, 294). What shapes are depicted on the grid? Does the grid depict a square? The truths about the individual pixels determine the answers to these questions. For example, if a square is depicted on the grid, that is because certain pixels are light and others are dark.

It is overwhelmingly plausible that the truths about meaning are not metaphysically basic; they are determined by some other kind of truth, in something broadly like the way that the truths about shape are determined by the truths about pixels. Theorists disagree about exactly what kinds of truths determine the truths about meaning: perhaps they are truths about the causal structure of our minds, truths about what we causally interact with, truths about what is in our environment, or some combination of these. (TE) is a contribution to this debate: it says that, in at least some cases, truths about things that happen later determine truths about meaning.

This claim may seem mysterious: how can what happens later affect what is the case now? (Is this some kind of backwards causation?) But in fact the phenomenon is ordinary. I intend to quit my job, and say: "This is last time I set foot in this office." I am engaged in a certain activity—entering the office—and I am attributing a particular feature to that activity—happening for the last time. The activity might have the feature, or it might not. Whether it does or not depends on what happens later (for example, whether I lose my nerve and come back tomorrow).

Views with this general structure are also familiar from other philosophical contexts. Consider *actual consequentialism*, the view that whether an action is right or wrong depends on its consequences (i.e., the consequences it in fact has, not those it might have been expected to have) (Moore, 2005; Singer, 1977). On this view, if I say, "Taking that money is wrong", I am attributing a certain feature to an action, and according to the actual consequentialist, whether the action has that feature depends on its consequences, hence on what happens later. Views with this structure can be found throughout the history of philosophy. Consider Aristotle's discussion of the view that whether a person is happy even in their youth depends on the entire course of her life:

> there is required [...] not only complete excellence but also a complete life, since many changes occur in life, and all manner of chances, and the most prosperous may fall into great misfortunes in old age, as is told of Priam in the Trojan Cycle; and one who has experienced such chances and has ended wretchedly no one calls happy.   (Aristotle, 1985, Nicomachean Ethics I.9, p. 1738)

Aristotle attributes this view to Solon. Say that a feature f is *solonic* if and only if whether something has f at a time t depends in part on what happens after t.[1]

---

[1] I introduced this terminology in Ball (2020b).

Being the last time I set foot in this office is uncontroversially solonic; the actual consequentialist claims that *being wrong* (and *being right*) are solonic, and Solon claimed that *being happy* is. The present view is that semantic features such as *referring to the products of a certain cultural tradition, applying only to objects that are beautiful*, and *meaning that the products of a certain cultural tradition can be disturbing*—and even *being true*, as used of sentences or assertions—are solonic.

It seems clear that neither Solon nor the consequentialists, much less the job quitter, are committed to backwards causation. Future events may make it the case that my action now is right or wrong, but they do not cause it to be right or wrong. What Solon and the consequentialists are committed to is a kind of *backwards non-causal determination*.

Some philosophers have claimed that it is possible that what happens later changes what happens before. (For example, Barlassina and Del Prete (2015) claim that it was true in 2002 that Lance Armstrong won the Tour de France, but that this was changed by a judgement of the Union du Cyclisme Internationale in 2012.) But the proponent of backwards non-causal determination is not as such committed to the claim that the future changes the past; plausibly, in the cases of Solon, consequentialism, and my setting foot in the office, the future determines the past without changing it. (My own view is that this is the most plausible description of the Armstrong case as well.) I will assume in what follows that non-causal determination does not involve change; proponents of the view that what happens at later times can change what happens at earlier times might attempt to develop an alternative version of temporal externalism based on this idea.

Any plausible metasemantic view needs a notion of non-causal determination. On almost everyone's reckoning, facts about meaning are not metaphysically basic; almost everyone agrees that words mean what they do only in virtue of our psychological states, what is in our local environment, what we do, or what we have done—and if meaning-related features are solonic, also in virtue of what we will do. And though many maintain the causal history of our uses of a word plays a metasemantic role, no one thinks that causal history *causes* the word to mean what it does; if causal history is metasemantically relevant, it makes words mean what they do in a non-causal way. There are, of course, interesting, deep, and difficult metaphysical questions about exactly what such non-causal determination consists in. (Supervenience or grounding—and what is ground anyway?—or something else?) But answering these questions would require a chapter (or a book) of its own, and the details matter little to our main themes. I therefore propose to take the notion of non-causal determination for granted, and to focus on issues that arise from the claim that how things are later non-causally determines how things are earlier.

Let me make some terminological stipulations to ease the discussion. I will abbreviate the noun phrase "non-causal determination" and the verb phrase "non-causally determines" *NCD*. One of the metaphysical issues that we are glossing over is the nature of the relata of the relation of NCD. I will say that *facts* NCD other facts (as when, according to Solon, the fact that a person will fall into great misfortune in old age NCDs the fact that they are not happy in youth), but I do not thereby intend to be making a substantive claim; I intend "facts" as I use it to be neutral as to the nature of these entities.

I will speak of the NCD of later facts by earlier facts as *forward NCD*, and the NCD of earlier facts by later facts as *backward NCD*. *Cross-temporal NCD* includes both forward and backward NCD.

2. The Metaphysics of Time

Exactly what we want to say about backward NCD will depend on our views about the metaphysics of time. The main question that will be relevant to our discussion is: what times exist? Eternalists respond that all times—past, present, and future—exist; all are equally real. There are a variety of alternatives to eternalism: notably presentism (the view that only the present exists), and "growing block" views on which the past and present exist but the future does not.

If eternalism is true, then understanding solonic properties and cross-temporal NCD is straightforward. If eternalism is true, then past and future objects (facts, events, etc.) exist—they are just as real as present objects—and since they exist, there is nothing to bar them entering into NCD relations. For example, the University of St Andrews advertises itself as *Scotland's first university*. The fact that St Andrews has that feature is NCDed by facts about the past—in particular, by the fact that no other university in Scotland was founded earlier. By the eternalist's lights, there is nothing mysterious here.

If eternalism is true, the future also exists; so facts about the future are also available to enter into NCD relations. According to the eternalist, there exist facts about my location at each point throughout my life—past, present, and future. And if these facts exist, they can enter into NCD relations. So there is nothing mysterious about them (for example) NCDing that this moment has the property of being the last time I set foot in this office.

The situation does not change when we turn our attention to metasemantics. Kripke (1980) defended a view of meaning on which (at least in many typical cases) the meaning of a name is determined by its causal connection to an initial use. For example, Kripke supposes that when I say "Barack Obama", the name picks out the person it does because my use is causally related to a "dubbing" or "initial baptism"—an occasion on which the name was introduced (presumably by the infant Obama's parents) to pick out that person. So on Kripke's view, facts about the past NCD facts about what "Obama" means now. But this is no more problematic than the facts about the past NCDing the fact that St Andrews is Scotland's first university. And crucially, by the eternalist's lights, backwards NCD should raise no additional problems. The facts about the future exist; why should they not NCD facts about the past and present? For instance, the end of my life exists to NCD whether I am happy now; and (crucially for our purposes) if our disputes resolve, that resolution exists in order to NCD what we mean now.

2.1 The Open Future

Our discussion so far focused on eternalism; but similar points could be made about other views. Presentists, for example, must engage in some moderately fancy footwork to make sense of any past- or future-directed claims. There are various strategies: some presentists claim that present things may have past- or future-directed "Lucretian" properties (perhaps, *being such that the University of St Andrews was founded in 1516*) (Bigelow, 1996), others claim that there may exist now true propositions about the past or the future (Crisp, 2007). But every presentist must have some strategy for explaining cases of forwards NCD. And if the presentist maintains that there are suitable truths about the future (for example, because some things have the relevant future-directed Lucretian properties, or because relevant propositions about the future are true), there is no reason why an analogous strategy should be more problematic for backwards NCD.

What would make the situation more complicated is a view that treats the past and the future *asymmetrically*: perhaps the past exists and the future does not, or perhaps, though neither exists, there are relevant presentist properties or propositions about the past but not the about the future. The problem is that many philosophers have found such an asymmetry plausible and well motivated. After all, while most views regard the facts about the past as fixed, many think that the future is still open. And if there is no fact of the matter about whether I'll come in to work tomorrow—not yet—then there is nothing that could make it the case that this is the last time I set foot in this office.

There are a variety of ways of thinking about the metaphysics of the open future, and a discussion of the details would take us too far afield from the issues that are the main focus of this book. I do not believe that the open future poses a distinctive problem for the metasemantic view defended here.[2] Any proponent of the open future must say something about our attitudes towards contingent near certainties such as *that the sun will rise tomorrow*. Presumably, the open future

---

[2] What might be a problem is a view on which the future is divided—for example, in which time splits into two, so that there are two distinct paths that are both my future. (Thanks to Roy Sorenson for raising this issue.) In this case, the temporal externalist might predict that meaning is pulled in multiple, incompatible directions. It is a good question whether divided time is a genuine possibility; see King (1995) for related discussion. Even if it is, it is not clear whether cases of this kind could generate a serious objection to temporal externalism; the temporal externalist might predict that meaning is indeterminate in these cases, but that verdict is not implausible. See Chapter 10, Section 9 for discussion of some related phenomena.

theorist regards it as open whether the sun will rise tomorrow; that is a contingent matter. Nonetheless, it is overwhelmingly likely that the sun will rise tomorrow in ways that make it rational to act on the assumption that it will. Even if it is not true that the sun will rise tomorrow, everyone should grant that our attitudes towards that proposition should be significantly different than our attitudes towards claims like *that this fair coin will land heads when I flip it*. I take it that in many cases, the facts about what I mean will be in the same category as *that the sun will rise tomorrow*: in many cases, there is little prospect of our beliefs and patterns of usage changing in ways that unexpectedly shape what we mean now. If the view predicts that in cases where there is significant uncertainty about our future beliefs and usage, we should not act confidently on the basis of claims about what we mean, that strikes me as plausible and unproblematic.

There is one further reason to think that the open future might be problematic for the purposes of the project of this book. I am presenting the metasemantic view I develop as an alternative to relativism (Chapter 9). But John MacFarlane (2003, 2008) argues that relativism is necessary for making sense of our our patterns of asserting and assessing claims about the future. I think that MacFarlane's case is not decisive, but I cannot address it in detail here. For now I will note only that even if MacFarlane is correct and the future is open, the result would be that claims about what we mean (like claims about future contingents) are true or false only as assessed at a particular time; temporal externalism can be understood within this framework, and the case against rival views (including relativist views about predicates of taste and related phenomena) would be unaffected.

I take the discussion to this point to have established that there is no deep metaphysical difficulty about temporal externalism; the view could be developed in ways that are compatible with a wide range of views about the nature of non-casual dependence and about the metaphysics of time.

3. Can the Future Explain the Past?

Even granting that the idea of backwards NCD is coherent, one might be worried about the idea that the future can *explain* the past. Perhaps not every kind of backwards explanation is problematic; after all, in granting the coherence of backwards NCD, we are (arguably) granting the coherence of a certain kind of backwards explanation: backwards constitutive explanation. For example, one way of explaining why 4 April 2008 was the last day I set foot in that office is by appeal to the fact that I left the office on that day and never returned. Still, what the temporal externalist is claiming is that intentional properties, such as the property of meaning *art*, or the property of having a belief or a desire with a particular content, are solonic—one has them in virtue of what happens in the future. These properties enter into psychological explanations: for example,

I went to the museum because I wanted to see art, or *Malcolm inferred that Moore doesn't know because he believes knowledge requires doubt*. Plausibly, psychological explanations of this kind are causal; we are saying (for example) that my desire to see art (presumably in conjunction with certain beliefs) *causally explains* my going to the museum. So the temporal externalist is committed to the claim that solonic properties figure in causal explanations.

This commitment might strike one as surprising. This section aims to make it plausible. The key claim is that familiar strategies for addressing related worries about mental causation—such as the worry that mental properties are excluded as causes by their neurobiological realisers, and the worry that intentional properties cannot be causes because having particular intentional properties depends on environmental factors—apply straightforwardly if temporal externalism is true. The upshot is that there is no unique problem about causation for temporal externalists.

Before turning to this, however, we need to get clear on the phenomenon. Many are sceptical of the possibility of backwards causation; that is, many think that it is impossible that an event which takes place at a later time be the cause of an event that takes place at an earlier time. The temporal externalist is not committed to backwards causation in this sense. What the temporal externalist is committed to is the existence of cases in which an event at an earlier time causally explains an event at a later time, and the earlier event has a property that features in this causal explanation in virtue of something that happens at a later time. In short, the picture is not:

e_2 at t_2 causally explains e_1 at t_1 (where t_2 is later than t_1).

It is rather:

e_1 at t_1 causally explains e_2 at t_2, in virtue of some feature p that some entity has at t_1, where the having of p at t_1 is NCDed by what happens at t_3 (where t_3 is later than t_2, and t_2 is later than t_1).

Or, in short:

e_1 at t_1 causally explains e_2 at t_2, in virtue of some feature p that some entity has at t_1, where p is solonic.

Call this *solonic causal explanation*. The temporal externalist is committed to solonic causal explanation.

Is this commitment problematic? Let's hope not: the kinds of cases that we have already considered show that appeals to solonic causal explanation are common. Consider, for example, the case of Barack and Michelle, discussed in the appendix to Chapter 6. In that case, Barack defended the view that to act freely is to have the ability to do what you want; Michelle objected that in that case an addict who desires a drug and takes it does so freely; Barack responded, "I take your point: the drug addict isn't free. So I was wrong to think that there is nothing more to freedom than the ability to do what you want. Real freedom requires not only doing what you want, but also having the desires that you want"; and Michelle agreed: "Ok, I was thinking that free will requires the ability to do otherwise. But now I see that isn't true."

Focus on the last two points. Barack attributes to Michelle the point that the drug addict isn't free. He concludes on the basis of considering this claim that his belief that to act freely is to do what you want is false, and adopts another view. In describing his reasoning, Barack is engaging in a kind of psychological explanation; he is saying: I used to believe that to act freely is to do what you want; I came to believe that an addict does not act freely, and that is inconsistent with the belief that to act freely is to do what you want; and so I gave up the belief that to act freely is to do what you want. This is a description of a causal process: Barack's having adopted one belief causally explains his adopting another, and so on.

In most cases, psychological explanations of this kind work because the causal transitions they describe track logical, or more broadly rational, relations between the contents of the attitudes. For example, if I believe that p and that *if p then q*, and I infer that q, that is a causal process; but our account of it in psychological terms depends on the fact that *that p* and *that if p then q* together entail *that q*.

Likewise with Barack's explanation of his transition in belief: it makes sense for him to give up the belief that to act freely is to do what you want, because that is inconsistent with the judgement that the addict does what they want but does not act freely. But that is the case only if 'act freely' is univocal in the two claims. And we have already argued that temporal externalism is the best (perhaps the only plausible) view that can deliver the result. Similar remarks apply to Michelle's explanation of her own change in belief.

So, our psychological explanations in this kind of case turn on temporal externalism, since temporal externalism is the only view on which the contents appealed to in these explanations stand in appropriate rational relations.

Of course, this does not show that our psychological explanations are correct. Some may worry that there is a deep problem about solonic causal explanations—that such 'explanations' cannot genuinely be explanatory, or place unacceptable demands on the metaphysics of causation. For example, even though solonic causal explanations do not strictly speaking involve backwards causation, it still may seem that some objectionable analogue of backwards causation is at work: how could properties possession of which depends in part upon what happens later be implicated in causation?

My strategy for addressing this worry is the following. Many views have it that whether we are in certain mental states depends on factors external to us—on our histories or environments. These views face analogous worries about the role of mental states in causal explanation. (If what mental states we are in is determined by factors outside of us and if those mental states play a role in causal explanation, then it may seem that there is an objectionable kind of action at a distance: how could properties possession of which depends in part upon what happens in the environment or in the distant past be implicated in causation?)

There are a number of strategies in the literature for resisting this line of argument. I will focus on one: Williamson's (2000) argument for the causal efficacy of knowledge. My aim is to show that it can easily extend to the temporal case. So temporal externalism has no distinctive problem about mental causation.

Williamson maintains that knowledge—clearly an extrinsic state, since it requires truth—is a better candidate cause of behaviour than belief in many cases, since in many cases we are interested in explaining behaviours that extend across time and involve interaction with the environment:

> Consider a causal explanation as simple as 'He dug up the treasure because he knew that it was buried under the tree and he wanted to get rich'. Note that the explanandum ('He dug up the treasure') makes reference to objects in the environment (the treasure) as well as to the subject's immediate physical movements. The internalist cannot substitute 'believe' for 'know' in the explanation without loss, for the revised explanans, unlike the original, does not entail that the treasure was where he believed it to be; the connection between explanans and explanandum is therefore weakened. (Williamson, 2000, 61–62)

Even true belief, Williamson maintains, would be a worse explanation. Suppose, for example, that the treasure hunter infers that the treasure is buried under the tree because they believe that it buried in the spot marked with an *X*, and that that spot is under the tree. But suppose that, although the treasure is under the tree, the *X* is not under the tree. In that case, the treasure hunter will believe, but not know, that the treasure is under the tree. If they look under the tree and see that the *X* is not there, then we would expect them to stop searching. In that case, true belief fails to explain why they dug up the treasure. An explanation that appeals to knowledge, on the other hand, would not fail.

Williamson concedes that in any given case, there might be alternative ways of giving a causally sufficient condition for the action: for example, one might give a complete physical description of the thinker and of their environment. But good explanations "capture significant generalizations" (Williamson, 2000, 81). The explanation in terms of knowledge will apply in a wide range of cases (including cases which are physically dissimilar): at least *ceteris paribus*, anyone who knows that the treasure is under the tree and wants the treasure will find it. The explanation in terms of the physical details misses this generalisation. It is overly specific, and so a worse explanation.

So Williamson's case for the causal efficacy of knowledge is that knowledge is more closely connected to the physically and temporally extended events that we are often interested in explaining than competing putative explanations, and does a good job of capturing significant generalisations. The case I want to make is that explanations in terms of the intentional properties posited by temporal externalism share these features.

Consider again Barack's explanation of his reasoning about free action. We described it in these terms: "I used to believe that to act freely is to do what you want; I came to believe that an addict does not act freely, and that is inconsistent with the belief that to act freely is to do what you want; and so, I gave up the belief that to act freely is to do what you want." The connection between the explanans and the explanandum is very close: setting aside cases of flagrant irrationality, we would expect anyone who comes to believe that addicts do not act freely despite doing what they want to believe that it is not the case that to act freely is to do what you want. This is a generalisation in itself. But it is also an instance of an even more significant generalisation, a generalisation that underlies: people do not typically believe inconsistent things, and if they detect an inconsistency, they will come to reject one of the inconsistent beliefs.

Again, we have argued that temporal externalism is the best way to deliver the result that one can change one's theoretical views so significantly without change of meaning or conceptual replacement; and this means that it is the only view that can deliver these straightforward explanations. This is, of course, not to say that it is impossible to give causally sufficient conditions for Barack's conclusion in other terms. For example, it is possible in principle to give a purely physical description of his brain through the reasoning process. But (as in Williamson's case) this would miss significant generalisations.

There are, of course, other strategies in the literature for making the case that externalistically determined contents might play a role in causal explanation. (For example, the notion of programme explanation discussed in Chapter 4 can be used in this way.) Many of these are available to the temporal externalist.[3] I therefore conclude that causation provides no distinctive obstacle to temporal externalism; on the contrary, there are reasons to think that the contents posited by temporal externalism are exceptionally good candidates to serve as causes. In the next

---

[3] It is true, however, that some strategies are not easily available to the temporal externalist; for example, it is hard to see how the temporal externalist could take up Dretske's (1991) idea that one's history provides a structuring cause.

section, we turn to a further objection often pressed against externalists of all stripes: that externalism prevents self-knowledge of what one thinks or means.

4. Self-Knowledge and Disquotation

Objections to the externalism that rely on claims about self-knowledge are very familiar, but they may seem particularly acute for the kind of temporal externalist view that I favour. In broad outline, the problem is that we all seem to be able to know what we are thinking and what we mean by introspection, without investigating the external world; but it is hard to understand how this is possible if what we are thinking and what we mean is determined by external factors.

The worry may seem to be particularly serious for the proponent of temporal externalist metasemantics, since on this view contingent facts about the future are the external factors that fix meaning, and it may seem that we are in a particularly bad epistemic position with respect to future contingents. So my first task is to make the case that if there is a problem about self-knowledge and temporal externalism, it is essentially the same as (and not qualitatively worse than) the problem facing other externalisms.

We began with a broad worry that there is a tension between the idea that meaning can be known introspectively and the idea that meaning is determined by the environment. There are various ways of developing this broad worry into a precise argument. Consider again a Putnam-inspired view of natural kind terms, on which what we mean by a word like "water" is determined in part by what substances are present in our environment. One way of developing the worry about introspective knowledge is to imagine a person who is unknowingly switched between an environment containing H_2O and an environment containing XYZ. On a plausible way of developing a Putnam-style view, such a switch may result in a change in meaning: the person who before the switch used "Water is wet" to make assertions that are true just in case H_2O is wet will eventually come to use "Water is wet" to make assertions that are true just in case XYZ is wet. Let's stipulate that the content of these latter assertions is *that twin-water is wet*. Crucially, this change may not be apparent on introspection; the chemically naive speaker may not know that she has been switched, and may not be aware of the difference between her previous environment and her present environment. For such a speaker, there seems to be no way of telling the difference introspectively, "from the inside", between thinking that water is wet and thinking that twin-water is wet, or between uttering "Water is wet" in order to say that water is wet and uttering a homophonic sentence in order to say that twin-water is wet.

This has seemed to several philosophers to pose a problem for the idea that we are in a position to know by introspection what we are thinking and what we mean.

One way of developing the worry is based on the idea that knowledge requires ruling out relevant alternatives:

Relevant Alternatives (RA) If (i) q is a relevant alternative to p and (ii) S's belief that p is based on evidence that is compatible with its being the case that q, then S does not know that p. (See Falvey and Owens, 1994, and McLaughlin and Tye, 1998, 353).

It is plausible that there is some true claim in the vicinity of (RA). If my belief that there is a rat in the garden is based on some evidence (the fact that I heard a rustle in the bushes, perhaps) that could just as easily have been a bird or the neighbour's cat, then I do not know that there is a rat in the garden. (RA) explains this: I could come to know only by getting evidence that would rule out the bird and the cat. The restriction to *relevant* alternatives is necessary to resist scepticism. At least on some conceptions of evidence, all of our evidence is compatible with its being the case that we are duped brains in a vat. If we nonetheless know ordinary empirical propositions, that is because the proposition that we are brains in vats is not relevant. Exactly what makes an alternative relevant is an interesting question, but we need not pause to attempt to work out the details; it is plausible that on any reasonable view, the proposition that I think that water is wet will be a relevant alternative to the proposition that I think that twin-water is wet (and vice versa) in the switching scenario.

Temporal externalism faces essentially the same problem; and it forecloses certain potential lines of response. For example, one line of resistance to this argument turns on the claim that the scenario in which we are switched between H_2O and XYZ environments is an extremely unusual one. If switching of this kind is necessary to raise alternatives to relevance, then self-knowledge is threatened only for thinkers who are switched. And if the conclusion we should draw from these considerations is that externalism predicts we can know what we mean, except in the scenario where we are unknowingly kidnapped and transported to different environments, one might find the threat to self-knowledge less than fearsome. Now, it is debatable whether the kinds of external factors that raise alternative meanings to the status of relevant alternatives are common or rare, if what we have in mind is the familiar kinds of externalist consideration developed by Putnam, Burge, Kripke, and others (see Ludlow, 1995). But regardless of the outcome of this debate, is quite plausible that temporal externalism makes alternatives relevant in a range of cases. Suppose we are discussing some matter of definition—say, whether gambling addiction is a disease—and suppose that, although we don't think that the debate will continue indefinitely, it is really unclear which how the debate will end. Then we are precisely faced with a scenario in which there are two (or more) alternative sets of facts that might fix meaning, we don't know which obtains, and the two possibilities are at the forefront of our attention. (I may be entertaining the possibility that you will convince me, wondering how I can rebut your arguments and defend my own position.) In this case, it seems hard to resist the idea that each outcome is a relevant alternative to the other.

Fortunately, there is a relatively standard line of response to these problems in the literature. This response points out that whether the switching case poses a substantial threat depends on exactly what we are supposed to be able to know by introspection. The proponent of this line of thought grants (what is fairly obviously true regardless of one's metasemantic views) that we cannot know by introspection that "water" as we use it is correctly applied to all and only aggregates of H_2O molecules. Knowing that requires empirical investigation. Nor can we know by introspection that (for example) "water" and "H_2O" are co-referential, or that "Water is wet" as we use it is true if and only if aggregates of H_2O molecules are wet. But there are some things that we can be entirely confident about on the basis of introspection, regardless of how the environment turns out—indeed that we cannot say or think falsely: things like (at the level of speech) " 'Water is wet' as I use it is true just in case water is wet", and (at the level of thought) "With this very thought, I am thinking that water is wet". These claims and thoughts cannot go wrong, roughly because (at the level of speech) whatever fixes the meaning of the mentioned sentence on the left-hand side of the biconditional also fixes the meaning of the used sentence on the right-hand side, so that the two cannot come apart; and likewise (at the level of thought) whatever fixed the content of the thought that I am thinking that water is wet also fixes the content of the embedded thought that water is wet, so that the two cannot come apart.

The response distinguishes between *disquotational* self-attributions of meaning—attributions like "water" as I use it means *water*, or "water is wet" as I use it is true if and only if water is wet—and *non-disquotational* self-attributions of meaning. It then observes that although externalism introduces the possibility of error with respect to non-disquotational self-attributions of meaning, it does not introduce the possibility of error with respect to disquotational self-attributions. On the contrary, those judgements seem to be (as Burge, 1988, says) *self-verifying*: they cannot be made falsely.

The idea, in short, is that I can capture the content of some part of my speech and thought—what I am saying, what I am thinking— by using the very words, the very cognitive representational capacities, that I use in that part of my speech and thought. A couple of points should be made. First, doing so is a distinct way of characterising what I mean; thinking, "With this very thought, I am thinking that water is wet" is not equivalent to any way of characterising what I am thinking in terms of "H_2O" thoughts, and does not depend on my having the ability to characterise what I am thinking in other terms. Second, characterisations of this kind are *substantive*. When one thinks "I am thinking that water is wet", one is thereby entertaining the thought that water is wet. This thought is contentful; it is not (for example) merely a mental image of some sounds that might have any content. And this arguably puts one in a position to tell a story on which disquotational self-attributions rule out relevant alternatives (see McLaughlin and Tye, 1998).

Nothing about this story has depended on the details of the metasemantic mechanisms that the externalist takes to determine meaning. The story works equally well for those who think that the causal history of our representations is metasemantically important, for those who think that the kinds in our environment are metasemantically important, and for those who think that the views of our linguistic peers are metasemantically important. And, importantly, the story works even if we think that facts about the future are metasemantically important. Even if this is the case, that fact would not make it possibile that our disquotational self-attributions are in error; as long as temporal externalist mechanisms determine the meaning of our higher-order representations and the representations that they are about in the same way, there is no possibility that the two will differ in content.[4]

There are many outstanding issues about the epistemic status of disquotational self-attributions of meaning: for example, it hardly immediately obvious that every self-verifying claim is easily known, and even if one has the feeling that it is known it is hardly immediately obvious *how* it is known; a further epistemological story is needed. And there are worries about the externalism and self-knowledge that are not straightforwardly addressed by the observations about disquotational self-attribution (e.g., Boghossian, 1997b).[5] I have nothing substantive to add to these debates, and this is not the place to try to resolve every question about knowing what we think and what we mean. What I want to conclude is only (i) that temporal externalism is not worse off with respect to these issues than other forms of externalism; and (ii) that temporal externalism can avail itself of the same resources as other forms of externalism in answering challenges about self-knowledge.

5. Vagueness, Persistence, and Meaning Change

I have claimed that in definitional disputes meanings remain constant throughout the dispute; for example, all parties to the dispute are using "art" with the same meaning, and this meaning does not change even when their views about what art is change. But surely meaning changes sometimes. "Madagascar" went from

---

[4] Presumably this is true even if the content we are self-attributing is indeterminate (for example, because the future is open); even in this case, I can use precisely the same representational resources in speaking and thinking as I use to talk about my own speech and thought; my disquotational self-attributions cannot come apart in content from my first-order thoughts and speech acts.

[5] See Jackman (2015) for discussion of some of these issues from a temporal-externalist friendly perspective.

referring to a part of the mainland to referring to an island (Evans, 1985); "gay" as we use it today does not mean the same thing that it meant in 1900 (Brown, 2000).

We have already provided some resources to begin to respond to objections of this kind. One motivation for my claim that meaning does not change is that it is important to vindicate our retrospective judgements about, and retrospective evaluations of, what we said and thought. If we say things like, "I used to think that art had to be beautiful, but now I see that I was wrong", that is a motivation for maintaining that the meaning of "art" as we use it has not changed. Since we do not say things like "People used to think that all gay people are happy, but now we see that that is wrong", there is no analogous motivation for thinking that the meaning of "gay" has not changed. On the contrary: we judge that utterances in 1900 of "All gay people are happy" are compatible with our own views, not in disagreement with what we believe. And these judgements, too, are something that our metasemantics should take into account: they can play a role in making it the case that "gay" as used then does not mean what "gay" means now. In short, the idea is that *retrospective reports and evaluations track sameness of meaning*.[6]

Here is a simple version of this kind of view. Let R and S range over representations, such as words (but potentially also mental representations such as concepts: see the discussion in Chapter 10, Section 1).

Retrospective Reports 1 (RR1) x's use of R at t_0 means the same as y's use of S at t_1

1. if y at t_1 is disposed to report x's use of R at t_0 using S; and
2. only if y is not disposed to reject reports of x's use of R at t_0 that use S.

RR1 handles the basic cases we have seen so far: in the case where I am inclined to say "I used to say that art had to be beautiful, but now I see that I was wrong", the first condition is met—I am using "art" to report on my prior use of "art"—so RR1 would predict that my meaning hasn't changed (despite my change in view). In the case where I am not inclined to say "People used to think that all gay people are happy, but now we see that that is wrong", the second condition is not met; I am disposed to reject reports using "gay" of speakers' use of "gay" 100 years ago. So RR1 would predict that meaning has changed.

RR1 does not provide individually necessary and jointly sufficient conditions. There will be cases in which one speaker is simply not aware of another and has no dispositions to report on them. In order to get an account that gives a verdict on every case, we would need to appeal to other criteria. We will not discuss the

---

[6] I am assuming here that interpersonal as well as intrapersonal retrospective reports matter. See Chapter 10, Section 6 for further discussion. See Ebbs (2000) for development of a related strategy.

possibilities here; even waiving this complication, RR1 is too simple, and we will discuss three complications that require modification of RR1 in what follows.

The first complication that motivates a modification of RR1 is that there may be cases in which y is simply wrong about x's practice. y is disposed to report x's practice in a certain way, but that is only because they are misinformed about x's attitudes or actions; if y knew the facts, they would change their mind. Worse, someone's practice of disquotational reporting may be simply unreasonable. It may appear random, not tracking any practice that we would recognise; or it may be superficial, relying on similarity in sound or appearance even when there are extreme differences in belief and underlying usage. Clearly, judgements like this should not be taken to bear on sameness of meaning. Therefore, RR1 should be replaced:

Retrospective Reports 2 (RR2) x's use of R at t_0 means the same as y's use of S at t_1

1. if y at t_1 *is sufficiently well informed about x's use of R at t_0* and is disposed to report that use with S, *and this disposition is reasonable*; and
2. only if in circumstances where *y is sufficiently well informed about x's use of R at t_0*, y is not disposed to reject reports of x's use of R at t_0 that use S, *and this disposition is reasonable*.

I would like to have a detailed systematic recipe for determining whether a disposition to report is reasonable or not, but I do not know how to provide one. Instead, I am going to take the notion of reasonableness for granted. To the extent that there is unclarity about whether a given disposition is unreasonable, there will be corresponding unclarity about whether meaning is the same, but since unreasonable dispositions are rare in practice, this seems like a consequence we can live with.

The second complication is that we need to restrict our attention to reports that take place in particular circumstances. As a number of philosophers have pointed out (e.g., Cappelen and Lepore, 2005), it is often permissible to disquotationally report oneself or others, even if the literal meaning of the words one uses does not exactly match the literal meaning of the words used in the speech act you are reporting. (To take a simple case, suppose that I say "Ansel is tall". "Tall" is context-sensitive—it picks out different properties in a conversation about skyscrapers than in a conversation about 7-year-olds. So, the proposition I express will depend on whatever subtle factors of my situation determine the standard one must meet to count as "tall". Nonetheless, you can report me as having said that Ansel is tall in a wide range of situations that differ with respect to these factors, and hence with respect to the standard one must meet to count as "tall".)

The phenomenon is an important one, but I still think that our disquotational reports are a critical source of evidence. This is because, even if such "loose" reports are possible in many circumstances, they are problematic in many others. One circumstance that makes such reports problematic is when we are trying to *evaluate* what someone said: whether they were right or wrong, whether they had good evidence for their claim, and so on. For example, let's call what I meant by "Ansel is tall" p_1, and what we would mean by "Ansel is tall" in the present context p_2; and let's suppose that p_1 is true and p_2 is false. Then if even if it is possible in some circumstances to report, "Derek said that Ansel is tall", it seems very problematic to say, "Derek said that Ansel is tall, but that is wrong"; after all, what I said was correct. Similarly, if my grounds for asserting p_1 were that his height significantly exceeds the height of other children in his class, and that these are good grounds for asserting p_1 but not for p_2, then it seems very problematic to say, "Derek said that Ansel is tall because he is taller than other children; but that is clearly no good reason to think that he is tall".

Now consider the kind of circumstance in which we have stressed the importance of disquotational reporting: we are engaged in a definitional dispute, looking back on a course of inquiry, evaluating our previous claims and the evidence for and against them. Call these *reasons-assessing circumstances*. Now reasons-assessing circumstances are precisely circumstances in which we have argued that it is important that disquotational reports track sameness of meaning.

The conclusion we should draw, therefore, is that RR2 can be modified to accomodate the flexibility in our reporting practice by restricting our attention to reasons-assessing circumstances.

Retrospective Reports 3 (RR3) x's use of R at t_0 means the same as y's use of S at t_1

1. if y at t_1 is sufficiently well informed about x's use of R at t_0 and *in reasons-assessing circumstances* y is disposed to report that use with S, and this disposition is reasonable; and
2. only if *in reasons-assessing* circumstances where y is sufficiently well informed about x's use of R at t_0, y is not disposed to reject reports of x's use of R at t_0 that use S, and this disposition is reasonable.[7]

---

[7] A referee objects that there are counterexamples to any view of this kind: suppose that at one time I use R with one meaning, and at a later time with a different meaning, but I do not notice the change. Then, I may be disposed to report my earlier usage of R using R; but by hypothesis the meaning of R has changed. I reply that the objection is question-begging: in any such case, if the meaning has genuinely changed, my persistence in reporting will be due to a failure to be sufficiently well informed or reasonable. If it is stipulated that I am well informed and reasonable, then I deny that the case is possible: in that case, it is not possible that the meaning has changed.

The third complication is that meaning change typically happens gradually. In 1200, "meat" applied to any solid food; by 2000, it applied only to the flesh of dead animals. I take it that we are not inclined to think retrospectively that our medieval ancestors were wrong to think that carrots were meat. The meaning of "meat" has changed. But it seems impossible to point to a specific time where the meaning change happened. (What year? Whose usage?)

So far, this is merely a question. But we can build these considerations into a line of argument against RR3. A speaker in 1201 would presumably be inclined to report uses of "meat" in 1200 disquotationally. By RR3, this would suggest that "meat" meant the same in 1201 as it did in 1200. Likewise, speakers in 1202 would be disposed disquotationally to report speakers in 1201; and this would suggest that "meat" meant the same in 1202 as in 1201, and hence (by the transitivity of sameness) the same in 1202 as in 1200. Likewise in 1203, and so on, year by year, until we can establish by this reasoning the obviously false conclusion that "meat" meant the same in 2000 as it did in 1200.

Now one response to this line of argument is that it is an instance of the sorites. Just as (say) colour terms are vague, such that it is impossible to locate the boundary between yellow and orange, likewise intentional language like "means *meat*" and "said that carrots are meat" are vague, such that it is impossible to locate the boundary between *meaning meat* and *meaning food*. And of course, there are a wide range of responses to sorites arguments in the literature; your favourite ought to be applicable in this case.

This may be the right response to the argument. I don't have much to add to the literature on vagueness, and so I won't comment further on particular versions of this strategy here. What I do want to point out is that this is not the only possible reaction to the case; there are other analogues of the argument in well-known philosophical literature—in particular, in the literature on persistence and personal identity. This analogue is the focus of discussion in the remainder of this chapter.

5.1 How Representations Persist

How do things persist? I am typing on a computer now; I typed on the same computer yesterday. But how should we think about the idea that today's computer is the same as yesterday's? And how should we think about the idea that I am the same person? To introduce some of the puzzles in this area, and to build up the apparatus we need to theorise about them, it will be helpful to borrow a familiar case of change (from Lewis, 1986, pp. 203–204): at t_0 I am sitting, and so have a particular shape. At t_1 I am not sitting, and so have a different shape. The metaphysician must give some account of this phenomenon that does not incoherently attribute both the property of sitting and the property of not sitting to one and the same object (in one and the same way). One plausible approach has it that the bearers of properties like *sitting* and *having such and such particular shape* are things that exist only for an instant: time-slices or *stages*. One and the same thing never has the property of sitting and the property of standing; the stage that sits is distinct from the stage that stands.

At this point, there are different ways in which the view has been developed.[8] One prominent view maintains that, in addition to the stages, there are objects that have stages as their parts. For example, my computer was here yesterday and still persists today. At every moment between yesterday and today, there is a computer-stage that exists only at that moment; but there is also an object that is composed of all of those stages. My computer is this temporally extended worm. Similarly, at each moment between my birth and my death, there is a person-stage; in addition to the stages, there is an object that is composed of them. I am this temporally extended worm. I (the worm) do not strictly speaking have the property of sitting, or the property of standing. Instead, it is my parts (the stages) that have those properties; I am sitting at t_0 in virtue of having a part that has the property of sitting.

Lewis claims that this style of view also has the potential to address other puzzle cases. It is very plausible that what matters to whether a person persists over time is relations of mental continuity and connectedness. For example, I judge that the person-stages who sat at this desk yesterday were me because I remember what those stages did, because I share with those stages many beliefs, interests, purposes, and character traits, and so on. But now consider the following case (adapted by Lewis from Parfit, 1971):[9]

> Consider Methuselah. At the age of 100 he still remembers his childhood. But new memories crowd out the old. At the age of 150 he has hardly any memories that go back before his twentieth year. At the age of 200 he has hardly any memories that go back before his seventieth year; and so on. When he dies at the age of 969, he has hardly any memories that go beyond his 839th year. As he grows older he grows wider; his callow opinions and character at age 90 have vanished almost

---

[8] For overviews of the debate, see Haslanger (2003); Hawley (2001); Sider (2001).
[9] Thinking of personal identity suggests other puzzle cases. A word can undergo *fission*: the English word "meat" and the Norwegian word "mat" (which refers to all food) descend from a common ancestor. Assuming that "meat" and "mat" do not have the same meaning, both cannot determine the meaning of that ancestor. In this case, there is no problem, since modern English speakers do not suppose that speakers hundreds of years ago were mistaken to regard carrots as "meat". But one can imagine a case in which a word undergoes fission, with the result that two distinct groups of speakers may each be inclined to retrospectively report their common ancestor. But I do not think that this kind of case poses a serious challenge to the temporal externalist's view, since in this case there is in effect a disagreement that has not resolved: if the two groups interact, they would dispute, and so we ought not to regard their inquiry as having reached a conclusion. This is therefore a case in which the temporal externalist needs make no definite prediction. However, the resources described in the following paragraphs could also be used to give an account of this case.

without a trace by age 220, but his opinions and character at age 220 also have vanished almost without a trace by age 350. [...] And so it goes.

(Lewis, 1983d, 65–66)

It would be natural for Methuselah to think that he was literally a different person at age 800 than he was at age 80. How can this be? After all, he is presumably the same person at 81 that he was at 80; there are strong psychological connections between stages at those times. And likewise he is the same person at 82 that he was at 81. And so on—there are no sharp breaks, no natural place to draw a cutoff between the person he was at 80 and the person he is at 800.

Lewis's account of the matter emphasises that a single stage can be a part of multiple worms. Following Lewis, suppose that there are sufficient connections between any two stages that are no more than 137 years apart, and insufficient connections between any two stages that are more than 137 years apart. Then every 137-year-long segment will be a person.

On this view, any stage will be a stage of many persons. This naturally raises issues about how to count persons. (Lewis poses the question as follows: "Methuselah spends his 300th birthday alone in his room. How many persons are in that room? There are infinitely many different 137-year segments that include all of Methuselah's stages on his 300th birthday" (1983d, 66).) Lewis's reply is that we ought "to deny that we must invariably count two nonidentical continuants as two" (1983d, 63). Instead, Lewis claims, we may count nonidentical continuants as one at a time if they share a stage at that time. As motivation, Lewis appeals to the fact that we apply similar methods in more quotidian cases:

If an infirm man wishes to know how many roads he must cross to reach his destination, I will count by identity-along-his-path rather than by identity. By crossing the Chester A. Arthur Parkway and Route 137 at the brief stretch where they have merged, he can cross both by crossing only one road. Yet these two roads are certainly not identical. (1983d, 63–64)

With this sketch of a view of persistence in hand, let's return to the issue about meaning with which we began. Simon Prosser (2020) points out that resources from the metaphysics of persistence of material objects can be applied to the metaphysics of representations.[10] In the remainder of this section, I want to make

---

[10] Prosser's focus is on a particular account of mental representations—the mental files view of Recanati (2012)—and on a different view of persistence than we have discussed—the stage theory of Hawley (2001); Sider (2001). But the basic insight can be adapted to other kinds of account. See also the discussion of Kaplan (1990) in Hawthorne and Lepore (2011).

use of Prosser's insight to sketch an account of the case of gradual meaning change that is compatible with temporal externalism.

It is plausible that words don't have stages in quite the way that people or computers do. But we can suppose a speaker at a time has a certain pattern of dispositions to use a word. A given pattern at a time is linked to patterns at other times in a number of ways, including by the kinds of reporting relations emphasised in RR3 and the discussion above. If RR3 was on the right track, then we can take the kinds of reporting relations considered there to link patterns into a temporally extended continuant. (Importantly, we need not restrict our attention to *retrospective* reports; we can consider reports of simultaneous or future speech acts as well.) One straightforward way to do this would be to allow each person's reporting dispositions to generate a continuant:

Report-Based Continuants *x*'s use of *R* at t_m is a part of the continuant generated by *y*'s use of *S* at t_n:

1. if *y* at t_n is sufficiently well informed about *x*'s use of *R* at t_m and *in reasons-assessing circumstances y* is disposed to report that use with *S*, and this disposition is reasonable; and
2. only if *in reasons-assessing* circumstances where *y* is sufficiently well informed about *x*'s use of *R* at t_m, *y* is not disposed to reject reports of *x*'s use of *R* at t_m that use *S*, and this disposition is reasonable.

Now the case of "meat" very much resembles the case of Methuselah; and the apparatus we have assembled puts us in a position to give a similar account. Any given use is not a part of a single word continuant in such a case. On the contrary: there may be many continuants.

The temporal externalist should say that it is continuants that are the primary bearers of meaning. To a first approximation, the temporal externalist view is that what a continuant means is determined by the dispositions associated with its final uses, the temporally latest uses that are parts of the continuant.

Uses get their meanings from the continuants of which they are a part. If a use is a part of only one relevant continuant, or if all of the continuants of which it is a part have the same meaning, then there is no problem about assigning a meaning. However, if a use is a part of many continuants that end up with different meanings—as is plausible for many borderline uses of a word like "meat"—then it is less clear what to say. (The situation is much like if Methuselah wonders: will I exist in 100 years? Some of the continuants of which the current Methuselah stage is a part will exist then, others will not. It is not clear whether Methuselah's question has a determinate, correct answer.)

One simple answer, which I think is appropriate in many cases, is that it is indeterminate what such intermediate uses of "meat" mean.[11] But for some purposes it may also be appropriate to adopt a more subtle view of meaning: uses have meanings only relative to continuants. We can consider a given borderline use of "meat" relative to a forward-stretching continuant—the continuant generated by later dispositions to report that use, which includes uses that occur long after users have come to apply "meat" only to animal flesh—and relative to that continuant, the use will mean *meat*; that is, it will be correctly applied only to animal flesh. Or, we can consider the same use relative to a backward-stretching continuant—the continuant that includes mostly uses that occurred before users had come to restrict "meat" from some foodstuffs, so that the borderline uses is one of the latest parts. Exactly what the content of this continuant will be depends on the details of the case; but we might imagine that relative to this continuant, the use means *food*; that is, it is correctly applied to any food.

When we interpret a speaker in this kind of situation, then, we have options: we can consider her use relative to the forward-stretching continuant or relative to the backwards-stretching continuant. This way of thinking of meaning has benefits. For example, it may be useful to be able to interpret a speaker as meaning different things, depending on our explanatory interests and purposes.

But thinking of our words (or, more seriously, thoughts) as having content only relative to a continuant—and, possibly, as having different meanings relative to different continuants—may come with costs as well. For example, it may require revision in how we conceive of rationality. Suppose that at a certain time I form a belief on the basis of an argument; perhaps I infer from the premise that so-and-so has free will to the conclusion that so-and-so could do otherwise. Now if my judgements and the judgements of my linguistic community, vary as time passes, it might turn out that my inference is a valid one relative to some continuants, and an invalid one relative to others; relative to one continuant I am making a good inference, relative to another I am making a mistake. This is a surprising consequence, and raises a number of questions. But it is of a piece with analogous revisions that have been proposed to the ways we conceive of the persistence of ourselves and things around us. Perhaps it is a consequence we can learn to live with.

---

[11] In effect, this amounts to a kind of supervaluationism: if every continuant of which a use is a part means X, then the use means X; if no continuant of which a use is a part means X, then the use does not mean X; otherwise the use is indeterminate in meaning.

6. Conclusion

This chapter began by explaining the idea that meaning can be backwards non-causally determined by later facts, defended the claims that this idea is compatible with a number of views of the metaphysics of time and that it poses no deeper problem about self-knowledge than other externalist views. It then discussed cases of meaning change. In many cases, our dispositions to report other uses track facts about meaning change. But in others, especially those where meaning change is gradual, these dispositions generate puzzles. I discussed two ways of resolving these puzzles: first, by associating them with sorites arguments and applying some theory of vagueness; second, by applying views that have been used to address analogous cases about the persistence of persons over time. There is more to be said about both possible resolutions, and I have not endorsed either view. But I hope that I have done enough to establish that these puzzles are not fatal to temporal externalism.

8
Contextualism, Relativism, and Metasemantics

The examples of definitional disputes on which we have focused thus far have presupposed that what is at issue when we are fixing the meaning of a word is something *constant* throughout our conversation, and also across other uses in our community. When we are arguing about art, we are (at least in the usual case) not thinking that we are using the word "art" with a novel meaning, unique to our conversation, and still less that we are discussing some idiosyncratic phenomenon of interest only to us now. On the contrary: we tend to presuppose that others are using the word "art" (and related words in other languages) with the same meaning, so that if we settle the definition, our conclusion will be relevant to future discussions and to evaluating the discussions of the past; if I decide that art is the product of a certain cultural practice, I will also think that Tolstoy and the ancient Greeks were wrong about art.

Not every discussion is like this. There are also words which seem designed precisely to make different contributions to semantics depending on the context in which they are used, and it is these words that will be our focus in this chapter.[1] If you and I each say "I am hungry", although there is an everyday sense in which each of our utterances of "I" means the same—we are both speaking English, and we are each using "I" to speak of ourselves—it is clear that our utterances differ semantically (my utterance is true just in case I am hungry, yours is true just in case you are hungry) and this is because "I" makes a different contribution to truth conditions when I use it than when you use it. (I use "I" to pick out myself, you use "I" to pick out yourself.)

The question of what makes it the case that "I" picks out what it does on each occasion of use is therefore a metasemantic question.[2] Perhaps in the case of "I", the answer to this question does not seem especially mysterious. But related questions in other cases are more difficult. What counts as "rich" if philosophers

---

[1] We revisit other sorts of case—in which a word is used in an idiosyncratic way for the purposes of a particular conversation—in Chapter 10.
[2] MacFarlane calls related questions *postsemantic* (e.g., MacFarlane, 2014, ch. 3). I have chosen to use *metasemantic* both because there is an established usage of the term "metasemantic" to talk about the question of how contextual parameters are fixed (e.g., Glanzberg, 2007), and because I want to stress the fundamental continuity of the processes by which the values of contextual parameters are fixed and the processes by which semantic values are fixed.

are at issue is one thing, what counts as "rich" if residents of Park Avenue are at issue is quite another, so that to say "Jane is rich" is to say something true in some conversations but not others. To say that someone is rich is to say that they are rich *by a certain standard*. But what makes it the case that a certain standard—the standard appropriate to evaluating philosophers, say—is the one relevant to a particular utterance of "Jane is rich"?

The view developed in Chapter 6 was that the conclusion of a debate can play a metasemantic role, implicitly defining words (such as "art") at issue in the debate in such a way that their meanings are determined throughout the debate. This chapter defends the view that the same mechanism plays a role in fixing the contribution of particular uses of words, including particular uses of many context-sensitive words—for example, the standard relevant to a particular utterance of "rich" or "flat". The view is plausible, I contend, because it is the best way of making sense of disputes involving context-sensitive vocabulary:

(23)   Tom: Jane is rich.
       Shiv: She is not; she can't afford a private island.

The view to be developed in this chapter and the next is that the interpretation of disputes of this kind depends on their resolution. Returning to (23), suppose the dialogue continues:

(24)   Tom: I see your point. I thought that Jane was rich, but she isn't. I was wrong.

The application of the methodology of the previous chapters to this case suggests that we take Tom's judgement seriously: his initial utterance of "Jane is rich" turns out to be false, and Shiv's challenge correct. But suppose instead the dialogue continues differently:

(25)   Tom: True, she can't afford a private island. But she is still rich: she makes far more money than most people. And have you seen her yacht?
       Shiv: Yeah, the yacht is nice. Ok, I take it back: she is rich after all.

Our methodology suggests taking Shiv's considered judgement seriously: Tom's initial utterance of "Jane is rich" turns out to be true, and Shiv's challenge a mistake.

As before, I will argue that the best theory will take claims like "If someone can't afford a private island, they are not rich", or "Jane is not rich" (in (24)), or "If someone owns a nice yacht, they are rich" (in (25)) as something like partial implicit definitions that play a metasemantic role. So in this sense, these disputes, too, ought to be thought of as definitional disputes (even though they are in most cases not giving real definitions). But (at least on the most natural way of imagining these cases), they do not fix the meaning of *every* use of "rich"; they are more or less irrelevant to later evaluations of whether particular countries (say), or corporations are rich—or even people, as evaluated in the context of some other conversation.

Cases of this kind are especially interesting because we also use gradable adjectives to talk about matters of taste:

(26) Philip: Richard Pryor is funny.
   Elizabeth: You're wrong. He is far too disgusting and offensive to be the slightest bit funny.

Disputes about what is funny (or tasty, sexy, cool, and so on) are especially puzzling because it looks as though each speaker is making a claim that they are in a position to know to be true; to a first approximation, anyone who has been exposed to Pryor's comedy is in a position to know whether it is funny (to them) or not. But this very fact makes it hard to understand how there could be a dispute here: what is at issue if both speakers are right?

There is a temptation to think that something is going wrong in debates like this, or that disputing about taste is fundamentally confused. I disagree: although some disputes about matters of taste involve misunderstanding or confusion (see Chapter 9, Section 4 for further discussion), conversations like (26) are common and seemingly reasonable. If someone is determined to regard such disputes as confused, I don't know how to refute them; but, for my own part, it seems to me that disputes of this kind *do* make sense, and are often important. As with other definitional disputes, there is therefore reason to look for a view that preserves Conservatism about Practice, at least across a range of cases.

There has been considerable discussion of cases of these kinds in the literature, and a thorough evaluation of how our metasemantic view handles all of the putative data about them (much less comparison of our view with alternatives) will require developing some simple formal tools. It is to this task that we now turn (Section (1)). In Section 2, we show how a range of metasemantic questions relate to this formal framework, and in Section 3, we show that extant answers to these questions in the literature—including views that focus on speaker intentions as well as relativist views—fare badly as accounts of disputes like (23) and (26). In the next chapter, I defend the temporal externalist alternative.

1. A Formal Framework

1.1 Two Representations of Context

What makes "I" as it is used on a particular occasion pick out a particular person? Two kinds of factors that will be involved in a complete answer. On the one hand, there is what every utterance of "I" has in common, no matter who is speaking; to a rough first approximation, we can think of this as a rule that says: *"I" picks out the speaker*. We can call this the *standing meaning* of "I". On the other, there are the facts about a particular speech situation; for example, the fact that Derek is speaking now.

If the meaning of "I" is something like a rule that tells us what "I" picks out in a speech situation, then the meaning of "I" is naturally represented by a function from speech situations to entities—roughly, the function that maps a situation to the person speaking in that situation. We can write this function "$\lambda s.$ the person speaking in s". To indicate that this function is our representation of the meaning of "I"—as we will say, the *semantic value* of "I"—we use double brackets notation:

(27) $[\![I]\!] = \lambda s.$ the person speaking in s.

To get beyond this rough sketch, we need to be more precise about how we are to represent speech situations. Following David Lewis (1980), we can represent a speech situation as a *location* in space and time, and also in the space of possibility—an ordered triple of an agent, a time, and a possible world, which Lewis calls a *context*. For any location-context $\mathscr{C}$, we will write $a_\mathscr{C}$ for the agent of $\mathscr{C}$, $t_\mathscr{C}$ for the time of $\mathscr{C}$, and $w_\mathscr{C}$ for the possible world of $\mathscr{C}$.

Lewis thinks that this is a good representation of a speech situation because it includes enough to do any metasemantic work that gets done at all. A context includes an entire world; it therefore includes any fact that could possibly be relevant to determining what utterances of "I", "that", etc. refer to.[3] Given this framework, it is easy to state a semantic value for some words; for example, "I":

(28) $[\![I]\!] = \lambda \mathscr{C}.a_\mathscr{C}$.

But it is very unclear how to state the semantic value of other words. What is the semantic value of "that"? Answering this question would require saying exactly what makes utterances of "that" pick out what they do, and this turns out to be no easy task. (What makes my utterance of "that" pick out my cardigan? The fact

---

[3] Liao (2012) raises worries about whether locations, construed in the way described, really do provide enough information to determine what utterances pick out. (For example: if time travel is possible, a single agent could be making two utterances at a single time and world, using "that" to refer to two different things; so a world, time, and individual do not give us enough information to determine the referent of each utterance.) His worries are good ones, but evaluating the possible responses to them would be a distraction from the main aims of this chapter. Our focus here will be on questions like: how do the facts about an utterance of "that" determine what that utterance picks out? Which facts are relevant? We are using Lewisian location contexts to represent the facts about an utterance that do the determining work (so that we will end up asking: how do facts about a location context determine what an utterance made in that context picks out?); we could ask the same questions, with no substantial change to the discussion, using whatever notion of context can accommodate Liao's examples.

that I'm pointing at it might be relevant, but I might be pointing to indicate the cardigan's colour or a particular button, and in any case I might not have pointed at all; my intentions might be relevant, but what if I distractedly point at my cardigan while intending to refer to my shirt, or (to adapt a famous example from Kaplan, 1996) to the picture of Spiro Agnew on the wall behind me?)

There is an alternative strategy for representing speech situations[4] that sidesteps this difficulty. (I emphasise that it does not really *solve* the difficulty but merely postpones it; we will return to the issue in Section 2.) Let a *list context* be an ordered sequence that contains an element for each context-sensitive expression in the language. To a first approximation, the element corresponding to each expression is the entity that that expression would pick out if uttered in a particular speech situation. (We will depart slightly from this first approximation as we go on, especially when we turn our attention to gradable adjectives.) For example, a context c might be a sequence consisting of an object for "I" to pick out (which we may write c_I), a day for "today" to pick out (c_{today}), an object for "that" to pick out (c_{that}), and so on; so that if I, speaking on 13 March 2017, use "that" to refer to my cardigan, the context will consist of me, 13 March, my cardigan, and so on.

If we are working with list contexts, it is trivial to write down semantic values for "I", "that", or indeed any context-sensitive expression:

(29) $[\![\mathbf{I}]\!] = \lambda c.c_I$.

(30) $[\![\mathbf{that}]\!] = \lambda c.c_{\text{that}}$.

Now every location context $\mathscr{C}$ will correspond to a list context, which represents what various context-sensitive expressions would pick out if uttered in the situation represented by $\mathscr{C}$.[5] When a location context $\mathscr{C}$ corresponds to a list context c, we write $\mathscr{C} \sim c$. The $\sim$ relation will be the focus of much of our discussion in this chapter.

---

[4] Also associated with Lewis, in early work (Lewis, 1970a), as well as Montague (1974b), Scott (1970), and more recently Braun (1996, 161).

[5] In many cases, a location context may not determine objects relevant to particular words. For example, consider location contexts in which no utterance is being made; if "that" refers to a particular object partly in virtue of a speaker's intentions, then (since in typical situations where no utterance is being made, agents are unlikely to have any relevant intentions) such location contexts will not determine a value for "that". In this case, we allow the list context to contain a "gap"; and typical list contexts may contain many such gaps. This won't matter much for our purposes; we focus on contexts in which utterances are in fact made. It might matter for some other purposes that have interested philosophers discussing these issues. For example, Kaplan (1977) was motivated in large part to develop a "logic of demonstratives" that captured the (putative) logical truth of such sentences as "I am here now". If (as is plausible) c_{here} or c_{now} are sometimes fixed at least in part by speaker intentions, hence gappy in cases where speakers have no relevant intentions, in our system "I am here now" will not be true in all contexts.

We could fill in this simple model in various ways.[6] But we have enough structure already to raise the questions we want to discuss.

2. Some Metasemantic Questions

One kind of metasemantic question—the kind that was our focus in Chapter 5—concerns *standing meaning*:

The Meta-Standing Meaning Question   What makes it the case that a word has the standing meaning that it does?

If we conceive of semantic value as our theoretical representation of standing meaning, then the Meta-Standing Meaning Question might look equivalent to the Meta-Semantic Value Question:

The Meta-Semantic Value Question   What makes it the case that an utterance has the semantic value it does?

In fact, however, once we have adopted the view that the semantic values of context-sensitive expressions simply point to the list context, the Meta-Semantic Value Question is not very interesting. Our semantic values are no longer representing facts like: *the standing meaning of "I" is a rule according to which an utterance of "I" refers to the speaker*. The semantic value of "I" just points to a particular element of the list context. All of the interesting questions will be about the list context.

Recalling Lewis's point (that since location contexts include a whole world, they include enough to determine anything semantic that gets determined at all), we can take it for granted that when an utterance is made, something about the location context in which it is made determines what any context-sensitive

---

[6] Here is one important way in which it might be developed. Kaplan (1977) famously distinguished two ways in which the truth or falsity of a sentence may depend on a situation in which it might be used. The focus of much of Kaplan's theorising was the notion of *content*. Content is Kaplan's representation of what is said; it is the object of speech acts like assertion and denial, and also of psychological states like belief. Kaplan's *contexts* are formal representations of situations in which an utterance might be made, and he claims that some sentences express different contents in different contexts; so the first way in which situations in which sentences might be used enter into Kaplan's theory is as a determinant of content. But contents, on Kaplan's view, are (or are representations of) truth conditions—they are true in some *circumstances* and false in others—so that we can evaluate whether an assertion of a content is true only given a circumstance at which to evaluate it. Determining the circumstance at which contents are evaluated is the second role that situations of utterance play. Kaplan therefore has two distinct lists of contextual parameters that play different roles in his system: context and circumstance. It is likely that the notion of content will play a crucial role in a detailed theory of communication. But for the purposes of this chapter, we need not go into these details, and we therefore ignore Kaplan's distinction.

expression contributes to the truth conditions of the utterance (to the extent that anything does), and hence determines the list context. But how? What is it about the location context me, 13 March 2021, the actual world that makes it the case that the list context relevant to my utterance includes my cardigan as the "that" parameter? More generally: we need an answer to the *Meta-List Question*:

Meta-List Question   What makes it the case that utterances of "I", "that", etc. pick out what they do? In other words: how does a location context determine a list context?

We should not expect a simple answer to the Meta-List Question, and not only because (as we have already suggested—Chapter 1, Section 5) metasemantics is, in general, complicated. Some views will see facts about standing meaning such as that an utterance of "I" refers to the speaker as parts of semantics (since they are conventionally encoded). As we have set out the issues here, facts about standing meaning of this kind play a role—alongside, perhaps, speaker intentions, facts about salience, and much else—in determining the list context that is relevant to a particular utterance. For some purposes, we might want a more fine-grained representation of what is going that would separate these things; but we need not introduce these details to illustrate the distinction between the different metasemantic views we will discuss.[7]

Put in terms of the notation introduced earlier, to say something about the relation between a location context and the list context that corresponds to it is to say something about the ~ relation: an answer to the Meta-List Question just is an account of the ~ relation. Different answers to the Meta-List Question—as we will say, different *meta-list theories*—will result in different predictions about the truth of utterances. And what we are saying now is that (for example) a plausible meta-list theory will include factors of different kinds. For example, a plausible account of what it is about a location context $\mathscr{C}$ that makes it the case that an utterance of "I" in $\mathscr{C}$ picks out Derek, hence that Derek is the value of c_I for the associated list context c, is that $\mathscr{C}$ is centred on Derek (that is to say, he is $a_\mathscr{C}$—the speaker); a plausible account of what it is about $\mathscr{C}$ that makes it the case that an utterance of "that" picks out my cardigan will allude to different sorts of facts about $\mathscr{C}$ (e.g., facts about the intentions of $a_\mathscr{C}$, what is salient in the context, and so on).

We have spoken of utterances of sentences being true or false, and of utterances of pronouns like "I" and descriptions like "the tallest member of my family" as picking out individuals. Call the truth value of an utterance of a sentence or the individual picked out by an utterance of a sub-sentential expression the *extension* of that utterance. Extension is a semantic notion—the extensions of sentences

---

[7] I'm grateful to Indrek Reiland for discussion of this point.

are truth values, and semantics (we have thus far supposed) is in the business of describing when and why sentences have the truth values they do. So one metasemantic question is:

The Meta-Extension Question What makes it the case that an utterance has the extension it does?

In the formal system we have sketched, extension corresponds to the result of applying semantic values to a list-context. So the Meta-Extension Question will be answered if we can answer the Meta-List Question and the Meta-Semantic Value Question.

Given the Lewisian assumption that location contexts provide the facts that answer all metasemantic questions (to the extent that they are answered at all), we get the following picture (where solid arrows represent the metasemantic determination relations, the nature of which we are investigating, and the joined dotted arrows represent a relation of determination by function application):

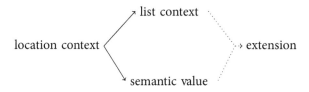

An answer to the Meta-Semantic Value Question would be an account of how the metasemantic determination represented by the solid downward-pointing arrow works. Our discussion of definition in Chapter 5 is a contribution to this project, and we will have more to say about it in subsequent chapters; but for the purposes of this chapter we are setting it aside. Our present focus is on the Meta-List Question. An answer to this question would be an account of the metasemantic determination relation represented by the solid upward-pointing arrow. That is what we turn to in the next section. We focus on gradable adjectives, with an eye towards understanding disputes such as (23).

3. Debating Gradable Adjectives

We're supposing that gradable adjectives like "flat" and "rich" are context-sensitive. Set in the formal framework of the previous section, this means that a list context c will contain (in addition to parameters that feed the semantic values of "I", "now", "that", etc.) a parameter that feeds the semantic value of "rich". A very simple way to implement this would be to let the list context contain a parameter c_{rich}, which provides a standard of richness—the degree to which something must be rich in order to count as "rich" in the context—and to let the semantic value of "rich" be something like (31)—a function which maps each context to a function that maps individuals to the truth value *true* just in case they are richer than a contextually specified standard:

(31) $\llbracket\mathbf{rich}\rrbracket = \lambda c.\lambda x.x$ is richer than c_{rich}.

3.1 Intentionalist Meta-Contextualism

A view of this kind makes developing a plausible answer to the Meta-List Question pressing. One driving idea of many approaches to the Meta-List Question for expressions like "that" is that the question is answered by appeal to some features of the speaker's psychological state—typically, her intentions. (There are a variety of views of this broad kind; see e.g. Grice, 1989b; Bach, 2008; Dowell, 2013; Viebahn, 2020, for different views on what intentions matter and what they do.) Call such views *intentionalist*. Intentionalism is at least a prima facie attractive view for "that"; after all, we often do use "that" intending to refer to particular things. But there is a complication involved in trying to adapt this kind of view into an answer to the Meta-List Question for parameters like c_{rich}: it's hardly clear that we have any intentions about standards of richness. Our initial presentation of the proposal abstracted away from the metaphysics of such things, but a better-developed version of the view would probably have to allude to mathematical objects—one well-known view in the literature has it that appeals to degrees on a scale, where a scale is an ordered, infinite set of points, and a degree is an interval on the scale (Kennedy, 1997; Kennedy and McNally, 2005)—and the supposition that we have intentions about things like this seems to be stretching the psychological facts.

Despite this, we can reconstruct an analogue of the intentionalist account even for parameters like c_{rich}.[8] In typical cases, we will have intentions or dispositions that our use of "rich" be such as to apply to certain things (say, Croesus, Ebenezer Scrooge, and Warren Buffett), and not to others (say, Bob Crachit and typical philosophy professors); often these will not be explicitly formulated, but can be elicited by appropriate questioning. And we can suppose that the standard of richness relevant to a conversation is our (theorists') representation of these intentions and dispositions; roughly, we will choose a value of c_{rich} which is such that for any object o, o is richer than c_{rich} if the speaker intends her use of "rich" to apply to o, and o is not richer than c_{rich} if the speaker intends her use of "rich" not to apply to o. With this understanding in mind, consider the following view:

---

[8] See King (2014) for more detailed discussion of this style of view.

Intentionalist Meta-Contextualism The value of the parameter c_{rich} of the list context is determined by the speaker's intentions and dispositions (i.e., by facts about the intentions and dispositions of $a_\mathscr{C}$ at $t_\mathscr{C}$ in $w_\mathscr{C}$, where $\mathscr{C} \sim c$).

The analogue of Intentionalist Meta-Contextualism may be an attractive view about c_{that}; but it is a bad view of c_{rich} because it cannot make sense of disputes like (23), much less its continuations in (24) and (25). Given Intentionalist Meta-Contextualism, on the most natural way of developing the scenario Tom is right—his assertion is true. (He intends "rich" as he uses it to apply to Jane, and that intention makes it the case that it does apply to Jane.) It is therefore hard to make sense of why Shiv would argue against him, why (in (24)) he feels the pressure of Shiv's argument and retracts his assertion, and so on. Of course, Shiv is right too; but it is hard to see how that helps make sense of what is going on. In fact, the fact that they are both right suggests that their views are not incompatible, and hence that they are not really disagreeing.

Now (as many have in effect pointed out), this kind of argument is not conclusive. After all, we argue in many ways about many things, and it's hardly clear that all of our disputes can be captured on the "canonical" model of *one person asserts the negation of what the other asserts, and at most one of these assertions is true.*

The response is correct as far as it goes, but it vindicates Intentionalist Meta-Contextualism only given a positive story what is going on that makes sense of the dispute. One kind of story would involve the kind of pragmatic reinterpretation that we discussed in Chapter 2 on this view, the dispute is about something metalinguistic—how to use the word "rich". But (as with the analogous position regarding our dispute about art) this view makes bad arguments good—a bribe may be a decisive reason to use the word "rich" in a certain way, but cannot settle the issue of whether Jane is rich—and good arguments bad—even if there are some cases in which the fact that Jane has a nice yacht constitutes a reason to use the word "rich" in a certain way, there are many relevant cases in which it does not.

An alternative story is more straightforwardly error-theoretic: perhaps the disputants are presupposing that they are using the words in the same way, so that they are really contradicting each other and at most one of their assertions can be true, even though in fact they are not using the words the same way, and their assertions are both true (Lopez de Sa, 2008). If correct, this claim would explain both their willingness to engage in dispute and our feeling that there is a disagreement. But something crucially important remains unexplained: namely, the continued existence of the presupposition that we are using words in the same way. Given Intentionalist Meta-Contextualism, the claim that Tom and Shiv are using "rich" in the same way, really contradicting each other, etc., is just obviously not true. The idea that speakers should so persistently stick to an obvious falsehood seems like something we should resist if we can.

3.2 Externalist Meta-Contextualism

If we deny that facts about the speaker's intentions (or, more generally, her psychology) at the time and world of utterance do the metasemantic work, then something external to the speaker's psychology must do it (if it is done at all):

Externalist Meta-Contextualism The value of the parameter c_{rich} of the list context is determined by facts about the situation external to the speaker's psychology (i.e., by facts that are not about the psychological states (e.g., intentions and dispositions) of $a_\mathscr{C}$ at $t_\mathscr{C}$ in $w_\mathscr{C}$, where $\mathscr{C} \sim c$).

Here we have many options. It might be held that some objective feature of the situation, or collection of features, more or less independent of psychological states of the speaker and audience—perhaps, the facts about the distribution of wealth in our society, or patterns of linguistic usage across the community, or metaphysical naturalness, etc.—fix the value of c_{rich}.[9] It is certainly possible that factors of this kind play some role. But the objections to this kind of view mirror the objections to analogous views about definitional disputes (such as the Argument from Spurious Evidence, Chapter 5, Section 3.2): if the truth of our claims depends on facts like these, it is unclear why we do not investigate these facts when we are trying to evaluate our claims, and unclear why we don't see them as providing decisive evidence.

Another type of view would have it that the psychological states (intentions and so on) of the audience, as well as those of the speaker, are relevant; so that if Shiv intends to use "rich" in such a way that Jane does not count as "rich", then the value of c_{rich} relevant to the interpretation *even of Tom's original utterance* is one that takes into account not only Tom's intentions but also Shiv's.

Now there are at least two ways of developing a view of this kind. The most straightforward of these would have it that the intentions (etc.) of someone other than the speaker (perhaps the intended audience, or perhaps actual hearers) at the time of utterance, make a difference to the value of c_{rich}. Like the versions of Externalist Meta-Contextualism that we have just rejected, this view is subject to a version of the Argument from Spurious Evidence; in particular, it entails that we should regard our evidence about our interlocutor's intentions as potentially decisive evidence for or against the truth of our claims like "Jane is rich". (We'll return to some related views in the next chapter.)

---

[9] For views of demonstrative reference broadly in this family, see e.g. Wettstein (1984); Gauker (2008); Stojnic et al. (2017). Gradable adjectives raise somewhat different issues; for example, pointing plays a prominent role in some theories of the reference of demonstrative pronouns like "that", but there is no clear analogue of pointing in the case of "tall" or "tasty".

3.3 Externalist Meta-Contextualism II: Relativism

The alternative way of developing the idea that not only the speaker's but also the audience's psychological states must be taken into account involves a more significant departure from the framework we have been working in so far. In particular, the view we will now consider rejects Lewis's idea that location context contain enough to do all the metasemantic work, so that whatever answers the Meta-Context Question must be drawn from the location context.

What could motivate rejecting this idea? Well, consider again disputes about taste. When Philip said, "Richard Pryor is funny", he spoke truly; but if his assertion is simply true, true once and for all, it is hard to make sense of Elizabeth's disputing it. What might help is if we could say that Philip's utterance is true from his perspective, but false from Elizabeth's; that would explain why it seems right for Philip to make the assertion in the first place, but also right for Elizabeth to reject it. But that means that determining the truth value—the extension—of an utterance requires looking not just at the location context associated with my utterance, but also at a *perspective* from which my claim is being evaluated.

Now we have two people—the original speaker, and the evaluator—and two location contexts, one corresponding to each of them. These two location contexts jointly fix the list context; in some cases (c_I, for example) the speaker's location context is most relevant, while in others (*perhaps* c_{rich}) the evaluator's location context is what matters. In short, we are replacing the idea that ~ is a relation between a single location context and a list context with the idea that ~ is a relation between two location contexts and a list context (so instead of $\mathscr{C} \sim c$, we will have $<\mathscr{C}_1, \mathscr{C}_2> \sim c$).

The resulting picture has it that the Meta-List Question must be answered by appealing not only to the location context centred on the utterance but also the location context centred on the evaluation:

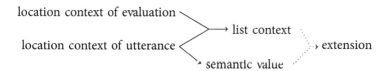

Views of this kind are called *relativist* in the literature, because (according to them) sentences get assigned a truth value only relative to a context of evaluation. This is a metasemantic claim; it is a claim about the structure of the correct meta-list theory. A relativist about "rich" can accept a semantic value like (31), as long as she insists that c_{rich} is determined (at least in part) by some facts about the context of evaluation—presumably the evaluator's intentions or something of the sort. Analogously, a view of this kind might give something like the following semantic value for "funny", likewise insisting that c_{funny} is determined by the evaluator's sense of humour:

(32) $[\![\textbf{funny}]\!] = \lambda c.\lambda x. x$ is funnier than c_{funny}.

Relativism is an improvement on the kinds of Externalist Meta-Contextualism we considered in the previous section. In particular, proponents of relativism make the case that they can make sense of some of the kinds of disagreements that we are considering by helping us provide an account of when it is appropriate to reject someone's assertion: we can reject previously made assertions just in case they are untrue relative to our context of evaluation (i.e., that we may in $\mathscr{C}_2$ reject an assertion of ϕ made in $\mathscr{C}_1$ just in case ϕ is untrue at the c such that $< \mathscr{C}_1, \mathscr{C}_2 > \sim c$) (MacFarlane, 2014).

But though relativist views may make sense of disagreement, and even of change of view in the face of disagreement, they do not make sense of *dispute*.[10] Tom and Shiv not only make assertions and disagree; they also offer arguments. And—despite the oft-quoted claim that there is no disputing about taste—I can likewise offer reasons for the claim that Richard Pryor is funny. (He brilliantly sends up the hypocrisy of the white establishment!) As Andy Egan puts the point:

> One thing that is pretty clear is that what is right about the aphorism, that there's no disputing about taste, is not that there's no disputing about taste. There's heaps of disputing about taste. People engage in disputes about which movies, music, paintings, literature, meals, furniture, architectural styles, and so on are good, beautiful, tasty, fun, elegant, ugly, disgusting, and so forth all the time. This is obvious to anyone who has watched dueling-movie-critics shows, read theater reviews, or negotiated with a group or partner about which movie or restaurant to go to, or which sofa or painting to put in the living room. (2010, 247)

Egan also points out that many of these disputes make sense, and it often happens that one party convinces the other. On the other hand, as Egan also emphasises, there is something right about the aphorism: many disputes about taste seem somehow defective. If you and I have both tried the chilli attentively, you liked it, and I hated it, then (it seems) there is just something wrong about spending time in dispute about whether or not it is tasty. (So the matter is not simple: we need to give an account of why the good disputes are good, but also why the bad disputes are bad.)

---

[10] In general, they do not even try. The most prominent recent relativist work, MacFarlane (2014) begins by developing a set of desiderata for a view of predicates of taste; these include some that we have also focused on (giving an account of assertion conditions, retraction conditions, and disagreement) but no mention at all is given of making sense of arguments or of the possibility of giving reasons for one's views.

Relativism, as we have presented it, is a schematic claim; it says that the context of evaluation is metasemantically significant, but it does not say exactly what aspects of the context of evaluation matter. Correspondingly, the relativist's options for making sense of disputes of this kind—of arguments, of giving reasons—will depend on the details of the metasemantic story she wants to tell— i.e., the details of her meta-list theory—and this is a matter about which relativists may disagree; moreover, an individual relativist may want to hold different views about different contextual parameters. But there are no promising options. The key problem with relativism is that there is no way of developing a detailed metasemantics within the relativist framework that makes sense of disputes involving gradable adjectives.

One strategy would be to add a relativist twist to the Intentionalist Meta-Contextualism discussed above. The most obvious possibility would be to let the intentions *of the evaluator* fix the value of c_{rich} or (perhaps less plausibly) c_{funny} in something like the way we had imagined the intentions of the *speaker* fixing the value: the evaluator will intend to treat some objects as "rich" and not to treat others as "rich", and these intentions will determine a value for c_{rich}. Then, what someone disputing about whether Jane is rich would hope to achieve would be to convince their interlocutor to intend to use or evaluate "rich" in certain ways.[11] But (as with non-relativist versions of Intentionalist Meta-Contextualism) this view makes our arguments seem misplaced. As we have already noted, the facts about the niceness of yachts do not seem likely to make me form any relevant intentions; and we might add (following on the discussion of definitional disputes in the previous chapter) that the kinds of considerations that might make me form intentions to apply "rich" in particular ways—practical considerations such as financial advantage or the avoidance of bodily harm—seem out of place, not like reasons to think that someone is rich or (at best) like the wrong kinds of reason.

An alternative adaptation of Internalist Meta-Contextualism would focus not on intentions but on some other psychological state. MacFarlane, for example, develops his semantics and metasemantics for "tasty" in terms of the notion of a *standard of taste*; on his view, each person's standard is analytically connected to what she likes and doesn't like. (As he says, "Roughly: if one knows a flavor and likes it, then that flavor is evaluated positively by one's tastes; if one dislikes it, then that flavor is evaluated negatively by one's tastes; and if one neither likes nor dislikes it, then the flavor is evaluated neutrally by one's tastes" (2014, 144); given our toy semantics, the idea would be that if one likes liquorice, one's standard determines a value for c_{tasty} that makes utterances of "Liquorice is tasty" evaluated at one's standard true, and so on.) Presumably MacFarlane would want to defend an analogous idea about "funny". But again, it is hard to see how this makes any

---

[11] This view is suggested by some of the discussion in Richard (2008).

sense of disputing about what is funny or tasty. If Philip tells Elizabeth, "No, Pryor *is* funny; he brilliantly sends up the hypocrisy of the white establishment", the MacFarlane-style view makes it very unclear what Philip aims to accomplish; his utterance is neither likely to change her standard of taste nor to change her judgements about what meets that standard (not, at least, if we suppose that she has really paid attention to Pryor's act).

The best-developed relativist attempt to make sense of what is going on in disputes about what is funny or tasty—Andy Egan's (2014)—involves some reconceptualisation of what is going on in disputes about taste. Egan points out that a big part of how we think of ourselves and our fellows is in terms of what we like and don't like. It matters to us whether we are mods or rockers, fans of pinot noir or fans of Pabst Blue Ribbon, goths or normcore philosophers; and it matters in our friendships and relationships whether our friends and relations share these proclivities. So, Egan claims, it makes good sense to think about our tastes and to try to get others to share them; and this is the point of these disputes. In his terminology, disputes about taste aim to bring it about that we're alike with respect to the self-attribution of properties such as (to a first approximation) *being disposed to laugh at Richard Pryor* or *being disposed to enjoy the taste of liquorice*. In our framework, this first approximation of Egan's view amounts (near enough[12]) to the combination of the following semantics and metasemantics:

(33) Semantics: $[\![\mathbf{funny}]\!] = \lambda c.\lambda x. c_{\text{funny}}$ would laugh at x.

(34) Metasemantics: The value of the parameter c_{funny} of the list context is the evaluator (i.e., $a_{\mathscr{C}_2}$, where $< \mathscr{C}_1, \mathscr{C}_2 > \sim c$).

The result is that if I say, "Richard Pryor is funny", then you should evaluate my utterance as true (and hence accept it) just in case you would laugh at Pryor—and you may reject it otherwise; Elizabeth should evaluate it as true just in case she would laugh at Pryor; and so on.

If that were all there is to Egan's view, we would have made very little progress at making sense of disputes. It makes little sense in general to try to convince someone who is familiar with Pryor's act that she does (or doesn't) find it amusing. In general, each of us is an authority on what amuses us; we neither need nor want further reasons to self-attribute the disposition to laugh at Richard Pryor, once we have seen Pryor's act and our response to it. There are certain exceptional cases—perhaps Pryor had an off night, perhaps I think you were distracted or in a bad mood—in which you've seen Pryor's act, think that you are not disposed to be amused by it, even though you are. (In general, if you were to see Pryor, you

---

[12] Egan himself develops this view within a somewhat different semantic framework, on which the semantic values of sentences are sets of centred worlds, and assertion is modelled in an Stalnakerian way. In the interest of maintaining focus, we set these details aside.

would be amused; the act you saw was just an exception.) But it seems clear that we dispute about taste even when we know that this is not what is going on. (This was a perfectly good instance of Pryor's act, you were in a perfectly ordinary mood and were not amused, and I know this; I still may think it was funny, and try to give you reasons to think so too.)

Still, this may suggest a more general recipe for making sense of disputes about taste. You are an authority about whether you were amused on a particular occasion, and unusual circumstances aside, it makes little sense to try to convince you that you were amused if you believe that you were not. But it may make sense to try to convince you that you *would have* been amused if circumstances had been different. Egan pursues a version of this strategy. What is at issue, he claims, in disputes about taste is dispositional and idealised in a variety of ways that may vary between different taste predicates. (For example, Egan claims that he doesn't like the cringe-inducing comedy of Ricky Gervais, but admits, "Perhaps my low cringe-tolerance is a failing, which would be done away with in the course of suitable comic idealization. So the idealized version of me, Egan+, will have a higher sympathetic pain tolerance than I now have, and will have different responses than the ones I have in my current, unidealized state" (2014, 87).) The suggestion is in effect that we should combine the relativist metasemantics in (34) with something like the following semantics:

(35)   Semantics: $[\![\mathbf{funny}]\!] = \lambda c.\lambda x.c_{\text{funny}}$ would laugh at x, if c_{funny} were idealised.

This helps make the dispute sensible in one respect. We are not authorities about the capacities and dispositions our idealised selves would have or lack; I might be able to adduce evidence that your idealised self would have or lack certain capacities or dispositions, thus giving you reason to self-attribute properties like *being disposed, after idealisation, to laugh at Richard Pryor*. (Egan notes that even this is too simple: laugh in what circumstances? idealised how? These details won't matter here.) But this advantage comes at a cost. First, it is not clear that a view of this kind makes sense of our confidence in making claims about what is funny. I know what makes me laugh as I am now; but I may well have no idea what would make ideal me laugh. (After all, I am nothing if not flawed; it would be surprising if idealisation doesn't result in some very big changes to my dispositions.) If claims about what is funny are claims about how I would react under idealisation, I should be much more circumspect in making them.

Second, as Egan points out, disputes about taste are often connected to practical matters: which movie we should see, which restaurant we should eat at, and so on. This would make sense if the dispute is focused on the self-attribution of dispositions to laugh or to enjoy certain tastes. But it makes much less sense once we have moved to *idealised* dispositions. If in my unidealised state I don't like Thai food, I am unlikely to want to go to a Thai restaurant, regardless of whether my idealised self would like it. So if our dispute about whether Thai food is tasty is a dispute about what our idealised selves would enjoy, that dispute bears on whether we should go to a Thai restaurant at most in a limited and indirect way.

Finally, it is not clear that we care enough about these properties to make them worth disputing over. Egan defends the idea that disputes about the self-attribution of properties are worth having by pointing to their role in social bonding, the formation of groups, and so on ("Very many groups and subcultures are defined, at least in part, by the common aesthetic sensibilities of their members (and the contrast between their shared aesthetic sensibilities and those of outsiders). Think of, for example, such subcultures as goths, punk rockers, ravers, trekkies, bikers, and so on" (2010, 260)); and it is certainly true that our tastes matter for these purposes—if we discover a shared passion for (say) the music of Taylor Swift, that may occasion a deep bond.

But suppose that I love Taylor Swift and you do not; and suppose that I can also prove that your idealised self would love Taylor Swift as much as I do. You might be surprised, interested in finding out what quirk of your psychology makes it idealise in this remarkable way. More likely, I suspect, you would just shrug; such idealisations seem pretty remote from anything you are likely to care about. It's hard to see us bonding or creating a subculture based around what our idealised selves would like rather than what we actually like.

In short, Egan is right that some of our arguments would make sense if we were disputing about what certain idealised versions of ourselves would enjoy; the things we say can often be construed as bearing on that question. And it may turn out that something like this is at issue in some disputes about taste. But in most cases, that question doesn't matter to us, so it seems an unlikely subject to be at the centre of so many "heaps" of disputes. Egan's view therefore fails to provide a satisfactory account of disputing about taste.

4. Conclusion

So much for the relativist version of externalist metasemantics. In what follows, we set aside the relativism, and return to Lewis's idea that a single location context gives us everything we could need to do any metasemantic work that gets done. The project of the next chapter is to give a better metasemantic theory, one that explains how we can sensibly argue about these matters, and why such arguments are senseless when they are.

9
Temporal Externalism, Context Sensitivity, and Matters of Taste

Our objective in this chapter is to give a meta-list theory—a variety of Externalist Meta-Contextualism—that does better than the alternatives we have considered so far. As we have already anticipated, the basic strategy will be the same as that we applied to definitional disputes: our considered judgements—those we arrive at in the end of a dispute—play a metasemantic role, determining what we meant all along.

We begin (Section 1) by outlining three desiderata on account of the relevant disputes. In Section 2, we turn to David Lewis's (1983c) account of accommodation—an account which has little-appreciated temporal externalist elements. Section 3 develops Lewis's account further into a view that mirrors the account of definitional disputes from Chapter 5. Section 4 applies the resulting account to disputes about taste. Disputes about taste, I will argue, are fundamentally continuous with other disputes involving gradable adjectives—disputes about what is tall and what is rich—and in particular, do not exhibit a distinctive phenomenon of faultless disagreement.

1. Three Desiderata

Let's try to sum up the conclusions we have arrived at, focusing first on those points where the views we have considered have stumbled.

1. Many disputes (not just disagreements, but (sometimes protracted) arguments that involve the giving and weighing of reasons) centrally involve context-sensitive terminology such as gradable adjectives. These disputes in some sense turn on the meanings of the relevant terminology, but the hypothesis that this is all that they are about fails to explain the way we argue.
2. We do not typically regard interlocutors' intentions, dispositions, or views as decisive evidence about the truth of our claims about what is rich, tall, funny, etc. On the contrary, we are comfortable making and defending judgements about matters of taste, even when we do not know our interlocutors' intentions, dispositions, or views, and even (in many cases) when we realise that those intentions, dispositions, and views differ from our own.

A further data point, to which we alluded briefly but which has not played a central role in our discussion so far, is that it is important to the successful conduct of debates of this kind that we can look back on and evaluate what we have said and how we have argued; for example, in (24) we imagined Tom saying, "I thought that Jane was rich, but she isn't. I was wrong", and in (25) we imagined Shiv saying, "Ok, I take it back: she is rich after all". (We also imagined Tom assessing Shiv's argument that Jane isn't rich because she can't afford an island as irrelevant—"True, she can't afford a private island. But she is still rich: she makes far more money than most people"—and we can imagine Shiv coming to agree with this assessment.)

 3. We can retrospectively assess our assertions and arguments.

It will not have gone unnoticed that these data points are very closely related to our targets in Chapter 5. There, we argued that the best way to make sense of analogous phenomena was by ensuring that meaning doesn't change over the course of a conversation, and we developed a theory on which our assertions can act as covert implicit definitions that play a role in fixing the meanings of our words. On this view, these covert implicit definitions fix meaning not only in a forward-looking way but also in a backward-looking way.

 It is a feature of the account to be developed that the same mechanisms are at work in the metasemantics of list-contextual parameters (in cases where we are disputing about whether something is tall or tasty) and the metasemantics of standing meanings (in cases where we are disputing about the nature of art or of freedom).[1] (That is why these cases of context sensitivity deserve to be regarded as a kind of definitional dispute.) This continuity is desirable for at least two reasons. First, to the extent that the data we have sought to explain are the same as regards the dispute about the nature of art and the dispute about whether Jane is rich, it is desirable that the explanation should take the same shape in both cases. And second, the structure of the view that we developed for standing meanings has already been partially anticipated in a famous and widely accepted view about the metasemantics of contextual parameters: namely, David Lewis's account of accommodation.[2] It is to Lewis's account that we now turn.

---

[1] Indrek Reiland suggests that there is reason to doubt that the same kinds of factors determine context-insensitive semantic meanings also determine the values of list-contextual parameters, since the former are a matter of convention while the latter are not. I reply that if context-insensitive semantic meanings are a matter of convention, then the content of certain conventions is sometimes determined by later facts. (This conclusion should not be surprising if the content of conventions is in part a matter of common knowledge or other mental states, and temporal externalism is true about the contents of mental states; see Chapter 10, Section 1.) And in this case, it should be no surprise that temporal externalist mechanisms are at work in both cases.

[2] Richard (1995) also endorses a temporal externalist view about contextual parameters. But he combines this with the idea that we also need to pay attention to the "local context", which is determined by facts at the time of utterance. This suggests a kind of relativist view, on which we can evaluate an utterance relative to parameters determined by the local context, or relative to parameters

TEMPORAL EXTERNALISM, SENSITIVITY, & MATTERS OF TASTE   153

2. Lewis on Accommodation

Lewis's (1983c) key idea is that many contextual factors relevant to determining the truth value of assertions— including assertions that are made using gradable adjectives such as "rich", "tall", or "hexagonal"—shift to make assertions true.[3] Suppose I say "France is hexagonal". Then whether what I say is true depends on whether I am using "hexagonal" strictly (so that only objects that very closely approximate a geometric hexagon in shape count as "hexagonal") or loosely (so that a wider range of objects, including those that differ substantially from a geometric hexagon, can count as "hexagonal"). The fact that my utterance of "France is hexagonal" is true only if I am using "hexagonal" loosely tends to make it the case that I *am* using "hexagonal" loosely; as Lewis puts it, the conversational score gets tends to become such that what we say is true. On the supposition that the semantics of "hexagonal" patterns with the other gradable adjectives we have seen so far, this amounts to the claim that my saying "France is hexagonal" tends to make the parameter of the list context associated with "hexagonal" ($c_{\text{hexagonal}}$) such that France is more hexagonal than $c_{\text{hexagonal}}$.

Lewis draws the following schematic lesson from these cases:

> If at time *t* something is said that requires component s_n, of conversational score to have a value in the range *r* if what is said is to be true, or otherwise acceptable; and if s_n, does not have a value in the range *r* just before *t*; and if such and such further conditions hold; then at *t* the score-component s_n, takes some value in the range *r*.   (1983c, 347)

The lesson is schematic because the "such-and-such further conditions" need filling in. The primary condition that Lewis discusses is that the parties to the conversation "tacitly acquiesce" (1983c, 339) rather than arguing or contesting the assertion. If you say "France is hexagonal", then whether the parameters of the list context shift so as to make it the case that your assertion comes out true depends on how I respond. If I reply, "Yes, and Italy is boot-shaped", then, Lewis thinks, the parameters tend to adjust so that both your assertion and my reply are true. But if I reply, "No, France is bordered by seas and rivers, which are not straight lines", then the parameters will not adjust (and your assertion will be false).

Put in our terms, one instance of Lewis's view would look like this:

---

determined by the global context. I do not think that the local context adds anything substantial to our understanding of the case, so I set Richard's view aside.
[3] The discussion in this section and the next builds on and develops ideas in Ball (2018a) and Ball and Huvenes (2022).

Lewisian Meta-Contextualism If at time t an assertion is made that requires component $c_{\text{hexagonal}}$ of the list context to have a value in the range r if the assertion is to be true; and if $c_{\text{hexagonal}}$ does not have a value in the range r just before t; and if such and such further conditions hold; then at t the list-context component $c_{\text{hexagonal}}$ takes some value in the range r.

In our discussion of definition, we treated assertions as (possibly covert, possibly partial) implicit definitions of some of the vocabulary used to make them; on the view we developed there, some assertions play a metasemantic role in that the words that compose the sentences used to make them take on the values required to make the assertions true. *Lewis's suggestion is precisely the analogue of this for contextual parameters.* On Lewis's view, assertions fix contextual parameters; some assertions play a metasemantic role—a role in a correct answer to the meta-list question—in that parameters of the list context relevant to the assertion take on the values required to make the assertion true.

So Lewis's view mirrors the view that some assertions are covert implicit definitions. In order to be clear both about the analogy and about the fact that the list context that is centrally at issue, we will call this *covert implicit parameter fixing*.

3. Temporal Externalist Meta-Contextualism: Beyond Lewis

Now, Lewis's suggestion won't do as it stands for exactly the reason that the traditional conception of stipulation—the conception on which stipulations play both an introductory role and a meaning-fixing role—fails. We called this traditional conception into question by considering Quine-style examples in which a stipulation that introduces a word is rejected in the course of further inquiry; we argued that the best way of understanding many such cases involves separating the introductory role of stipulation from the meaning-fixing role, so that the initial stipulation that introduces the word need not fix its meaning, and some assertion that takes place later in the conversation can fix the meaning even of prior uses.

I want to defend the analogous position about covert implicit parameter fixing, and on very similar grounds. Lewis has already stepped away from the idea that whatever we say goes; on his view, an assertion does list-fixing work only if interlocutors acquiesce. But this is too simple because the conversation will proceed beyond the interlocutors' first response. Consider the difference between the continuation of Tom and Shiv's disagreement in (23)—which begins with Tom asserting that Jane is "rich" and Shiv rejecting this assertion—in (24) and in (25).

In (24), Tom accepts Shiv's correction. In this case, both Tom and Shiv agree that Tom's initial assertion ("Jane is rich") is false and Shiv's correction ("She is not!") is true. Since this is the considered view of all parties to the conversation, our meta-list theory should vindicate it. In (25), on the other hand, Tom rejects Shiv's correction, and Shiv comes to agree with his rejection. In this version of the case, all parties agree that Tom's initial assertion is true and Shiv's correction is false. And again, since this is the considered view of all parties to the conversation, our meta-list theory should vindicate it.

Lewis's proposal does vindicate this view of (24). On Lewis's view, since Shiv objects to Tom's initial assertion, "such-and-such further conditions" do not obtain, and there is no reason to think that contextual parameters adjust so as to make Tom's assertion true. But the same is true of (25); there, too, Shiv objects, and so Lewis's view provides no reason to think that Tom's assertion is true. So Lewis's view fails to make the desired prediction about (25).

A better view would look past Shiv's initial reaction to the final resolution of the dispute. Whether an assertion plays a list-fixing role is determined by what happens at the end of the debate—by considered judgements, opinion once all the evidence is in:

Temporal Externalist Meta-Contextualism If at time t an assertion is made that requires component c_{rich} of the list context to have a value in the range r if the assertion is to be true; and if c_{rich}, does not have a value in the range r just before t; then: (i) if the considered judgement of the parties to the conversation is that the assertion is true; then at t c_{rich} takes some value in the range r; but (ii) if the considered judgment of the parties to the conversation is that the assertion was not true then at t c_{rich} takes some value outside the range r.

I claim that Temporal Externalist Meta-Contextualism can explain the three data points with which this section began. The data points were these:

1. Many disputes (not just disagreements, but (sometimes protracted) arguments that involve the giving and weighing of reasons) centrally involve context-sensitive terminology such as gradable adjectives. These disputes in some sense turn on the meanings of the relevant terminology, but the hypothesis that this is all that they are about fails to explain the way we argue.
2. We do not typically regard interlocutors' intentions, dispositions, or views as decisive evidence about the truth of our claims about what is rich, tall, funny, etc. On the contrary, we are comfortable making and defending judgements about these matters, even when we do not know our interlocutors' intentions,

dispositions, or views, and even (in many cases) when we realise that those intentions, dispositions, and views differ from our own.
3. We can retrospectively assess our assertions and arguments.

The third data point is accommodated straightforwardly given Temporal Externalist Meta-Contextualism: there is no problem about retrospective evaluations, since there is no meaning change. When we look back and say, "I said that Jane was rich, but I was wrong", what we say can be simply and straightforwardly correct.

The second data point is also relatively easy to handle. When we say, "Jane is rich", we are simply trying to speak truly. If our interlocutors tacitly acquiesce, or if we win the argument—and assuming that we are right about Jane's income and savings—then the assertion is true, just as we took it to be. If our interlocutors object, and convince us, then we are wrong—the world has turned out to be otherwise than we initially believed, our assertion a mistake. So we can be convinced that we were wrong. Our confidence is appropriate to the extent that we are justifiably confident that we won't be convinced that we were wrong. There is no spurious evidence here, since we can't look into the future to determine whether we will change our mind. This means that it is appropriate to make and defend the claim that Jane is rich to the extent that we have good reasons—reasons that make us justifiably confident that our interlocutors won't object, or that we can convince them if they do.

The first data point requires more discussion. It is clear that Temporal Externalist Meta-Contextualism vindicates the idea that our disputes in some sense turn on how we use words—the outcome of these debates plays a meaning-fixing role—and equally clear that it vindicates the idea that our disputes are not just about how we should use words—when we resolve the dispute, what we end up agreeing on is not merely metalinguistic, but an ordinary, first-order claim—for example, that Jane is rich. But it may be less clear that Temporal Externalist Meta-Contextualism makes sense of our disputes.

In the appendix to Chapter 5, we proposed three constraints on an account of a dispute. First, we must predict that speakers make the assertions they do for recognisable reasons; we must be able to give a plausible account of what they are trying to accomplish in speaking in the way that they do. Second, although speakers sometimes speak falsely, they typically behave in ways that show that they still regard their assertions as bound by norms of truth; for example, they may apologise if their assertions are shown to be untrue. An account should not predict that speakers routinely disregard these rules; it should not predict that speakers routinely act as though they were not bound by them at all. (Similar remarks could be made for whatever norms we think are plausible.) Third, we ought to respect speakers' informed and considered views.

To see how we can meet these constraints, let's look more closely at the exchange that begins (23):

(23) Tom: Jane is rich.
Shiv: She is not; she can't afford a private island.

At this point, Tom and Shiv have conflicting intentions about what counts as "rich" for the purposes of the conversation. Temporal Externalist Meta-Contextualism predicts that neither intention is decisive; either could turn out to be correct, depending on how the dispute proceeds. If Tom concedes (as in (24)), then both Tom and Shiv agree that Shiv's objection is a good one. In that case, Temporal Externalist Meta-Contextualism predicts that the meaning of "rich" is such that the objection is in fact a good one; if someone can't afford a private island, then that is a good reason to think that they are not "rich". But if Tom pushes back and Shiv concedes (as in (25)), then both Tom and Shiv will agree that Shiv's objection was a bad one. In that case, Temporal Externalist Meta-Contextualism predicts that the meaning of "rich" is such that the objection is in fact a bad one; if someone can't afford an island, that is at most a weak reason to think that they aren't "rich". So Temporal Externalist Meta-Contextualism accords with the informed and considered views of the parties to the dispute about which arguments are good and which are bad. We are meeting the third constraint.

The dialogue also shows how we are meeting the second constraint: although someone speaks falsely on either way of developing the dialogue, that person also retracts their assertion, so that no norm is disregarded.

What of the first constraint? Stepping back for a minute from metasemantics, what is the point of a well-conducted dispute? What are we trying to accomplish? Here is a naive answer: one is trying to get one's opponent to adopt a certain belief, and (at least in the case of an honest, well-conducted debate), to do so on good grounds, for good reasons. This answer is a reasonable first attempt if our disagreement is purely empirical, and nothing metalinguistic—no matters of definition, no values of contextual parameters—is at issue. And the key point is that *the Temporal Externalist Meta-Contextualist can take exactly this answer on board in definitional disputes too.* By her lights, disputes about what is (e.g.) rich of the type we have been considering look exactly like ordinary empirical disputes: they are a matter of giving and evaluating reasons for a claim.

4. The Metasemantics of Predicates of Taste

Our temporal externalist view looks attractive for the metasemantics of gradable adjectives like "rich" and "tall". But our discussion of relativism raised another sort of case—predicates of taste—that may seem to raise quite different issues. Many theories of disputes about taste seem to presuppose that whatever is going on with disputes about what is funny or tasty is quite different than what is going on with disputes about what is rich or tall.

I want to defend the contrasting position: the semantic and metasemantic differences between predicates of taste and other gradable adjectives are, for the purposes of theorising about disagreement and dispute, entirely insignificant. Typical predicates of taste—"funny", "delicious", "awesome", and so on—are, after all, gradable adjectives.[4] Recall our very simple semantics for "rich":

(36) $[\![\mathbf{rich}]\!] = \lambda c.\lambda x.x$ is richer than c_{rich}.

We will need to add a wrinkle to this very simple story to accommodate all of the data. But I contend that—with our metasemantic theory in place—even the very simple style of semantics can handle the phenomena that have been of interest in philosophical discussions of predicates of taste. We can accommodate disputes about taste, the phenomena associated with "faultless disagreement", and much else, on the hypothesis that the semantics of "funny" and "tasty" are as simple as (37) and (38)—given our metasemantics:

(37) $[\![\mathbf{funny}]\!] = \lambda c.\lambda x.x$ is funnier than c_{funny}.

(38) $[\![\mathbf{tasty}]\!] = \lambda c.\lambda x.x$ is tastier than c_{tasty}.

Or so this section argues.

What are the phenomena of interest? Let's begin with one that has already entered our discussion:

Putative Desideratum A Accommodate the phenomenon of *faultless disagreement*.

Following Kölbel (2004) and Lasersohn (2005), many discussions of predicates of taste focus on the idea that two parties to a dispute about a matter of taste may genuinely, canonically disagree, contradict each other, and so on, even though neither is wrong. (So the phenomenon is not meant to be, for example, merely that if I prefer pickles to olives and you prefer olives to pickles, we disagree (in some relatively weak, non-canonical sense) even though neither of us is wrong; it is meant to be that when I say "Olives are tasty and pickles are not" and you say "Pickles are tasty and olives are not", you are contradicting me, saying the negation of what I said, and neither of us is wrong.)

We may take as further evidence for Putative Desideratum A another fact that has already entered our discussion: that in many cases, engaging in arguments, giving reasons for one's views, and so on, seems futile or misguided. Once it has

---

[4] This point is emphasised in Glanzberg (2007), who also defends the idea that many puzzles about predicates of taste can be resolved by attention to metasemantics, though he does not anticipate the temporal externalist view developed here.

been established that Philip has attended to the relevant features of Pryor's comedy and likes it, Elizabeth has attended to the relevant features and doesn't like it, one may feel that there is nothing more to say. (And if Elizabeth is trying to say it, she is making a mistake.) This is the wisdom in the old saying that there is no disputing about taste: it's not that people don't do it, it's that (in some cases anyway) they shouldn't.

Putative Desideratum B Make sense of the fact that in some cases disputes about matters of taste are problematic, not sensible, not something we should bother with.

Relativism is designed to satisfy Putative Desideratum A, and we have argued that relativism makes it hard to see how any disputes about taste are sensible, so it also satisfies something stronger than Putative Desideratum B. Now, we have already rejected the relativists' account. So what do we say about the desiderata?

Well, suppose Philip tells Elizabeth, "Richard Pryor is funny". Applying our temporal externalist metasemantics for parameters of the list context, we can see that if Elizabeth agrees, the c_{funny} parameter of the list context relevant to Philip's utterance will be set in such a way that Pryor counts as "funny" and the utterance will be true. But suppose Elizabeth disagrees (keep in mind that we're assuming that Elizabeth is familiar with Pryor's act and doesn't like it). At this point, there is some temptation to say that we have a case of faultless disagreement, and therefore that it would be pointless to continue the discussion. But I contend that this conclusion is too quick: until we have seen Philip's reaction—and indeed the rest of the conversation—we are in no position to say whether Philip and Elizabeth are both right, and we are also in no position to say whether there is a canonical disagreement. The facts that do relevant meaning-fixing work are simply not in place. In particular, I claim that any development of the conversation will fall into one of three categories:[5]

(a) Not faultless: one or the other party to the conversation is wrong.
(b) No (genuine, canonical) disagreement: the parties to the conversation are talking past each other and any disagreement is merely verbal. (In this case it is possible that neither party is wrong.)
(c) Indeterminate: it is not determinate whether the dispute is substantive (and not faultless) or (potentially faultless but) merely verbal.

---

[5] This claim is broadly consonant with the view developed in Stojanovic (2007, 2012). Stojanovic also argues that there is no faultless disagreement, on the grounds that once the relevant contextual parameters are settled, it will turn out that disagreements are either not faultless or not genuine. But Stojanovic assumes that the relevant contextual parameters are set by speaker intentions and other features. Her view is therefore subject to the objections discussed in the previous chapter.

So (on my view) there are cases of genuine disagreement about matters of taste. (These are the cases of type (a).) But these are not cases in which the disagreement is faultless; they are cases in which one or the other party is wrong, and in typical cases will even come to admit their mistake. And these are also not cases in which dispute is faulty or misguided; on the contrary, they are cases in which the dispute reaches a natural conclusion.

There are also cases in which dispute is faulty. (These are the cases of type (b).) In these cases, the parties to the dispute are likely to agree that further argument would be senseless or futile. So we will vindicate Putative Desideratum B, at least to the extent it ought to be vindicated: we will predict that disputes about taste don't make sense precisely in those cases in which the disputants themselves would (in looking back on the dispute) judge that their disputes didn't make sense.

And there are—or at least, there may be[6]—cases which do not resolve into one or the other of these. (These are the cases in which the conversation ends without either party convincing the other.)

So there are cases that are faultless, cases where there is disagreement, and cases where it is not determinate whether there is faultlessness or disagreement. But there are no cases of faultless disagreement. So Putative Desideratum A is incorrect and should be rejected.

In order to substantiate these claims, I want to take a step back to reconsider some of the conclusions we have reached already about definitions and non-taste gradable adjectives. In Chapter 5, we considered a dispute about art that we imagined to begin when you made a claim to the following effect: "Conceptual 'art' is not art", and I responded along the lines of, "No, conceptual art is art". Now there is some temptation to say that there is a genuine—even canonical—disagreement here (am I not asserting exactly what you are denying?); and there is also some temptation to say that neither of us is at fault (I am using "art" to pick out the products of a certain cultural tradition (which includes conceptual art); you are using "art" to pick out objects created with a certain intention (which conceptual art is not)). But we argued that the situation is not so simple: there are cases in which our dispute involves canonical disagreement, but these are cases in which one of us is wrong; and there are cases in which we are each right, but these are cases in which we are talking past each other. (There may also be cases which do not determinately fall into either of these kinds.) Which kind of case we are in depends on how our debate pans out—on whether one of us manages to convince the others, or we decide that we have been speaking past each other all along.

We have seen the same pattern with non-taste gradable adjectives; and I want to argue that the situation is the same with predicates of taste. Consider three ways

---

[6] We leave open the possibility that in some or all such cases, some further metasemantic factor over and above the mechanisms of implicit definition discussed here intervenes to make things determinate—see chapter 10, Section 9 for discussion.

that Philip and Elizabeth's dispute about whether Richard Pryor is funny might conclude. First, the disputants might give up the dispute, not simply in the sense that they stop talking about it (e.g., for lack of time) while continuing to believe each other mistaken—we will consider that case in a moment—but in the sense that they acknowledge and accept each other's position:

Case A   After various considerations for and against the claim that Pryor is funny, Philip concludes: "Well, he may not be funny to *you*, but he is funny to *me*."

There are several things to notice about this way of developing the scenario. First, Philip is not conceding his original claim. (It would be very odd, for example, for him to say something like "He is funny to me, but I was wrong when I said that he is funny".) But, second, he is also dropping his objection to Elizabeth's response; he is, in effect, accepting what she said. (It would be very odd, for example, for him to say "He may not be funny to you, but you were wrong when you said 'He isn't funny'".)

This combination of attitudes only makes sense if his original assertion and Elizabeth's response are not really inconsistent. It is natural (given the metasemantic resources we have been developing) to see Philip's conclusion as not simply acknowledging an antecedently existing but unnoticed fact (that his initial assertion and Elizabeth's initial response were in fact consistent), but as going towards making it the case that the initial assertion and response are consistent. It will succeed in making it the case if Elizabeth concurs. (It is unclear (to me at least) what we should say if she continues to argue; most plausibly this should be regarded as a case of indeterminacy.)

In cases of this kind, the parties to the dispute take themselves to be faultless, and also take there to have been no genuine disagreement; and Temporal Externalist Meta-Contextualism is designed to vindicate precisely these judgements. In this case, the idea will be that in Philip's original utterance, "funny" means something like *funny to Philip*, and in Elizabeth's original utterance, "funny" means something like *funny to Elizabeth*.

A second way that the case might play out is that one party may concede the other's point and retract their own. For example:

Case B   Philip says something like: "I see what you mean; he is rather crude. He makes me laugh, but he really isn't funny." Alternatively, (after further argument) Elizabeth says: "Fine, if you say so, but I have to say, I just don't get why it's funny."

Many people find it somewhat odd to admit that one laughs at something that isn't funny, or that something that one doesn't get is funny. But these uses are easy enough to understand and not terribly unusual; "I don't get why it's funny" is easy to find online, and while some of these uses seem to be intended to suggest that it really isn't funny, others are clearly presupposing that it really is funny. "It makes me laugh but it isn't funny" is similarly easily googleable. Uses of predicates of taste that involve adopting the standards of others (including, as Philip is perhaps doing, standards that involve a degree of idealisation) are continuous with uses that involve only our own standards. It may be in a single conversation that we begin defending the claim that something is "funny" by appealing to the fact that it makes us laugh, while later acknowledging others' tastes, or idealisations, as relevant to our assertion. Alternatively, we may also resolutely refuse to do so, regarding the fact that it makes us laugh as entirely sufficient to think it "funny". Both paths are open to us; which one we take determines what we mean and have meant all along.

The attitudes of the disputants in Case B contrast quite strongly with their attitudes in Case A. Here, the conceder is retracting his or her initial assertion. (If Philip responds as indicated, he no longer wants to defend the claim that Pryor is funny. It would be quite reasonable and natural for him to say, "I was wrong".) As before, our metasemantic perspective suggests that we should regard this as playing a role in making it the case that the speaker means what he or she does. If Philip concedes, his concession goes towards making it the case that when he said "Richard Pryor is funny", he meant something along the lines of *funny to a scrupulous audience* or *funny to me, were I morally ideal*. By his own lights, in this case, the assertion he thereby made was false. Likewise if Elizabeth concedes; she will take her original objection to be mistaken (perhaps it is just wrong; perhaps it gives some reason to think that Pryor isn't funny, but not a sufficient reason) and Philip's assertion to be correct. As before, our methodology is to attempt to vindicate judgements like these; in this case we should do it by letting the judgements fix the value of the list-contextual parameters relevant to the assertions that the speakers are looking back on.

There is at least one more possible outcome of the dispute to consider:

Case C   The dispute may simply end, with no conclusion reached. (Perhaps Philip gets bored and changes the subject; perhaps Elizabeth has to catch a bus and just leaves.)

In this case, there is no covert implicit parameter fixing. Unless some other metasemantic factor steps in, the parameter will not take a determinate value. Further, it will not be determinate whether the value of the parameter relevant to Philip's assertion is the same as the value of the parameter relevant to Elizabeth's assertion. So it is not determinate whether they are (canonically) disagreeing.

It may reasonably be objected at this point that we have failed fully to capture the data. In the cases of disputes involving gradable adjectives that were *not* about matters of taste (such as Tom and Shiv's dispute about whether Jane is rich), it seems that Tom and Shiv do not disagree about who is richer than whom; if asked to place people in order from the richest to the least rich, they would produce the same ordering. Their dispute seemed to turn on where in this ordering to locate the cutoff between those objects that count as "rich" and those that do not. But the dispute between Philip and Elizabeth does not seem to be like this. Philip and Elizabeth do not merely disagree about where to locate a cutoff on an agreed scale; they disagree about the scale, about what is funnier than what. As Peter Lasersohn puts the point:

> What seems crucial for disagreements over taste is not the location of the cutoff point, but the assignment of degrees. Different people may assign markedly different degrees of fun or tastiness to the same items, and may differ radically in the relative order of these items on the fun or tastiness scale; but no objective 'matter of fact' would seem to select any one of these assignments or orderings as the correct one. (Lasersohn, 2008, 308)

So we may add to our list of apparent desiderata:

Putative Desideratum C Make sense of the fact that (unlike disputes involving "tall" or "rich", which are mostly a matter of determining a cutoff point on an uncontroversial and objective scale) disputes about taste are very often a matter of determining not only the cutoff point but also the ordering of entities on the scale. (Or in other words: even when it is controversial who is tall, it is uncontroversial who is taller than whom. But it is very often controversial what is tastier than what.)

Now something is right about Putative Desideratum C: it's true that we often disagree not only about what is tasty or funny but what is tastier or funnier than what. And this is a fact that our theory must come to grips with. But what is wrong with Putative Desideratum C is the claim that there is a sharp distinction between predicates of taste and other gradable adjectives in this respect. "Rich" is an obvious case. It is by no means clear how to order the retiree on a fixed income who owns outright an expensive home, the infant who stands to inherit a fortune on her 18th birthday, the young founder of a Silicon Valley start-up with nothing in the bank but stock options worth a mint on paper, the executive with high income but no savings, and so on; in each case, we can argue not only about who is rich but about who is richer than whom. And the same is true even in more straightforward cases: Mount Everest rises 8,850 metres above sea level, more than any other earthly peak, and so is standardly accorded the title of tallest mountain; but the top of Mauna Kea, despite being only 4,205 metres above sea level, is some 10,210 metres above the sea floor. It is easy to find online discussions of which mountain is taller (e.g., Melina, 2010).

It is one thing to acknowledge that gradable adjectives are not unique with respect to the feature that Lasersohn observes, and another to give an account of what is going on. In order to get into the details, we will need to be somewhat more precise about the semantics. A standard view of the semantics of gradable adjectives has it that the semantic values of gradable adjectives crucially involve *measure functions*—functions from individuals to degrees on a scale, where a scale is an infinite, linearly ordered set of points, and a degree is an interval on the scale. On this view, the semantic value of a word like "rich" will map an object to a degree of richness, and compare this degree to a threshold degree determined by the context. Letting δ_{rich} be a measure function from objects to the scale associated with "rich", the semantic value of "rich" will be:

(39) $[\![\text{rich}]\!] = \lambda c.\lambda x.\delta_{rich}(x) \geq c_{rich}$.

On this semantics, the measure function δ_{rich} maps entities onto the scale, and so determines how entities are ordered with respect to the scale.

There might be different views about the place of δ_{rich} in our semantic theory. On one view, δ_{rich} is a contextual parameter.[7] On this view, settling the value of δ_{rich} would be a matter of covert implicit parameter fixing. On another view, δ_{rich} is part of the semantic value of "rich", not a contextual parameter. On that view, if the resolution of debates about how entities ought to be ordered with respect to the scale—i.e., debates where the parties agree on the facts about income, savings, and so on, and disagree about what is richer than what—are to play a metasemantic role, it must be a matter of covert implicit definition rather than covert implicit parameter fixing; the resolution of the debates would play a role in answering the Meta-Semantic Value Question rather than the Meta-List Question. Since broadly similar temporal externalist mechanisms are in operation in either case, I need not attempt to determine which of these views is correct.

This may be the best analysis of many relevant cases, but there are alternatives if they are wanted. Michael Glanzberg (ms), for example, argues that predicates of personal taste require two distinct contextual parameters: in addition to what he calls the "standard value" (along the lines of c_{rich}), there is also an "experiencer"

---

[7] For example, some authors maintain that aesthetic adjectives (including predicates of taste) are typically *multidimensional* in that multiple dimensions or factors are relevant to possession of the feature attributed by the adjective. As Stojanovic and McNally write, "The beauty of a place (and thus whether it is beautiful) might depend on the (ir)regularity of the terrain, the sort of vegetation found there, the color of the sky, etc." (Stojanovic and McNally, 2017, 21). Arguably, if one settles the relative importance of the different dimensions for the purposes of a conversation, one will thereby have settled what function $\delta_{beautiful}$ is relevant, and to the extent that the relative importance of these dimensions varies between conversations it might be reasonable either to treat $\delta_{beautiful}$ as a contextual parameter, or to let the dimensions be contextual parameters and $\delta_{beautiful}$ be determined by them. In either case, I would argue that temporal externalist mechanisms apply to the parameter or parameters.

Stojanovic and McNally postulate a connection between multidimensionality and the phenomenon described in Putative Desideratum C. I am sceptical, since (as I have shown) that phenomenon occurs with respect to words such as "tall" and "rich", which are less naturally thought of as multi-dimensional and do not satisfy the tests for multidimensionality described in Sassoon (2013).

parameter (c_E).[8] If this is right, then the semantic values of predicates of taste will be something along the lines of:

(40) $\llbracket\textbf{funny}\rrbracket = \lambda c.\lambda x.\gamma_{\text{funny}}(c_E)(x) \geq c_{\text{funny}}.$

where γ_{funny} is a function that maps an experiencer (c_E) and an entity (x) to a degree, where the degree represents (something like) the extent to which the entity amuses the experiencer.

On this semantics, a debate about what is funny might play a role in fixing the semantic value of either of the two contextual parameters. If we agree in relevant respects about what is funnier than what, the resolution of a debate about whether something is funny may play a role in fixing the value of c_{funny}. (Many online debates about the sitcom *Friends* take something like this shape; it is widely agreed that *Friends* is moderately amusing but not hilarious, and disputed whether *Friends* is funny.) But if (like Philip and Elizabeth) we disagree even about what is funnier than what, the resolution of our debate may play a role in fixing the value of c_E. For example, in case A, Philip's response goes towards making it the case that the value of c_E in the context relevant to his original utterance of "Richard Pryor is funny" is Philip himself. In case B, by contrast, Philip's response goes towards making it the case that the value of c_E relevant to his original utterance is something else—perhaps an idealised version of Philip. Since Philip's tastes differ from ideal-Philip's tastes, this will result in a different ordering of entities on the scale of funniness. So on a Glanzberg-style semantics, the resolution of debates about how entities ought to be ordered with respect to the scale can be a matter of covert implicit parameter fixing.

5. Conclusion: The Explanatory Role of Metasemantics

The best account of disputes about taste—and other disputes involving context-sensitive vocabulary—does not need to complicate pragmatics or to adopt relativism. Once we take on board a temporal externalist metasemantics, we can see why disputes about taste make sense, even given a simple semantics. But even if one were not satisfied with temporal externalism, there is a lesson to be drawn from this: attention to metasemantics can play an important explanatory role. Semantic and pragmatic views therefore cannot be evaluated independently of metasemantics.

---

[8] One of Glanzberg's main aims is to defend the idea that the two parameters differ metasemantically. This may be so—a variety of metasemantic mechanisms may be at work in any particular case—but I maintain that both are subject to covert implicit parameter fixing.

10
Temporal Externalism: Choice Points

We have now defended Temporal Externalism in definitional disputes, including in cases where context-sensitive vocabulary is at issue:

Temporal Externalism (TE) Facts about what happens at later times can play a role in determining the meaning of our words (and the contents of our mental states) at earlier times. In particular, definitional disputes can play a role in determining meaning, even though they do not involve change of meaning.

Views that endorse TE can be developed in a variety of ways, and different varieties of TE will be subject to different possible objections. This chapter is a map of some of the conceptual terrain, indicating some choice points where theorists may disagree. (The map may be of interest even to those who reject TE, as similar choice points will arise for a range of metasemantic theories.) I will explain and motivate my own preferred path through the choices; but my hope is that even many of those who found some aspect of the discussion so far objectionable will find a view that resists their objections here.

1. Issue 1: To What Meaning-Bearing Entities Does TE Apply?

Many sorts of thing can be thought of as meaningful or representational. Perhaps the most obvious are linguistic entities—words, sentences, discourses, and the like. These were our main focus in Chapters 5 and 9. There are other kinds of representations—photographs, for example—to which the kinds of arguments we have been considering do not seem to apply; and although it might be possible to develop a version of TE about (say) the representational content of diagrams, maps, or works of art, considering these cases in detail would take us too far from our main concerns.

What does matter to understanding disputes is the representational content of our mental representations: thoughts, beliefs, desires, and so on. Some views that endorse the idea that the meanings of words are determined in part by facts external to the speaker deny that the representational contents of thoughts are so determined (e.g., Putnam, 1975). Others maintain that the meanings of words are determined by different external facts than the contents of thoughts (e.g., Sawyer, 2020a). On either style of view, it might turn out that TE is true of linguistic representations but not mental representations, or (for views structurally like Sawyer's) vice versa.

The considerations we have used to motivate TE in Chapter 5 commit us to thinking that TE is also true of mental representations. For we stressed the importance of retrospective evaluations of what was said, such as (41):

(41)   I said that art had to be beautiful, but now I see that I was wrong.

But of course, we can equally make such evaluations of what was thought:

(42)   I used to think that art had to be beautiful, but now I see that I was wrong.

We used examples like (41) to motivate the idea that the conclusion we reach in our dispute about art plays a role in determining what the word "art" meant all along. Examples like (42) establish a similar conclusion at the level of thought: the thought that the subject had at the beginning of the conversation—the thought expressed by her initial utterances of "Art has to be beautiful"—is inconsistent with the thought that she has at the end of the conversation—the thought expressed by "It's not the case that art has to be beautiful". If thoughts are mental representations, and they are composed of concepts that correspond at least roughly to words of natural language, then we should say that the word "art" expresses the same concept (which retains the same content) throughout the conversation. In short, we should endorse *Thought–Language Parallelism*:

Thought–Language Parallelism   The same future factors that play a role in fixing the meaning of our words also play that same role in fixing the contents of our thoughts.

Other considerations may seem to tell against Thought–Language Parallelism. Sarah Sawyer (2020a) argues that what she calls *Sainsbury's puzzle* (Sainsbury, 2014) shows that the contents of thoughts must be determined in a different way than the meanings of words. The puzzle takes the form of a dilemma. Linguistic practices regarding the words "whale" and "fish" have changed over time: long ago, people were disposed to utter sentences like, "Whales are fish"; now they are not. Now either "whale" and "fish" mean the same now as they did long ago, or they don't. But if they mean the same now as they did long ago, then people long ago were in error; their judgements and dispositions to apply the words did not make the words mean something appropriate to their views. But if they do not mean the same, then it seems that people long ago were correct, we now are also correct, and there is no disagreement between us; and, to the extent that we are inclined to say that people in the past were wrong to say that whales were fish, this may strike us as counterintuitive. As Sawyer puts the point, "To say that it does [mean the same now as it did long ago] fails to accommodate the fact that meaning is determined by use; but to say that it doesn't fails to accommodate the fact that there is substantive disagreement across the two times" (2020a, 385).

Sawyer uses the dilemma to motivate a view on which the meanings of words are determined by idealised facts about use—as Sawyer puts it, "the linguistic meaning of a term at a time can be understood as the characterization of the relevant subject matter that members of the linguistic community would settle on at that time were they to reach reflective equilibrium in the context of a dialectic" (2020a, 383)—while the contents of thoughts are fixed by "relations to objective properties" (2020a, 387). That is, Sawyer maintains that different facts fix the meanings of words and the contents of thoughts:

Thought–Language Divergentism Different factors fix the meaning of our words than fix the contents of our thoughts.

Both aspects of Sawyer's view are problematic. The view of linguistic meaning fails to make sense of retrospective evaluations like (41) in many cases. As Sawyer describes the meaning-determining dialectic, it is "an honest, open debate, shorn of all subjective elements, in which participants aim for a characterization of the subject matter through reason and reflection on actual and hypothetical cases, deferring to the most competent as and when appropriate" (2020a, 383–384). Crucially, this dialectic is meant to be limited by current actual use: "The dialectic is not to be understood as involving maximal reflection on the subject matter, as this would inevitably extend the discussion beyond actual use to what was perceived to be ideal future use. Rather, the relevant notion is to be understood as full reflection within actual empirical and theoretical boundaries" (2020a, 383–384).

With this in mind, consider the case of same-sex marriage. It is plausible that speakers engaging in a Sawyerian dialectic in 1960 would have settled on a view of marriage according to which the meaning of "marriage" is such that same-sex couples cannot be married—that would be the most natural way to respect the "theoretical boundaries" provided by use at that time. And it is plausible that speakers engaging in a Sawyerian dialectic in 2020 would settle on a view of marriage according to which same-sex couples can be married. So Sawyer predicts that the meaning of "marriage" has changed. But speakers in 2020 might truly say, "In 1960, we said that same-sex marriage was impossible, but we were wrong", and it is hard to see how this could be true if meaning has changed. (True, Sawyer will claim that the contents of our thoughts about marriage has not changed; but that does not explain the data, since the claim is about what was said. Sawyer might reply that the said-that report is true in virtue of the contents of our thoughts, but if so, it is not very clear what theoretical work is left for Sawyer's notion of meaning to do.)

Sawyer's view of thought content is also problematic; it fails to provide a satisfying account of how the content of thought is determined in the cases we have focused on. Perhaps Sawyer's view is plausible in some cases; there might well be "objective properties" that can explain why our "water" thoughts latched onto H_2O.[1] But what objective properties can explain why our "art" thoughts latched onto the phenomena they do (rather than other candidate phenomena)? There are no natural kinds here, and it's hard to believe that *the products of a certain cultural tradition* is more apt to be meant than *objects produced with certain aesthetic intentions*—or any number of other possibilities. Sawyer's view of thought content would leave meaning massively underdetermined in cases where there is no especially salient objective phenomenon, or where there are multiple candidate objective phenomena; and many or most of the cases where there is dispute are like this. In short, even if Sawyer's view works in cases where a natural kind or similarly objectively privileged phenomenon is in the picture, it is not applicable to the cases that we are most interested in (see discussion of the Inapplicability Objection in Chapter 5, Section 3.2).

Now one thought available to Sawyer in order to solve this underdetermination worry would be to endorse TE about thought contents. In cases where there is no unique salient objective property, the Sawyerian might maintain that the contents of our thoughts are partly determined our decisions in the course of theorising, while still insisting that they are also fixed in part by objective properties. The result would be a version of TE that endorses Thought–Language Divergentism.

If I were convinced that there were a significant theoretical role for a notion of linguistic meaning distinct from the notion of thought content to play, I would endorse this version of TE. But this is not my view. I maintain that Thought–Language Divergentism is not well motivated. Sawyer's dilemma about Sainsbury's puzzle was: "To say that [the meaning of 'whale' has not changed] fails to accommodate the fact that meaning is determined by use; but to say that it [has changed] fails to accommodate the fact that there is substantive disagreement across the two times" (2020a, 385). But I suggest that the first horn of the dilemma is misleading; one can maintain that the meaning has not changed while at the same time insisting that meaning is determined by use. On the view I recommend, "whale" means the same now as it always did, and this meaning is determined by the view we arrive at in the end of our inquiry. Although this does require giving up

---

[1] I myself would think that TE has a home even here; it turned out that "water" picks out a natural kind, but it might have turned out (compatibly with our practices before the year 1700) that "water" picks out a superficial kind—not H_2O, but any clear, odourless (etc.) liquid. (Thanks to Patrick Greenough for discussion of this kind of case.) But Sawyer's view that objective chemical properties play a privileged role is commonly held in the literature and I will grant it for the sake of discussion.

the claim that meaning is determined by use understood as requiring that what we mean at a particular time is determined by our dispositions to use the word *at that same time*, it does not require giving up the claim that meaning is determined by use in a more extended sense—what we mean is determined by our entire pattern of use over time, including our future use.[2] This is my preferred view: TE combined with Thought–Language Parallelism.

2. Issue 2: How Much Does Meaning Vary?

In Chapter 1, we introduced the idea that some theoretical projects might best be understood as revisionary with respect to semantics: they aim to change what our words mean. Chapter 2 discussed one contemporary version of this view: the view that definitional disputes involve metalinguistic negotiation. On any such view, the result of a definitional dispute will often be a change in meaning; and on one version of the view, the parties to the dispute are already using key words implicated in the dispute with different meanings.

Any view of this style will accept some version of the following principle:

Meaning Variationism People who differ with respect to the sentences they accept—especially sentences of the kind that are likely to be regarded as definitional or analytic truths—thereby differ with respect to what they mean.

Meaning Variationism suggests that either in interpersonal cases (I say "Art must be beautiful", you say "It's not the case that art must be beautiful") or in intrapersonal cases (I used to say "Art must be beautiful", now I say "It's not the case that art must be beautiful")—or perhaps most plausibly, in both—typical differences in view amount to differences in meaning; in the interpersonal case, you and I mean something different by "art", and in the intrapersonal cases, what I mean has changed.

In Chapters 2, 5, and 6, I argued that there is relatively little variation in meaning across time and across speakers. Of course, meanings do change (see the discussion in Chapter 7), and occasionally the best diagnosis of disagreements is one on which the participants are speaking past each other (as in some of the disputes about taste discussed in Chapter 9). But in general, disputes about matters of definition do not involve any variation in meaning: both speakers mean the same thing by the words that are central to the dispute despite their differences in view, and if someone changes her mind, that does not typically result in change of meaning.

---

[2] See Collins (2005) for related discussion.

Meaning Sameness Parties to a definitional dispute typically mean the same thing by their words, and the meanings of words do not typically change over the course of or as a result of the dispute.

The view that I prefer incorporates Meaning Sameness; defending that claim was a main aim of Part I. But it would be possible to combine TE with views on which meaning change is much more widespread. Consider, for example, the view defended in Peter Ludlow's *Living Words*, according to which words typically have standing meanings that do not determine an extension; instead, "we adjust or modulate their meanings on a conversation-by-conversation basis" (2014, 2). Ludlow begins the book with the following example:[3]

> Quite often people ask me how many books I've written. When they do (for example, on airplanes), I pause and say, "well...it depends on what you mean by 'book.'" I have edited several volumes of previously published work by others. Do these edited volumes count as books? Some people (most non-academics) say yes, and others say no. I have written a couple of eBooks; do they count as books? But wait, one isn't published yet. And the one that is published is only about fifty pages long. Book? Again the answer I get varies. Was my Columbia University dissertation a book? By the way, it was "published," with minor revisions, by the University of Indiana Linguistics Club. Book? The same book? What about drafts of books that are sitting on my hard drive? Are they books? Is a co-authored book a "book I wrote?" It takes a few minutes of asking these questions before I can answer and tell my conversational partner whether I have written two or three or six or ten books. (2014, 1)

Ludlow's idea is that there is a variety of things that one might mean by the word "book"; exactly which one means is determined in the course of conversation, and will often vary between different conversations.

There is considerable room for discussion about how widespread the phenomenon that Ludlow is seeing here really is. But whatever one's view, it is extremely plausible that we sometimes depart from this standard meaning and use words in an idiosyncratic way. This is true even in cases closely related to the great philosophical disputes we considered in Chapter 5: parents may debate what is or is not to count as "art" in the course of deciding which of a child's productions to keep and which to throw away, and such a debate may in no way presuppose that the conclusions reached will be relevant to other conversations.[4] (If we decide that this one is art because it looks like a bird, we should not conclude on that

---

[3] See Jackman (2015) for discussion of related views from a temporal-externalist friendly perspective.
[4] Thanks to Andy Egan for suggesting this case.

basis that Tolstoy is wrong about art.) Even in academic contexts, we may make stipulations only for the purposes of a certain conversation or work. And even if an author intends to advance a once-and-for-all definition of art that will govern many conversations across the community, past and future, it may be that her proposed definition is accepted by no one else—and despite this, the best way of making sense of her writings may be to take her use of "art" to be governed by her proposed definition.

Sometimes, then, meaning varies between conversations. And sometimes, a dispute is purely local: we disagree about what is "art" in a sense that is relevant only for present purposes. Ludlow's picture of what goes on in these cases is a version the metalinguistic negotiation picture that we rejected in Chapter 5: two parties begin the dispute meaning different things; the dispute is really about what they will go on to use the word to mean ("I think it is important to understand that when we engage in debates about personhood we are in point of fact engaged in a debate about the proper modulation of the term 'person'" (Ludlow, 2014, 56–57).) So, according to Ludlow, the debate is about the word, not some worldly phenomenon. But if that view is wrong, what is going on when (for example) parents are disputing whether a particular work is art?

Many of the same considerations we appealed to in Chapter 6 also apply in this case. Crucially, parties to disputes of this kind can support their views with arguments. And it would be natural of them to report their own past views in ways that we have argued track sameness of meaning. For example, we can imagine Ludlow's airplane interlocutor early in the conversation asserting, "PhD dissertations are books", but later revising his view (perhaps after realising that most PhD dissertations are not published), and concluding: "I used to think that a PhD dissertation was a book, but now I see that I was wrong". Likewise, we can imagine the art-sorting parent beginning with the view that *that* is "art" because it looks vaguely like a flower, but revising her view after reflecting that it could easily be a chance splatter. She might report: "I was thinking that everything that looked a certain way was art, but now I think that that was a mistake."

These facts will motivate temporal externalism: "book" and "art" are used in a distinctive way in these cases, a way particular to the conversations in which they occur, but they are used with the same meaning throughout these conversations, and their meaning is determined in part by judgements arrived at in the end of the conversation.

The same considerations may provide reasons to think that "book" and "art" as used in a particular conversation do not mean what they mean in other conversations. After all, it would be strange for the art-sorting parent to say, "I used to think that art had to be the product of a certain cultural tradition, but now I see that I was wrong: this smudge of handprints is clearly art."

There is, of course, much more to be said. But the case for temporal externalism can be made regardless of how variable we take meaning to be. Those who, with

Ludlow, think that meaning varies all the time will see temporal externalism as operating primarily at the level of uses within the context of a particular conversation. Those who see debates as long-lasting will see temporal externalism as giving an account of how long-lasting meanings are determined.

3. Issue 3: How Revisionary Can We Be?

Suppose that we introduce a word for a phenomenon, and go on to develop clear dispositions to apply or withhold the word in a wide range of cases. And suppose further that a situation arises about which we are just not sure whether or how to apply the word; it is a case that we had simply failed to consider, and nothing in our antecedent patterns of usage seems to dictate how we ought to go on.

A relatively modest version of TE would have it that TE applies in cases like this: our stipulations, dispositions, usage, often leave certain cases open; and in these cases our later judgements determine what we meant all along. We can close what we had left open; but if our stipulations, usage, or dispositions determines that a word is applicable in a particular case, it is applicable and we cannot change this (without change of meaning).

Gap-Closing Temporal Externalism (GCTE) Facts about later times can fix meaning at earlier times, but only in those cases in which there is no antecedent fact that can do the meaning-fixing work.[5]

Candidate cases of this type have sometimes seemed to arise in the history of science. Hartry Field writes:

> Consider the use of the term "heavier than" by pre-Newtonians. Did it stand for the relation of having greater mass than, or for the relation of having greater weight than? In pre-Newtonian physics there was no distinction between the weight of an object and its mass; and since the term "heavier than" was applied almost exclusively in the context of objects at the surface of the earth where there is a near-perfect correlation between mass and weight, there is little in the pre-Newtonian use of the term that could have settled the matter. (2001, p. 278)

Field proposes the case as one in which it is indeterminate which relation "heavier than" picks out; he proposes an account of *partial designation* on which "heavier than" partially designates the relation of having greater weight than, and partially designates the relation of having greater mass than. Perhaps Field's view gives a

---

[5] I take this to be the view defended in Jackman (1999, 2005); see Chapter 1 for further discussion.

good description of some ways the case might be developed. But suppose (as seems possible) that Newtonians debated the issue: perhaps some maintained that an elephant in space would be heavier than a mouse on Earth, while others denied this. One can imagine giving reasons on either side of the dispute, that eventually one side convinces the other, and that the parties go on to retrospectively evaluate their positions: "I used to think that to be heavier than required having greater mass, but now I see that I was wrong." In that case TE would provide an attractive way of making sense of the dispute, the arguments, and the retrospective judgements.

In other cases, our theorising does not simply close gaps but seeks to overturn aspects of our previous belief and usage. We have already discussed cases of this kind—the *atom* case discussed in Chapter 5 is one example—but for a plausible real-life case, one might consider the first proponents of the possibility of same-sex marriage. It may be that deeply entrenched beliefs, dispositions, and patterns of usage were entirely and consistently arranged against them in every one of their peers; perhaps prior to argument everyone regarded same-sex marriage as a conceptual impossibility, and every clue we could gather at the time would lead us to conclude that it was built into the meaning of "marriage" that only men can marry women and only women can marry men.[6]

A more ambitious version of TE would encompass these cases as well:

Revisionary Temporal Externalism (RTE) Facts about later times can fix meaning at earlier times. Even in cases where antecedent facts appear to settle a matter of meaning, these can be overturned by later facts.

The considerations that we used to motivate temporal externalism in Chapter 5 extend straightforwardly to (RTE). Even if we explicitly attempt to stipulate that atoms are indivisible, we might later judge that we were mistaken; even if everyone's judgements and behaviours all the time indicated that they took it to be a necessary, analytic truth that same-sex marriage is impossible, we might later judge that we were all mistaken all along. Thus (RTE) is my preferred view.

---

[6] See, for example, US Supreme Court Chief Justice John Roberts's dissent in Obergefell v. Hodges (the case that legalised same-sex marriage across the US), which focuses in large part on claims such as: "marriage 'has existed for millennia and across civilizations.' [...] For all those millennia, across all those civilizations, 'marriage' referred to only one relationship: the union of a man and a woman" (2015, 4), and "the fundamental right to marry does not include a right to make a State change its definition of marriage. And a State's decision to maintain the meaning of marriage that has persisted in every culture throughout human history can hardly be called irrational" (2015, 2).

4. Issue 4: In Virtue of What Is TE True?

According to TE, future facts play a role in determining what we mean. But—as with any view about what makes it the case that we mean what we do—we might wonder: why do future facts matter to meaning? In virtue of what is it the case that future facts, rather than (say) present dispositions or facts about the present environment, that matter?

There are a variety of ways in which this kind of question might be answered. On one kind of view, it is ultimately certain facts about us, now—for example, about how we are disposed to use a word—that determine what makes it the case that we mean what we do. One version of this idea would have it that the relevant factor is our dispositions to make judgements about how our words could correctly be applied if the world turned out to be a certain way.[7] For example, I might judge that my word "water" is correctly applied to H_2O (and not XYZ) if I find out that H_2O is the dominant substance in the lakes and rivers around here, but that that word applies to XYZ (and not H_2O) if I find out that XYZ is the dominant substance in the lakes and rivers around here. Crucially, the view is not that dispositions (alone) determine what we mean; it is rather that dispositions determine what determines what we mean. In the example we are considering, what I mean would be determined in part by facts about my environment (what substance is in the lakes and rivers); but the fact that those external facts determine what I mean is itself determined by my dispositions to make judgements about what "water" would apply to various cases.

We have called the theory of what determines what we mean *metasemantics*. The theory of what determines what determines what we mean—in other words, what determines which metasemantic theory is true—can be called *meta-metasemantics* (Cohnitz and Haukioja, 2013). We might defend a meta-metasemantic theory on which factors internal to us, now (such as dispositions) determine what metasemantic theory is true; and compatibly with this, we might defend a metasemantic theory on which external factors determine what we mean.

This style of view is compatible with temporal externalism (Haukioja, 2020), since we might be disposed to judge (say) that "art" (as we use it now) is correctly applied to so-called "conceptual art" if the world turns out to be such that we all come to judge that *Fountain* is art, to apply the word "art" to "conceptual artworks", and so on; but that "art" (as we use it now) is not correctly applied to so-called "conceptual art" if the world turns out to be such that we all come to judge that *Fountain* is not art, to decline to apply the word to "conceptual artworks", and so on. In that case, what we mean would be determined in part by our later practice, and the fact that our later practice determines what we mean is itself determined

---

[7] See Cohnitz and Haukioja (2013), Haukioja (2020) for a related view; and see also the view developed in Chalmers and Jackson (2001); Chalmers (2007).

by our dispositions. In short, the following is a prima facie defensible combination of views:

Temporal Externalism + Dispositionalist Meta-Metasemantics Facts about later times play a role in determining what we meant at earlier times, and facts about later times play this role because of dispositions we have at the earlier times.

However, it is not clear that this view does justice to the motivations we have considered for endorsing TE. Consider the following case:

Confidence, then Change In 2022, Barack is supremely confident that free will is the ability to do what one wants; so confident that he is disposed to judge that "free" is correctly applied only to those people who have the ability to do what they want no matter what he or others come to think about freedom. After many years of discussion, Barack's dispositions change; in 2027, he re-evaluates the evidence and comes to think that free will is the ability to do otherwise. He says, "I once said that free will is the ability to do what one wants, but I now think that I was wrong."

Barack's 2022 dispositions would not suggest that future facts ought to be relevant to what he means (in 2022). But plausibly, the kind of argument for TE that we gave in Chapter 6 can be brought to bear on this case; and if we take that argument seriously, then we ought to reject dispositionalist meta-metasemantics. We showed in Part I that many ways we argue for and against our positions in definitional disputes, as well as our practices of retrospective reporting and evaluation, motivate Meaning Sameness. Given Meaning Sameness, Barack's 2022 utterances of "Free will is the ability to do what one wants" and his 2027 utterances of "Free will is not the ability to do what one wants" are inconsistent. But considerations of charity motivate preferring a metasemantic view that makes his later utterances true over a metasemantic view that makes his earlier utterances true.[8]

Considerations of charity are doing crucial work here. If we are open to the possibility of attributing to ourselves error and irrationality then this style of argument for TE will get no purchase. For example, if we are happy to think that Barack is just making a mistake in *Confidence, then Change*—perhaps the meaning of his words and the contents of his thoughts just changes between 2022 and 2027, and he is incorrect in 2027 when he thinks his earlier view was wrong—then we will find no convincing argument for TE in this kind of case. It is only if we think that we ought to take Barack's later views especially seriously, so that we ought to do our best to vindicate them as the products of a rational process, that the kinds of considerations that we brought to bear against alternative pictures of what is

---

[8] At least if his latter utterances are made on the basis of judgements formed in reasonable ways. We'll return to this qualification in Section 8.

going on (Chapters 2, 5, and 8) and in favour of temporal externalism (Chapters 6 and 9) get off the ground.

This suggests the following view:

Temporal Externalism + Charity Facts about later times play a role in determining what we meant at earlier times, and we ought to believe that facts about later times play this role because it is the best way of interpreting us so that our definitional disputes and inquiries are reasonable and make sense.

Temporal Externalism + Charity does not directly address the meta-metasemantic question of in virtue of what it is the case that facts about later times play a meaning-determining role. But it suggests that one place to look for an explanation of why temporal externalism is true is in the explanation of why we ought to interpret people charitably (see Glüer, 2006; Pagin, 2006, for discussion).

5. Issue 5: Which Future Facts Matter?

There are a variety of different views on which facts external to the speaker play a role in determining the content of that speaker's representations. Some views emphasise physical facts about a speaker's environment; the classic example is Putnam's view about the significance of chemical kinds in Putnam (1975). Other views emphasise facts about other speakers; Putnam's claim that there is a *division of linguistic labour* (according to which the meanings of words as used by ordinary speakers depend on the beliefs and abilities of scientific experts) is a classic example here too.

One might analogously develop a range of views consistent with TE about which future facts matter. Perhaps broadly physical facts can matter—what natural or chemical kinds are in the future environment. Whatever our judgement about this, these are not the kinds of case that we have focused on. The previous section sketched an argument for TE which was motivated by the idea that our theory of meaning ought to interpret us charitably in such a way that our retrospective evaluations of what we thought and said, our ways of arguing, and also our later assertions and judgements, are reasonable and not systematically in error; and that the best way of doing requires making those later judgements and assertions correct. If this is our motivation, then the future facts that play a role in determining what we mean are our judgements and assertions. It is the fact that I judge (for example) that art is the product of a certain cultural tradition that makes it the case that "art" as I use it and have used it all along is correctly applied to products of a certain cultural tradition.

Naturally, this view raises further questions: whose judgements matter—only one's own or the judgements of others (experts) in one's community? Do all judgements matter or only certain privileged (analytic) ones? Do the judgements have to be made on particular grounds or in particular circumstances? The remainder of this section maps the theoretical terrain.

6. Issue A: Whose Judgements Matter?

Our version of temporal externalism maintains that future judgements play a role in determining what we mean. But a variety of views would be compatible with this claim; it might be that my future judgements (and no one else's) determine what I mean, or it might be that the future judgements of scientific experts or others do the work. And it might be that different views are appropriate in different cases.

Let's start with the most individually-focused view. If we consider a dispute about some matter of taste, such as those discussed in Chapter 9, it seems plausible that the judgements of the individual are what really matters. If I very firmly judge that chocolate is terrible and not at all tasty, and nothing can sway me in this judgement, it may be that all the world stands against me; still, it seems plausible that, as I use the word "tasty", I can speak truly when I say "Chocolate is not tasty". So it seems that in this kind of case, there is little room for the judgements of my community to make a difference:

Individual Temporal Externalism   Facts about later times can fix meaning at earlier times. But the only facts about later times that can play a role in determining what a particular speaker means are facts about that speaker's own judgements.

Now one might worry that even in a dispute about what is funny or tasty, Individual Temporal Externalism is a mistake, since it doesn't do justice to the contribution of one's interlocutors. After all, we have suggested throughout Part I that the temporal externalist mechanisms work best when the parties to the conversation reach agreement (or agree that they have been talking past each other). Shouldn't we then prefer the following view?

Individual/Interlocutor Temporal Externalism   Facts about later times can fix meaning at earlier times. But the only facts about later times that can play a role in determining what a particular speaker means in a particular conversation are facts about the judgements of that speaker and the judgements of other parties to that conversation.

It is not clear to me whether we should prefer Individual Temporal Externalism to Individual/Interlocutor Temporal Externalism. Even the Individual Temporal Externalist will admit that in some cases one's interlocutors influence what one means by convincing one to make a certain judgement. That does not show that the interlocutors' views themselves determine what one means, according to the Individual Temporal Externalist; it only shows that interlocutors can causally influence one's own views, which determine what one means. The Individual Temporal Externalist might maintain that reaching agreement is important only because it is an indication that all of the evidence has been evaluated and each party has reached a considered view, at which point they are unlikely to change their minds.

The cases where Individual Temporal Externalism and Individual/Interlocutor Temporal Externalism are likely to differ are cases where the discussion ends without a resolution—for example, where one of the parties to the conversation has to leave and the conversation is never resumed. In that case, the Individual Temporal Externalist is likely to rule that the parties to the dispute mean different things by their words; after all, each party comes to a different conclusion. Therefore, the Individual Temporal Externalist is likely to rule that the dispute is merely verbal (since the speakers end up making different judgements, if each speaker's judgements determine what that speaker means, they will most likely end up meaning different things). It is open to the Individual/Interlocutor Temporal Externalist to reject this conclusion, since she might maintain that the views of each interlocutor are relevant to what the other means; she might therefore think that the crucial word is indeterminate in meaning for both speakers.

For my own part, I have no strong view about which of these verdicts is correct. But in other kinds of case, I would maintain that neither Individual nor Individual/Interlocutor Temporal Externalism is sufficient to do justice to the phenomena. In many cases, it is natural to think that our disagreements last over time, even across generations; if we arrive at a certain view of art or of marriage, it is natural to think that figures in the past who held different views were wrong, that their beliefs and utterances were false. Moreover, it is often crucial to understanding our views and arguments to be able to relate them to the views and arguments of the past. We want to be able to say that those who thought that conceptual art was not really art were making a mistake, and to be able to evaluate whether the arguments they mustered for their position had any force at all; we want to be able to say that those who thought that same-sex marriage was ruled out by definition were mistaken, their views false. And (we have argued) that requires that we mean the same by "art" and by "marriage" as they did. Given the arguments of Part I, that suggests that we should view our judgements as fixing what speakers in the past meant. So, in these cases, we ought to endorse a form of Social Temporal Externalism:

Social Temporal Externalism Facts about later times can fix meaning at earlier times. The facts about later times that can play a role in determining what a particular speaker means include facts about that speaker's linguistic community, potentially including facts about the judgements in the community in the distant future, after the speaker dies.

That is the view I would defend. But it leaves open several questions. First, there is the question of *voluntarism*. Can I opt out of the social practice? Is there something I can do to stipulate that only my own use matters? We return to this issue below.

Second, there is the question of exactly which of my linguistic peers matter. Is it a particular group with special expertise—and if so, in what does this expertise consist?[9] Or is it my entire linguistic community (or, perhaps more realistically (given that the entire community agrees only in rare cases), a substantial enough part of my community)? In short, should we accept a version of Expertise Temporal Externalism?

Expertise Temporal Externalism   Social Temporal Externalism is true, and the judgements of experts are especially important in the determination of meaning.

I suspect that different views may be appropriate in different cases. (For example, it is plausible that experts of some variety play a special role in fixing the meaning of scientific vocabulary, but less plausible that experts play a special role in fixing the meaning of other kinds of words.) But nothing we have said so far commits us to a particular view, and attempting to resolve this issue would likely take us far from our main concerns. I therefore leave questions associated with Expertise Temporal Externalism open for further work.

7. Issue B: Which Judgements Matter? Analyticity and Holism

The defence of TE in Chapter 6 focused on disputes about matters of definition, and arrived at the view that our later judgements in these disputes can determine what we meant all along. Setting out the dispute in this way presupposes that some judgements are matters of definition—analytic, in the sense that they determine the meaning of some constituent term or concept.[10] We argued there that this conception of analyticity does not have problematic metaphysical or epistemic consequences. What the temporal externalist proponent of the analytic/synthetic distinction is proposing is simply this:

Analyticity Temporal Externalism   Facts about later times can fix meaning at earlier times. The facts that matter are our judgements about a particular class of sentences—the *analytic* sentences.

---

[9] See Ball (2020a) for some relevant discussion.
[10] See Ball (2020c) for further discussion of this *metasemantic* conception of analyticity.

But one might still be sceptical: how can we tell whether a given judgement is analytic? Is there some principled way of determining whether a judgement is a matter of definition or merely empirical?

If there is no line to be drawn between those judgements that play a meaning-fixing role and those that do not, then we must accept either that all judgements play such a role or that none do. To claim that none do would be to give up on Judgement TE. But the view that all judgements play a meaning-fixing role—often called *holism* in the literature—is available to a proponent of Judgement TE. On this view, the sum of all of our judgements at the end of inquiry play a role in determining what we meant all along.

Holistic Temporal Externalism   Facts about later times can fix meaning at earlier times. The facts that matter include all of our judgements.

I do not have a principled recipe for determining which judgements are analytic or matters of definition, and which are not. But nor am I convinced that we need to accept holism if we lack such a recipe. As Grice and Strawson (1956) observe, there is widespread agreement on which judgements are analytic and which are not, and this makes it plausible that we are tracking a genuine distinction:

> those who use the terms "analytic" and "synthetic" do to a very considerable extent agree in the applications they make of them. They apply the term "analytic" to more or less the same cases, withhold it from more or less the same cases, and hesitate over more or less the same cases. This agreement extends not only to cases which they have been taught so to characterize, but to new cases. In short, "analytic" and "synthetic" have a more or less established philosophical use; and this seems to suggest that it is absurd, even senseless, to say that there is no such distinction. For, in general, if a pair of contrasting expressions are habitually and generally used in application to the same cases, where these cases do not form a closed list, this is a sufficient condition for saying that there are kinds of cases to which the expressions apply; and nothing more is needed for them to mark a distinction.   (Grice and Strawson, 1956, 142–143)

Grice and Strawson maintain on these grounds that there is an analytic/synthetic distinction. Of course, this does not in itself establish that the distinction has the metasemantic significance that we have accorded it. (It is possible that there is a real distinction between the examples we judge to be analytic and the examples we judge to be synthetic, but that that distinction is not especially relevant to metasemantics, since the analytic examples play no special role in determining the meaning of words they contain.)

Why, then, should we think that there is a privileged subset of judgements that play a metasemantic role? One answer would rely on a phenomenon that we have already discussed: the fact that the parties to a dispute may sometimes conclude that we were speaking past one another all along. If I insist that free will requires the ability to do otherwise and am unmoved by any argument to the contrary, and you insist that free will requires only the ability to do what you want and are likewise unmoved by any challenge, then we may well conclude that we simply mean different things by "free will". If we persistently disagree in our judgement about some peripheral case, it is much less likely that we will come to the conclusion that we mean different things. It is natural to suppose that our judgements about whether we mean different things and are merely talking past each other will strongly correlate with our judgements about what is analytic and what is not.[11] And if that is so, we have some reason to think that our judgements about sameness and difference of meaning, and our practices of treating people as genuinely engaging or failing to communicate, are tracking our judgements about analyticity. And to the extent that we want to vindicate these judgements, we should maintain that the analytic truths are crucial to the determination of meaning.

Let's not pretend that this brief discussion settles the matter. My preference is for Analyticity TE; but Holistic TE strikes me as a contender that has not decisively been ruled out.

8. Issue C: How Must Judgements Be Arrived At?

In the cases we have discussed, we arrive at the conclusions we do in broadly reasonable ways: we consider the evidence and are convinced by arguments which seem to us to best survive our scrutiny. But we form beliefs for lots of reasons, good and bad; in addition to evidence and arguments, we cannot ignore the role of bias, wishful thinking, delusion, interlocutors' charisma, coercion, torture, or brainwashing.

We may find the idea that later judgements formed on the basis of bias or brainwashing determine what we mean now difficult to swallow, even if we think it plausible that our considered opinions play a meaning-fixing role in cases where these judgements are formed on the basis of good reasons. The worry is especially acute for those who endorse Revisionary TE. We may wonder: suppose the world is conquered by a racist dictator who (through a mix of charisma, propaganda, and brainwashing) manages to make it the case that we all share his racist views. Could that make it the case that (for example) the meaning of the word "person"

---

[11] It is worth noting again that the temporal externalist has flexibility here; we can admit that different speakers (even experts) may disagree about analytic matters while meaning the same thing, so long as they (or, given Social TE, their community) converges on a judgement in the long run.

is such that even now what we think when we say "All humans are persons" is false?[12]

There are several issues here that need to be disentangled. One is: *can we resist the metasemantic impact of future events?* For example, if we anticipate the rise of the racist dictator and believe that we will likely be brainwashed in the future, can we now draw a line in the sand to the effect that what we mean now by "person" cannot be affected by our future judgements? For example, can I simply stipulate that *by "person", I now mean such and such, and no future action or judgement can override this stipulation*?

Exactly what resources we have to answer these questions will depend in part on what variety of TE we endorse. For example, even if we set the possibility of brainwashing or irrationality aside, the proponent of Social TE may worry that my own judgements might get swept aside if a great majority of my peers coalesce around a view that I reject. By contrast, the proponent of Individual TE can maintain that, as long as I can stick firm to my judgement, there is no risk that the judgements of others will determine what I mean. But the cases of irrationality and brainwashing raise a challenge for every view. Can we opt out of the determination of meaning by future facts? The proponent of Voluntaristic TE says yes:

Voluntaristic Temporal Externalism   Facts about later times can fix meaning at earlier times. But a speaker at time *t* can choose whether facts about times later than *t* determine what she means at *t* or not.

Nothing we have said so far commits us to the truth or to the falsity of Voluntaristic TE, and I doubt that a single answer will be plausible in every case. It is difficult to know how to interpret someone who wants to resist the effects of their future

---

[12] Other views with a similar structure have faced similar lines of objection. For example, consider the Peircian pragmatist view that truth is belief at the end of inquiry. Peirce considers the objection that what we believe at the end of inquiry could be fixed by problematic means, but simply denies that this is possible. As Cheryl Misak puts the point:

> No acceptable account of truth can hold that beliefs permanently settled by torture are true by virtue of their settledness. Surely we aim for more than stubborn or immovable belief. And if we were to get a stubborn belief by adopting a specious method, then those beliefs would not be true simply by virtue of being stubborn. What if a totalitarian state, a religion, or the faggot and rack were successful in settling belief permanently—would this belief be true?
>
> Peirce answers "yes", but argues that such methods are in fact unable to settle belief permanently. His argument, which can be found in the 1877 "The Fixation of Belief", is that the only method that is able to result in true beliefs is the method that, prima facie, we want to affirm—the method of science and reasoning. That is, true beliefs are not "merely" going to be permanently settled upon. They would in fact be settled in a way which we all think is admirable.   (Misak, 2004, 56–57)

I find Peirce's view incredible. *Perhaps* torture is unable to fix belief in a permanently settled way. But bias and other less than "admirable" traits and methods are endemic to human cognition; a future in which we form no beliefs on these bases is next to impossible to imagine, and I see no reason to think that beliefs formed on the basis are going to be less permanent.

judgements; exactly what verdict seems most plausible is likely to depend in part on exactly how these judgements are formed. For example, we may want to give more weight to our attempts to resist the potential metasemantic force of future brainwashing than to attempts to resist the potential metasemantic force of judgements formed on the basis of reasonable arguments and evidence.

A second issue is: should we allow that judgements arrived at in a bad way can do meaning-determining work at all? Or should we insist that only those judgements formed in a responsible way matter? In short, *do our judgements play a metasemantic role even if they are arrived at in an epistemically problematic way?*

If we think that only judgements formed in a responsible way can play a metasemantic role, then we will endorse some version of Virtue Temporal Externalism:

Virtue Temporal Externalism   Facts about later times can fix meaning at earlier times. The facts that matter are our judgements; but these judgements only matter if they are formed in an epistemically responsible way.

A defender of Virtue TE should say more about the relevant notion of epistemic responsibility; but we will not undertake this task here. Instead, we will try to characterise some of the considerations that might tell for and against Virtue TE.

A first point regards one of the main arguments for TE in Chapter 5. The cases we considered there involved a speaker changing her mind. At one time, she makes an assertion of something she takes to be a definitional claim:

(43)   Free will requires the ability to do otherwise

At a later time she retracts that assertion, and puts forward a definitional claim inconsistent with it.

(44)   I said that free will requires the ability to do otherwise, but I was wrong. Free will doesn't require the ability to do otherwise.

(45)   Free will is the ability to do what you want.

No plausible view can preserve the truth of (43), (44), and (45): (44) is true only if "free will" means the same in all three utterances, but if "free will" means the same, then (43) and (45) are inconsistent. And we argued that, in this kind of scenario, we should prefer a view that preserves the truth of (45) to a view that preserves the truth of (43). After all, (45) reflects the speaker's considered judgement, her view once all the evidence is in; it seems uncharitable to rule this view false on the basis of (43), her judgement prior to considering the full range of evidence.

This style of argument has very little force when applied to cases where judgements are formed in an epistemically irresponsible way. There, the speaker's later judgement is not her *considered* judgement, her judgement once all the evidence is in; it is her swayed or forced judgement, one not based on evidence at all. It may be more charitable in this kind of case to prefer her *earlier* judgements (at least, on the assumption that these were formed in a responsible way).

If that is correct, it constitutes an argument in favour of Virtue TE. But it is important that we apply the argument cautiously. Arguably, we make judgements on bad grounds and form opinions in epistemically irresponsible ways all the time. Many of even our most cherished views may be tainted by implicit biases. Virtue TE would threaten to make a range of our views untrue in ways we may find problematic. For example, it may be that most of us assign people of certain races or genders somewhat more credibility than they really deserve; we are a little bit more ready to believe their testimony than we ought to be. If so, then it may be that very many of the beliefs we have formed on the basis of testimony are less than fully virtuous. And if testimony feeds into belief formation in a wide range of cases, Virtue TE would mean that very many of our judgements cannot play a meaning-fixing role. This threatens to undermine the potential benefits of temporal externalism: if our judgements do not play a meaning-fixing role, then the kind of account of our arguments and considered judgements offered in Chapter 5 and Chapter 9 won't be possible.

The proponent of Virtue TE therefore has work to do in order to try to establish some boundaries: under what circumstances are our judgements metasemantically efficacious? How bad can a method for forming beliefs be if beliefs formed by means of it are to be capable of determining meaning? I do not have well-worked-out answers to these questions, and so will leave the development of Virtue TE for future work.

9. Issue D: What If There Are No Settled Judgements?

The cases we focused on in Chapter 5 tended to involve convergence: at the end of the debate, all parties came to agree (or at least, to agree that the dispute was merely verbal). But in other cases, we may never reach an agreement. We can consider a variety of different scenarios: we have a brief exchange which ends inconclusively and we never revisit the topic; we go on talking but neither side convinces the other; the world ends before the conversation can play out.

TE as such does not deliver predictions about these kind of cases, and is not committed to any particular view about these cases. TE is a partial metasemantic theory (see Chapter 1, Section 5). It is the claim that future facts sometimes make a difference to meaning; in cases where the relevant kind of facts fail to obtain, the proponent of TE could think that it is indeterminate what we mean, or that some present fact is sufficient to fix meaning (even though it would not have been sufficient had different future facts obtained). It is plausible that no single account will work in every case. In some cases, it may be very plausible that there are other facts—speaker intentions or facts about the environment—that can do the relevant metasemantic work. In other cases, this may be much less clear; and in such cases, the most plausible verdict is likely to be that there is a significant degree of indeterminacy.

One version of this kind of worry is worth drawing attention to explicitly. We have already discussed the idea that some definitional disputes—for example, about truth and paradox—seem characteristically intractable. In Chapters 3 and 4, we discussed theorists who think that the seeming fact that we have made little progress in resolving the disputes shows that our methodologies are problematic and need to be changed. An alternative attitude towards at least some ongoing disputes is that it is important that the dispute continue without being resolved; the disputing itself is playing some important role.

Perhaps the most prominent development of this idea has it that there exist *essentially contested words or concepts*: that is, words or concepts "the proper use of which inevitably involves endless disputes about their proper uses" (Gallie, 1956, 169). Gallie proposes a detailed theory about the features that an essentially contested concept must have; the most crucial features for our purposes are that essentially contested concepts signal something we value, and that each user of the concept "recognizes the fact that [their] own use of it is contested by those of other parties, and that each party must have at least some appreciation of the different criteria in the light of which the other parties claim to be applying the concept" (Gallie, 1956, 172).

Of course, it is very plausible that many of the definitional disputes that we have discussed meet these criteria, and indeed "art" is one of Gallie's key examples. However, it is not clear that this establishes that there are debates that are genuinely impossible to resolve. If a concept meets Gallie's criteria, it would be natural to describe it as *contested*. But it is compatible with this that the contestation will be resolved. In order to show that there are *essentially* contested concepts, it would have to be shown that these concepts cannot cease being contested while remaining the concepts they are; in other words, that the debates cannot be resolved without changing the concepts. In my view, the case that there are essentially contested concepts has simply not been made. On the contrary: we already suggested that there are reasons to think that progress has been made in many cases, and can be made in others. (See Chapter 4 for further discussion.)

Even if this is wrong, there is a further reason to doubt that there is a serious objection to temporal externalism here. Suppose that some disputes are genuinely unresolvable in the way the proponent of essentially contested concepts would suggest. In this case, the temporal externalist mechanism would not determine what the words at the centre of those disputes mean. But this seems like a plausible verdict on the case: after all, the parties to the dispute regard themselves as disagreeing with each other in a way that suggests that they mean the same thing by their key terms; but different aspects of their practice pull in different ways, so that the resolution of the dispute that would fix meaning is not in place. In short, even if there were essentially contested concepts, and even if the temporal externalist rules such concepts indeterminate in content, that verdict is plausibly correct.

10. Conclusion

This chapter has presented a menu of possible temporal externalist views. We have defended a particular path through these options: temporal externalism applies to both thought and language (Thought-Language Parallelism); although meaning change is possible, there is relatively little variation in meaning across time (Meaning Constancy); and we can determine meaning in a way that makes our antecedent judgements false (Revisionary TE). The future facts that make a difference to meaning are facts about judgements and beliefs—not just our own beliefs but the beliefs of members of our community, including future members (Social TE). We also raised issues about whether experts play a privileged role (Expertise TE), about whether judgements can determine meaning only if they are formed in certain ways (Virtue TE), and about what happens when no conclusion is reached; but our discussion of these issues was less decisive.

Even readers who remain doubtful about temporal externalism may draw something from the treatment of disputes about definition described in this book: metasemantics has underappreciated explanatory potential. Attending to possible ways in which what we think and mean can be determined can help explain how people engage with each other and how inquiry into definitional matters can reasonably be conducted. Whether or not the temporal externalist view defended here is correct, the potential of metasemantics to contribute to our understanding of these issues—and the potential for presuppositions about the range of possible metasemantic views to hinder our understanding—should not be ignored. In each case, the right metasemantic view can help explain what is going on, without the need to go relativist or to invoke complicated pragmatic stories about what is communicated and why.

Those who find temporal externalism, and in particular Revisionary Temporal Externalism, attractive can draw a further conclusion about the methodology of inquiry. We need not be bound by our previous views and the ways we have talked in the past; change in view, even about matters of definition, need not amount to change of subject. Appeals to ordinary language or folk usage need not faze the revisionist; her views could be novel but still correct. We should simply do what epistemically responsible agents have always done: follow the arguments, believe on the basis of the best reasons we can, and change our minds as appropriate.

Bibliography

Ambrose, A. (1942/1952). Moore's 'proof of an external world'. In Schilpp (1952), pages 395–417.
Ambrose, A. (1970). Three aspects of Moore's philosophy. In Ambrose and Lazerowitz (1970), pages 80–88.
Ambrose, A. (1992). Linguistic approaches to philosophical problems. In Rorty (1992), pages 147–155.
Ambrose, A. and Lazerowitz, M., editors (1970). *G.E. Moore: Essays in Retrospect*. George Allen and Unwin Ltd., London.
Anderson, E. (2004). Uses of value judgments in science: A general argument, with lessons from a case study of feminist research on divorce. *Hypatia*, 19:1–24.
Aristotle (1985). *The Complete Works of Aristotle, Volume Two*. Princeton University Press, Princeton. Jonathan Barnes, editor.
Aristotle (1995). *Selections*. Hackett Publishing Company, Cambridge. Terence Irwin and Gail Fine, editors.
Ayer, A. J. (1940). *The Foundations of Empirical Knowledge*. MacMillan, London.
Bach, K. (2008). On referring and not referring. In Gundel, J. and Hedberg, N., editors, *Reference: Interdisciplinary Perspectives*, pages 13–58. Oxford University Press, Oxford.
Ball, D. (2018a). Lewisian scorekeeping and the future. *Croatian Journal of Philosophy*, 18:375–384.
Ball, D. (2018b). Semantics as measurement. In Ball, D. and Rabern, B., editors, *The Science of Meaning*, pages 381–410. Oxford University Press, Oxford.
Ball, D. (2020a). Metasemantic ethics. *Ratio*, 33:206–219.
Ball, D. (2020b). Relativism, metasemantics, and the future. *Inquiry*, 63:1036–1086.
Ball, D. (2020c). Revisionary analysis without meaning change; or, could women be analytically oppressed? In Burgess et al. (2020), pages 35–58.
Ball, D. and Huvenes, T. T. (2022). A puzzle about accommodation and truth. *Philosophical Studies*, 179:759–776.
Bantegnie, B. (2020). What are the debates on same-sex marriage and on the recognition of transwomen as women about? On anti-descriptivism and revisionary analysis. *Inquiry*, 63:974–1000.
Barker, C. (2002). The dynamics of vagueness. *Linguistics and Philosophy*, 25(1):1–36.
Barlassina, L. and Prete, F. D. (2015). The puzzle of the changing past. *Analysis*, 75:59–67.
Beall, J., Glanzberg, M., and Ripley, D. (2017). Liar paradox. In Zalta, E. N., editor, *The Stanford Encyclopedia of Philosophy*. Metaphysics Research Lab, Stanford University, fall 2017 edition.
Belleri, D. (2017). Verbalism and metalinguistic negotiation in ontological disputes. *Philosophical Studies*, 174:2211–2226.
Bigelow, J. (1996). Presentism and properties. *Philosophical Perspectives*, 10:35–52.
Boghossian, P. (1997a). Analyticity. In Hale, B. and Wright, C., editors, *A Companion to Philosophy of Language*, pages 331–368. Blackwell, Oxford.
Boghossian, P. (1997b). What the externalist can know a priori. *Proceedings of the Aristotelian Society*, 97:161–175.

Borg, E. (2004). *Minimal Semantics*. Oxford University Press, Oxford.
Braun, D. (1996). Demonstratives and their linguistic meanings. *Noûs*, 30:145–173.
Brown, J. (2000). Against temporal externalism. *Analysis*, 60:178–188.
Burge, T. (1977). Belief de re. *Journal of Philosophy*, 74:338–362.
Burge, T. (1979). Individualism and the mental. In Ludlow and Martin (1998), pages 21–84. Originally published in *Midwest Studies in Philosophy*, 4, 1979.
Burge, T. (1986). Intellectual norms and the foundations of mind. *Journal of Philosophy*, 83:697–720.
Burge, T. (1988). Individualism and self-knowledge. *Journal of Philosophy*, 85:649–663.
Burgess, A. (2006). *Identifying Fact and Fiction*. PhD thesis, Princeton University.
Burgess, A., Cappelen, H., and Plunkett, D., editors (2020). *Conceptual Ethics and Conceptual Engineering*. Oxford University Press, Oxford.
Burgess, A. G. and Burgess, J. P. (2011). *Truth*. Princeton University Press, Princeton.
Bybee, J. S. (2002). Memorandum for Alberto R. Gonzalez, Counsel to the President. Available online at https://nsarchive2.gwu.edu/NSAEBB/NSAEBB127/02.08.01.pdf, accessed 29 June 2023.
Cappelen, H. (2018). *Fixing Language*. Oxford University Press, Oxford.
Cappelen, H. (2020). Conceptual engineering: The master argument. In Burgess et al. (2020), pages 132–151.
Cappelen, H. and Lepore, E. (2005). *Insensitive Semantics: A Defense of Semantic Minimalism and Speech Act Pluralism*. Blackwell, Oxford.
Carey, S. (2009). *The Origin of Concepts*. Oxford University Press, Oxford.
Chalmers, D. (2007). Two-dimensional semantics. In Lepore, E. and Smith, B., editors, *Oxford Handbook of the Philosophy of Language*, pages 574–606. Oxford University Press, Oxford.
Chalmers, D. and Jackson, F. (2001). Conceptual analysis and reductive explanation. *Philosophical Review*, 110:315–361.
Chalmers, D. J. (2011). Verbal disputes. *Philosophical Review*, 120(4):515–566.
Chihara, C. (1979). The semantic paradoxes: A diagnostic investigation. *Philosophical Review*, 88:590–618.
Chomsky, N. (1986). *Knowledge of Language*. Praeger, New York.
Clark, A. and Chalmers, D. (1998). The extended mind. *Analysis*, 58:7–19.
Cohnitz, D. and Haukioja, J. (2013). Meta-externalism vs meta-internalism in the study of reference. *Australasian Journal of Philosophy*, 91:475–500.
Collins, J. (2015). Truth and language, natural and formal. In Achourioti, T., Galinon, H., Martínez Fernández, J., and Fujimoto, K., editors, *Unifying the Philosophy of Truth*, pages 85–105. Springer Netherlands, Dordrecht.
Collins, J. M. (2005). Temporal externalism, natural kind terms, and scientifically ignorant communities. *Philosophical Papers*, 35:55–68.
Crisp, T. (2007). Presentism and the grounding objection. *Nous*, 41:90–109.
Davidson, D. (2001). Truth and meaning. In *Inquiries into Truth and Interpretation, second edition*, pages 17–42. Oxford University Press, Oxford.
Davies, S. (2005). Definitions of art. In Gaut, B. and Lopes, D. M., editors, *The Routledge Companion to Aesthetics, second edition*, pages 227–240. Routledge, London.
Davison, N. (6 October 2017). Why can't we cure the common cold? *The Guardian*. https://www.theguardian.com/news/2017/oct/06/why-cant-we-cure-the-common-cold, accessed 29 June 2023.
Dean, J. (2003). The nature of concepts and the definition of art. *Journal of Aesthetics and Art Criticism*, 61:29–35.

Donnellan, K. (2012). The contingent a priori and rigid designators. In *Essays on Reference, Language, and Mind*, pages 147–171. Oxford University Press, New York.
Dowell, J. (2013). Flexible contextualism about deontic modals: A puzzle about information-sensitivity. *Inquiry*, 53:149–178.
Dretske, F. (1991). *Explaining Behavior*. MIT Press, Cambridge, MA.
Ebbs, G. (2000). The very idea of sameness of meaning across time. *American Philosophical Quarterly*, 37:245–268.
Ebbs, G. (2002). Leaning from others. *Nous*, 36:525–549.
Egan, A. (2010). Disputing about taste. In Feldman, R. and Warfield, T., editors, *Disagreement*, pages 247–286. Oxford University Press, Oxford.
Egan, A. (2014). There's something funny about comedy: A case study in faultless disagreement. *Erkenntnis*, 79:73–100.
Eklund, M. (2002). Inconsistent languages. *Philosophy and Phenomenological Research*, 64:251–275.
Eklund, M. (2007). Meaning-constitutivity. *Inquiry: An Interdisciplinary Journal of Philosophy*, 50:559–574.
European Commission (2010). Commission Regulation (EU) No 731/2010 of 11 August 2010 concerning the classification of certain goods in the Combined Nomenclature. http://eur-lex.europa.eu/eli/reg/2010/731/oj.
Evans, G. (1985). The causal theory of names. In *Collected Papers*, pages 1–24. Oxford University Press, New York.
Falvey, K. and Owens, J. (1994). Externalism, self-knowledge, and skepticism. *Philosophical Review*, 103:107–137.
Field, H. (2001). Indeterminacy, degree of belief, and excluded middle. In *Truth and the Absence of Fact*, pages 278–306. Oxford University Press, New York.
Fine, K. (1994). Essence and modality. *Philosophical Perspectives*, 8:1–16.
Frankfurt, H. G. (1969). Alternate possibilities and moral responsibility. *Journal of Philosophy*, 66:820–839.
Frankfurt, H. G. (1971). Freedom of the will and the concept of a person. *Journal of Philosophy*, 68:5–20.
Gallie, W. (1956). Essentially contested concepts. *Proceedings of the Aristotelian Society*, 56:167–198.
García-Carpintero, M. and Kölbel, M., editors (2008). *Relative Truth*. Oxford University Press, New York.
Gauker, C. (2008). No tolerance for pragmatics. *Synthese*, 165:359–371.
Gellner, E. (1959). *Words and Things*. Victor Gollancz, London.
Glanzberg, M. (2007). Context, content, and relativism. *Philosophical Studies*, 136:1–29.
Glanzberg, M. (2016). Not all contextual parameters are alike. Available on his website at https://michaelglanzberg.org/wp-content/uploads/2018/06/parametersaredifferent June16-1ra1yfv-1.pdf.
Glüer, K. (2006). The status of charity I: Conceptual truth or a posteriori necessity? *International Journal of Philosophical Studies*, 14:337–359.
Greaves, H. (2013). Epistemic decision theory. *Mind*, 122:915–952.
Grice, H. and Strawson, P. (1956). In defense of a dogma. *The Philosophical Review*, 65:141–158.
Grice, P. (1989a). Logic and conversation. In Grice (1989d), pages 22–40.
Grice, P. (1989b). Meaning. In Grice (1989d), pages 213–223.
Grice, P. (1989c). Prolegomena. In Grice (1989d), pages 3–21.
Grice, P. (1989d). *Studies in the Way of Words*. Harvard University Press, Cambridge, MA.

Harman, G. (1986). *Change in View*. MIT Press, Cambridge, MA.
Haslanger, S. (2003). Persistence through time. In Loux, M. J. and Zimmerman, D. W., editors, *The Oxford Handbook of Metaphysics*, pages 315–354. Oxford University Press, Oxford.
Haslanger, S. (2012). Gender and race: (what) are they? (what) do we want them to be? In *Resisting Reality: Social Construction and Social Critique*, pages 221–247. Oxford University Press, Oxford.
Haukioja, J. (2020). Semantic burden-shifting and temporal externalism. *Inquiry*, 63:919–929.
Hawley, K. (2001). *How Things Persist*. Oxford University Press, Oxford.
Hawthorne, J. and Lepore, E. (2011). On words. *Journal of Philosophy*, 108:447–485.
Heikkinen, T. and Järvinen, A. (2003). The common cold. *The Lancet*, 361(9351):51–59.
Heim, I. and Kratzer, A. (1998). *Semantics in Generative Grammar*. Blackwell, Oxford.
Hobbes, T. (1996). *Leviathan*. Cambridge University Press, Cambridge.
Jackman, H. (1999). We live forwards but understand backwards: Linguistic practices and future behavior. *Pacific Philosophical Quarterly*, 80:157–177.
Jackman, H. (2004). Temporal externalism and epistemic theories of vagueness. *Philosophical Studies*, 117:79–94.
Jackman, H. (2005). Temporal externalism, deference, and our ordinary linguistic practice. *Pacific Philosophical Quarterly*, 86:365–380.
Jackman, H. (2015). Externalism, metasemantic contextualism, and self-knowledge. In Goldberg, S., editor, *Externalism, Self-Knowledge and Skepticism*, pages 228–247. Oxford University Press, New York.
Jackman, H. (2020). Temporal externalism, conceptual continuity, meaning, and use. *Inquiry*, 63:959–973.
Jackson, F. (1998). *From Metaphysics to Ethics: A Defense of Conceptual Analysis*. Oxford University Press, New York.
Jackson, F. and Pettit, P. (1990). Program explanation: A general perspective. *Analysis*, 50:107–117.
Juhl, C. (2009). Pure and impure stipulation. *Philosophy and Phenomenological Research*, 79:637–652.
Kant, I. (1997). *Critique of Pure Reason*. Cambridge University Press, Cambridge.
Kaplan, D. (1977). Demonstratives: An essay on the semantics, logic, metaphysics, and epistemology of demonstratives and other indexicals. In Almog, J., Perry, J., and Wettstein, H., editors, *Themes From Kaplan*, pages 481–564. Oxford University Press, New York.
Kaplan, D. (1990). Words. *Aristotelian Society Supplementary Volume*, 64:93–119.
Kaplan, D. (1996). Dthat. In Martinich, A., editor, *The Philosophy of Language, third edition*, pages 292–305. Oxford, New York.
Kennedy, C. (1997). *Projecting the adjective: The syntax and semantics of gradability and comparison*. PhD thesis, University of California Santa Cruz.
Kennedy, C. and McNally, L. (2005). Scale structure, degree modification, and the semantics of gradable predicates. *Language*, 81:345–381.
Kim, J. (1998). *Mind in a Physical World*. MIT Press, Cambridge, MA.
King, J. C. (2014). The metasemantics of contextual sensitivity. In Burgess, A. and Sherman, B., editors, *Metasemantics*, pages 97–118. Oxford University Press, New York.
King, P. J. (1995). Other times. *Australasian Journal of Philosophy*, 73:532–547.
Kölbel, M. (2004). Faultless disagreement. *Proceedings of the Aristotelian Society*, 104(1):53–73.
Kripke, S. A. (1980). *Naming and Necessity*. Harvard University Press, Cambridge, MA.

Kripke, S. A. (1982). *Wittgenstein on Rules and Private Language*. Harvard University Press, Cambridge, MA.
Larson, R. and Segal, G. (1995). *Knowledge of Language*. MIT Press, Cambridge, MA.
Lasersohn, P. (2005). Context dependence, disagreement, and predicates of personal taste. *Linguistics and Philosophy*, 28(6):643–686.
Lasersohn, P. (2008). Quantification and perspective in relativist semantics. *Philosophical Perspectives*, 22(1):305–337.
Lazerowitz, M. (1942/1952). Moore's paradox. In Schilpp (1952), pages 369–394.
Lazerowitz, M. (1964). *Studies in Metaphilosophy*. Routledge and Kegan Paul, London.
Lewis, D. (1970a). General semantics. *Synthese*, 22:18–67.
Lewis, D. (1970b). How to define theoretical terms. *The Journal of Philosophy*, 67:427–446.
Lewis, D. (1972). Psychophysical and theoretical identifications. *Australasian Journal of Philosophy*, 50:249–258.
Lewis, D. (1980). Index, context, and content. In *Papers in Philosophical Logic*, pages 21–44. Cambridge University Press, New York.
Lewis, D. (1983a). Languages and language. In Lewis (1983b), pages 163–188.
Lewis, D. (1983b). *Philosophical Papers, Volume I*. Oxford University Press, New York.
Lewis, D. (1983c). Scorekeeping in a language game. In Lewis (1983b), pages 233–249.
Lewis, D. (1983d). Survival and identity. In Lewis (1983b), pages 55–77.
Lewis, D. (1984). Putnam's paradox. *Australasian Journal of Philosophy*, 62:221–236.
Lewis, D. (1986). *On the Plurality of Worlds*. Blackwell, New York.
Lewis, D. (1999). Reduction of mind. In *Papers in Metaphysics and Epistemology*, pages 291–324. Cambridge University Press, New York.
Liao, S. (2012). What are centered worlds? *Philosophical Quarterly*, 62:294–316.
Locke, J. (1690/1894). *An Essay Concerning Human Understanding, Volume II*. Clarendon Press, Oxford.
Longino, H. (1994). In search of feminist epistemology. *The Monist*, 77:472–485.
Lopes, D. M. (2014). *Beyond Art*. Oxford University Press, Oxford.
Lopez de Sa, D. (2008). Presuppositions of commonality: An indexical relativist account of disagreement. In García-Carpintero and Kölbel (2008), pages 297–310.
Ludlow, P. (1995). Externalism, self-knowledge, and the prevalence of slow switching. *Analysis*, 55:45–49.
Ludlow, P. (2014). *Living Words: Meaning Underdetermination and the Dynamic Lexicon*. Oxford University Press, Oxford.
Ludlow, P. and Martin, N., editors (1998). *Externalism and Self-Knowledge*. CSLI, Stanford.
MacFarlane, J. (2003). Future contingents and relative truth. *Philosophical Quarterly*, 53:321–336.
MacFarlane, J. (2008). Truth in the garden of forking paths. In García-Carpintero and Kölbel (2008), pages 81–102.
MacFarlane, J. (2014). *Assessment Sensitivity: Relative Truth and its Applications*. Oxford University Press, Oxford.
Maguire, B. and Woods, J. (2020). The game of belief. *The Philosophical Review*, 129:211–249.
Malcolm, N. (1942/1952). Moore and ordinary language. In Schilpp (1952), pages 343–368.
Malcolm, N. (1949). Defending common sense. *The Philosophical Review*, 58:201–220.
Malcolm, N. (1970). G.E. Moore. In Ambrose and Lazerowitz (1970), pages 34–52.
Margolis, E. and Laurence, S. (2007). The ontology of concepts—abstract objects or mental representations? *Nous*, 41:561–593.

Matthen, M. (1999). Evolution, Wisconsin style: Selection and the explanation of individual traits. *British Journal for the Philosophy of Science*, 50:143–150.

McGinn, C. (1991). Can we solve the mind-body problem? In *The Problem of Consciousness*, pages 1–22. Blackwell, Cambridge, MA.

McLaughlin, B. and Tye, M. (1998). Externalism, twin earth, and self-knowledge. In Wright, C., Smith, B. C., and Macdonald, C., editors, *Knowing Our Own Minds*, pages 285–320. Oxford University Press, New York.

Melina, R. (2010). Which mountain is the tallest in the world? *LiveScience*. https://www.livescience.com/32594-which-mountain-is-the-tallest-in-the-world.html, accessed 29 June 2023.

Millikan, R. G. (1989). Biosemantics. *Journal of Philosophy*, 86:281–297.

Misak, C. (2004). *Truth and the End of Inquiry: A Peircean Account of Truth*. Oxford University Press, Oxford.

Montague, R. (1974a). *Formal Philosophy*. Yale University Press, New Haven.

Montague, R. (1974b). Pragmatics and intensional logic. In Montague (1974a), pages 119–147.

Moore, G. (2005). *Ethics*. Oxford University Press, Oxford.

Neander, K. (1988). What does natural selection explain? Correction to Sober. *Philosophy of Science*, 55:422–426.

Neander, K. (1995). Pruning the tree of life. *British Journal for the Philosophy of Science*, 46:59–80.

Ogden, C. and Richards, I. (1946). *The Meaning of Meaning, eighth edition*. Harcourt, Brace, and World, Inc., New York.

Oxford English Dictionary (2021). the, adj., pron.2, and n.1. In *OED Online*. Oxford University Press. https://www.oed.com/view/Entry/200211, accessed 10 March 2021.

Pagin, P. (2006). The status of charity II: Charity, probability, and simplicity. *International Journal of Philosophical Studies*, 14:361–383.

Parfit, D. (1971). Personal identity. *Philosophical Review*, 80(1):3–27.

Patterson, D. (2009). Inconsistency theories of semantic paradox. *Philosophy and Phenomenological Research*, 79:387–422.

Plunkett, D. and Sundell, T. (2013). Disagreement and the semantics of normative and evaluative terms. *Philosophers' Imprint*, 13(23).

Plunkett, D. and Sundell, T. (2021). Metalinguistic negotiation and speaker error. *Inquiry*, 64:142–167.

Priest, G. (2006). *In Contradiction: A Study of the Transconsistent*. Oxford University Press, Oxford.

Prior, A. (1960). The runabout inference ticket. *Analysis*, 21:38–39.

Prosser, S. (2020). The metaphysics of mental files. *Philosophy and Phenomenological Research*, 100:657–676.

Putnam, H. (1975). The meaning of 'meaning'. In *Mind, Language, and Reality: Philosophical Papers, Volume 2*, pages 215–271. Cambridge University Press, New York. Originally published in *Minnesota Studies in the Philosophy of Science*, 7, 1975.

Putnam, H. (1978). *Meaning and the Moral Sciences*. Routledge, London.

Quine, W. V. O. (1960). *Word and Object*. MIT Press, Cambridge, MA.

Quine, W. V. O. (1966). Carnap and logical truth. In *The Ways of Paradox and Other Essays*, pages 100–125. Random House, New York.

Railton, P. (1989). Naturalism and prescriptivity. *Social Philosophy and Policy*, 7:12–14.

Recanati, F. (2012). *Mental Files*. Oxford University Press, Oxford.

Richard, M. (1995). Defective contexts, accommodation, and normalization. *Canadian Journal of Philosophy*, 25:551–570.
Richard, M. (2008). *When Truth Gives Out*. Oxford University Press, Oxford.
Richard, M. (2020). The a-project and the b-project. In Burgess et al. (2020), pages 358–378.
Roberts, J. (2015). Obergefell v. Hodges. available online at https://supreme.justia.com/cases/federal/us/576/14-556/, accessed 29 June 2023.
Robinson, R. (1954). *Definition*. Oxford University Press, Oxford.
Rorty, R., editor (1992). *The Linguistic Turn: Essays in Philosophical Method*. The University of Chicago Press, Chicago.
Rosen, G. (2015). Real definition. *Analytic Philosophy*, 56:189–209.
Rouse, J. (2014). Temporal externalism and the normativity of linguistic practice. *Journal of the Philosophy of History*, 8:20–38.
Sainsbury, R. (2005). *Reference Without Referents*. Oxford University Press, New York.
Sainsbury, R. (2014). Fishy business. *Analysis*, 74:3–5.
Sainsbury, R. M. (2009). *Paradoxes*. Cambridge University Press, Cambridge.
Sassoon, G. W. (2013). A typology of multidimensional adjectives. *Journal of Semantics*, 30:335–380.
Sawyer, S. (2020a). Thought and talk. In Burgess et al. (2020), pages 379–395.
Sawyer, S. (2020b). Truth and objectivity in conceptual engineering. *Inquiry*, 63:1001–1022.
Scharp, K. (2013a). *Replacing Truth*. Oxford University Press, Oxford.
Scharp, K. (2013b). Truth, the liar, and relativism. *Philosophical Review*, 122:427–510.
Schiffer, S. (1996). Contextualist solutions to scepticism. *Proceedings of the Aristotelian Society*, 96:317–333.
Schilpp, P. A., editor (1942/1952). *The Philosophy of G.E. Moore, second edition*. Tudor Publishing Company, New York.
Scientific American (2017). Are mathematicians finally satisfied with Andrew Wiles's proof of Fermat's Last Theorem? Why has this theorem been so difficult to prove? *Scientific American*. https://www.scientificamerican.com/article/are-mathematicians-finall/, accessed 29 June 2023.
Scott, D. (1970). Advice on modal logic. In Lambert, K., editor, *Philosophical Problems in Logic: Some Recent Developments*, pages 143–173. D. Reidel, Dordrecht.
Shah, N. (2006). A new argument for evidentialism. *The Philosophical Quarterly*, 56:481–498.
Shoemaker, S. (2003). Functionalism and qualia. In *Identity, Cause, and Mind, expanded edition*, pages 184–205. Oxford University Press, New York.
Sider, T. (2001). *Four-Dimensionalism: An Ontology of Persistence and Time*. Oxford University Press, New York.
Sider, T. (2011). *Writing the Book of the World*. Oxford University Press, New York.
Singer, M. G. (1977). Actual consequence utilitarianism. *Mind*, 86:67–77.
Sober, E. (1995). Natural selection and distributive explanation: A reply to Neander. *British Journal for the Philosophy of Science*, 46:384–397.
Spicer, F. (2008). Are there any conceptual truths about knowledge? *Proceedings of the Aristotelian Society*, 108:43–60.
Stock, K. (2003). Historical definitions of art. In Davies, S. and Sukla, A. C., editors, *Art and Essence*, pages 159–176. Praeger, London.
Stock, K. (2009). Definition of 'art'. In Davies, S., Higgins, K. M., Hopkins, R., Stecker, R., and Cooper, D. E., editors, *A Companion to Aesthetics, second edition*, pages 231–234. Wiley-Blackwell, Oxford.

Stojanovic, I. (2007). Talking about taste: Disagreement, implicit arguments, and relative truth. *Linguistics and Philosophy*, 30:691–706.

Stojanovic, I. (2012). Emotional disagreement. *Dialogue: Canadian Philosophical Review*, 51:99–117.

Stojanovic, I. and McNally, L. (2017). Aesthetic adjectives. In Young, J. O., editor, *The Semantics of Aesthetic Judgements*, pages 18–37. Oxford University Press, Oxford.

Stojnic, U., Stone, M., and Lepore, E. (2017). Discourse and logical form: Pronouns, attention and coherence. *Linguistics and Philosophy*, 40:519–547.

Stoljar, D. (2017). *Philosophical Progress: In Defense of a Reasonable Optimism*. Oxford University Press, Oxford.

Stoneham, T. (2003). Temporal externalism. *Philosophical Papers*, 32:97–107.

Tanesini, A. (2006). Bringing about the normative past. *American Philosophical Quarterly*, 43:191–206.

Tanesini, A. (2014). Temporal externalism: A taxonomy, an articulation, and a defence. *Journal of the Philosophy of History*, 8:1–19.

Tarski, A. (1933). The concept of truth in the languages of the deductive sciences. In *Logic, Semantics, Metamathematics, papers from 1923 to 1938*, pages 152–278. Hackett, Indianapolis.

Thomasson, A. L. (2016). Metaphysical disputes and metalinguistic negotiation. *Analytic Philosophy*, 57(3):1–28.

Travis, C. (2008). Annals of analysis. In *Occasion-Sensitivity: Selected Essays*, pages 65–93. Oxford University Press, Oxford.

Tye, M. (2006). Absent qualia and the mind-body problem. *The Philosophical Review*, 115:139–169.

van Fraassen, B. C. (1980). *The Scientific Image*. Oxford University Press, Oxford.

van Inwagen, P. (1975). The incompatibility of free will and determinism. *Philosophical Studies*, 27:185–199.

Viebahn, E. (2020). Ways of using words: On semantic intentions. *Philosophy and Phenomenological Research*, 100:93–117.

Walton, K. (2007). Aesthetics—what? why? and wherefore? *The Journal of Aesthetics and Art Criticism*, 65:147–161.

Wat, D. (2004). The common cold: A review of the literature. *European Journal of Internal Medicine*, 15(2):79–88.

Way, J. (2016). Two arguments for evidentialism. *The Philosophical Quarterly*, 66:805–818.

Wettstein, H. K. (1984). How to bridge the gap between meaning and reference. *Synthese*, 58:63–84.

Whitehead, A. N. and Russell, B. (1963). *Principia Mathematica, second edition*. Cambridge University Press, Cambridge.

Williamson, T. (2000). *Knowledge and its Limits*. Oxford University Press, Oxford.

Williamson, T. (2007). *The Philosophy of Philosophy*. Blackwell, Oxford.

Wilson, M. (1982). Predicate meets property. *The Philosophical Review*, 91:549–589.

Wittgenstein, L. (1953). *Philosophical Investigations*. Blackwell, Oxford.

Index

accommodation 153–7
adjectives, gradable 127, 134–6, 141, 157–8, 160–5, 173–4 (*see also* disputes about taste)
Ambrose, Alice 10
analyticity 103–4
analytic/synthetic distinction 180–2
appropriateness 39–42, 43
argument argument 28–30
argument from spurious evidence, the 84
Aristotle 112
Ayer, A. J. 9–10

Bradley, F. H. 10
Burge, Tyler 62–3, 84–8, 92–3
Burgess, Alexis 60

Cappelen, Herman 31–4, 38, 42, 43
  Master Argument 32–5
  Prudential Argument 33
Carnap, Rudolf 35 (*see also* Ramsey-Carnap-Lewis Metasemantics)
causation 57, 83, 112, 114, 118–20 (*see also* solonic causal explanation *and* non-causal determination)
  causal explanation 53–5, 56, 119
  efficacy of knowledge 119–20
  mental 56, 117, 119
Chalmers, David 42–43
charity
  and interpretation 9–10
  temporal externalism 97–100, 176–7
Chomsky, Noam 60–1
Clark, Andy 42–3
competence
  Chomskian account of 60–1
  conceptual role account of 49–50, 59–60
  Fregean account of 60
  and inconsistent concepts 49–50
  interpretation account of 61–3
conceptual engineering 5, 31–45
  ambitious vs. anodyne 32
  distinctness from theorizing 34–5, 38
conservatism about practice 3, 5–6, 18, 31, 46–7, 67

context 136–41
  list 138–41
  location 137–41
consequentialism 112–3

definition
  of concepts 75n.5
  covert implicit 94–6, 100, 102, 103–4
  descriptive 75–7, 78–80
  nominal 74–5, 78–80, 104
  real 74–5, 80–4
  stipulative 75–7, 92, 94, 96, 104
Determination of Meaning by Theory 39
disagreement, faultless 158–60
dispute
  about taste 136, 149, 158–63, 165 (*see also* adjectives, gradable)
  verbal 22–4, 25–8, 29, 31
disquotation
  reports 126–7
  self-attribution 123–4

Egan, Andy 148–50
Eklund, Matti 53–5, 57, 59–61
essentially contested words/concepts 186–7
explanation
  constitutive 53–6
  programme 56–8
  selectional 58–9

Field, Hartry 173–4
Frege, Gottlob 60

Gallie, W. B. 186
Glanzberg, Michael 164–5
Grice, Paul 6–8, 10, 181

Haslanger, Sally 40n.2, 42, 44
Hobbes, Thomas 72–3, 77

inapplicability objection 82–4
incoherence/inconsistency, of words or concepts 5–6, 46–66, 79, 167

Jackman, Henry 12–7
Jackson, Frank 56–8, 72–3, 78–9

Kant, Immanuel 73
knowledge
  causal efficacy of 119–20
  concept of 78–9
  norm 107
  self-knowledge 121–4
Kripke, Saul 84, 114

Lasersohn, Peter 163
Lazerowitz, Morris 10
Lewis, David 35–6, 40, 41n.3, 42, 129–30, 137, 153–5 (*see also* Ramsey-Carnap-Lewis Metasemantics *and* Meta-Contextualism, Lewisian)
Ludlow, Peter 171–3

MacFarlane, John 116
Malcolm, Norman 3–9, 17, 21–2
meaning, (*see also* semantics)
  change 21–30, 124–5
  indeterminacy of 14–6
  sameness 3, 8, 9–11, 125–8, 171–3
  and truth-conditions 7–8
  and use 6–8, 17
  variationism 170
metalinguistic negotiation 10–1, 21–30, 107, 170, 172
metaphysics of time 114–5
  of open future 115–6
metasemantics 11–2, 82–4, 87–8, 100–2, 113
  meta-extension question 141
  meta-list question 140–1, 142, 145, 155, 164
  meta-standing meaning question 139
  meta-semantic value question 139, 141, 164
Meta-Contextualism
  Externalist 144, 145–50, 155–7
  Intentionalist 142–143
  Lewisian 154
  Temporal Externalist 154–7, 161
meta-metasemantics 175
  dispositional 176
Moore, G. E. 4, 10

naturalness, metaphysical 15–6
non-causal determinism (NCD) 113–7
  backwards 113, 116–7
non-distinctiveness 64–6
normative meaning-giving characterisations 85–8
norms of assertion 107, 109

paradox 46–67
  hardness of 48–67
  non-distinctiveness of 64–6

Patterson, Douglas 60–1
persistence
  metaphysical 128–30
  of representations 128–32
Pettit, Philip 56–8
Plunkett, David 22–3
practices
  linguistic, metaphysics of 13–4
pragmatics 8, 9–11
presentism 115
programme explanation 56–8
Prosser, Simon 130–1
Pull Hypothesis, the 49
Putnam, Hilary 121, 177

Quine, Willard van Orman 91–2, 95

Ramsey-Carnap-Lewis Metasemantics (RCL) 35–40
  and Appropriateness 39, 40–2, 43
  Determination of Meaning by Theory 38–9
  Platitudes 36–7
Ramsey, Frank 35 (*see also* Ramsey-Carnap-Lewis Metasemantics)
reasons-assessing circumstances 127–8
relativism 116, 145–50, 159
revisionism about practice 5, 31–2, 46
Russell, Bertrand 67, 94

Sawyer, Sarah 167–70
Sainsbury, R. M. 48, 58, 167
Scharp, Kevin 61–3
selection explanation 58
semantics, characterization of 7–8
Sober, Elliott 59
solonic causal explanation 117–8
solonic features 112–3
speech situations 137–8
stipulation 90–6
Sundell, Tim 22–3

temporal externalism 3, 11–8, 71, 90–110, 151–87 (*see also* meta-contextualism)
  analyticity 180–1, 182
  and appropriateness 40–2
  expertise 180
  gap-closing 173–4
  holistic 181–2
  individual 178–9, 183
  individual/interlocuter 178–9
  meaning-sameness 96
  revisionary 174, 182
  social 179–80
  and meaning variationism 170, 171

   virtue 184–5
   voluntaristic 183–4
thought-language divergentism 168–9
thought-language parallelism 167, 170
Travis, Charles 7n.5

Walton, Kendall 81
Williamson, Timothy 119
wrong kind of reason 26–8, 31

zebras 12–7